Comparative Perspectives on Privacy in an Internet Era

Carolina Academic Press
Global Papers Series

Edited by
Russell L. Weaver and Steven I. Friedland

Comparative Perspectives on Privacy in an Internet Era

GLOBAL PAPERS SERIES
VOLUME VII

Edited by

Russell L. Weaver
PROFESSOR OF LAW & DISTINGUISHED UNIVERSITY SCHOLAR
UNIVERSITY OF LOUISVILLE, LOUIS D. BRANDEIS SCHOOL OF LAW

Jane Reichel
PROFESSOR OF ADMINISTRATIVE LAW
STOCKHOLM UNIVERSITY FACULTY OF LAW, SWEDEN

Steven I. Friedland
PROFESSOR OF LAW & SENIOR SCHOLAR
ELON UNIVERSITY SCHOOL OF LAW

CAROLINA ACADEMIC PRESS
Durham, North Carolina

Library of Congress Cataloging-in-Publication Data

Names: Privacy Discussion Forum (3rd : 2017 : Uppsala, Sweden) | Weaver,
Russell L., 1952- editor. | Reichel, Jane, editor. | Friedland, Steven I.,
editor.
Title: Comparative perspectives on privacy in an Internet era / edited by
Russell L. Weaver, Jane Reichel, Steven I. Friedland.
Description: Durham, North Carolina : Carolina Academic Press, LLC, [2018] |
Series: The global papers series ; Volume VII
Identifiers: LCCN 2018030818 | ISBN 9781531009571 (alk. paper)
Subjects: LCSH: Privacy, Right of--Comparative studies--Congresses. | Data
protection--Law and legislation--Comparative studies--Congresses. |
Internet--Law and legislation--Comparative studies--Congresses. | Privacy,
Right of--Sweden--Congresses.
Classification: LCC K3264.C65 P753 2017 | DDC 342.08/58--dc23
LC record available at https://lccn.loc.gov/2018030818

eISBN 978-1-5310-0958-8

Carolina Academic Press, LLC
700 Kent Street
Durham, North Carolina 27701
Telephone (919) 489-7486
Fax (919) 493-5668
www.cap-press.com

Contents

Series Note

The Global Papers Series involves publications of papers by nationally and internationally prominent legal scholars on a variety of important legal topics, including administrative law, freedom of expression, defamation and criminal law. The books in this series present the work of scholars from different nations who bring diverse perspectives to the issues under discussion.

Russell L. Weaver*
Jane Reichel**

Introduction

In their landmark 1890 article, *The Right to Privacy*,[1] Samuel Warren and Louis Brandeis sounded the alarm regarding increasing societal encroachments on the right to privacy. Today, with the dawn of the internet era, nineteenth-century technologies and encroachments seem quaint. While the internet has enabled many things, including the ability to communicate more effectively, it has also made it more difficult for individuals to protect their privacy. As Edward Snowden's disclosures revealed, the U.S. National Security Agency (NSA) conducted a massive cybersurveillance that swept up staggering amounts of personal information, including telephone records, emails, text messages, etc. Presumably, other nations are engaged in similar operations. At the same time, businesses mine personal data in order to obtain information regarding their customers' preferences, and more effectively market their products. Moreover, social media companies and internet service providers collect large amounts of information regarding their users' lives.

In 2017, the Privacy Discussion Forum convened at Uppsala University Faculty of Law (Sweden) for the third Privacy Discussion Forum. The event brought together scholars from many different countries to examine privacy issues. Participants were allowed to examine these issues through a variety of lenses, including (but not limited to) Tort, Constitutional Law & Administrative perspectives, as well as from the perspective of media intrusions on individual autonomy, as well as governmental and private uses of information (not only collection issues, but also distribution and use issues). However, a central theme of the discussions was the challenges to privacy created by the internet. The forum produced an interesting array of papers which are published in this book.

---

* Professor of Law & Distinguished University Scholar, University of Louisville, Louis D. Brandeis School of Law.

** Professor in Administrative Law, Stockholm University Faculty of Law, Sweden, previously Uppsala University Faculty of Law.

1. 4 HARV. L. REV. (1890).

Professor Luke Milligan's contribution to the forum is entitled *Freedom from Fear*. In that article, he discusses Warren and Brandeis' article, *The Right to Privacy*.[2] Milligan contends that the Warren and Brandeis view of privacy was multi-dimensional, including both a "breadth" dimension and a "depth" dimension. The "breadth" dimension prohibits government from engaging in physical trespasses, as well as from intruding on individual privacy via other unjustifiable means. The "depth" dimension includes a right to be free of the fear of being subjected to injury. While he notes that the breadth dimension is reflected in the U.S. Supreme Court's interpretation of the Fourth Amendment, as extending to non-physical invasions of privacy, he argues that the depth dimension remains undeveloped. He references the Court's holding in *Clapper v. Amnesty International USA*,[3] where the Court held that "the Fourth Amendment is not violated by mere threats or attempts to conduct unreasonable searches or seizures. Nor is it violated by a vast surveillance scheme which just happens to spare the individual claimant." As a result, the plaintiffs in *Clapper* were unable to establish standing to sue because they could not show that the government was actually surveilling them. In other words, under the Court's current interpretation of the Fourth Amendment, there is no protection against the *fear* of unreasonable searches and seizures. There is only protection against actual searches and seizures.

Viewing the matter from an originalist perspective, Milligan argues that the right to be free from fear was very much on the minds of the founding generation. He notes that the Fourth Amendment guarantees "the people" the right to be "secure" in their persons, houses, papers, and effects, and he argues that there are good historical reasons to define the term "secure" as including the right to be free from fear. In making this argument, he resorts to dictionary definitions and historical materials. After mapping out his arguments, he contends that this broader definition of the Fourth Amendment, as including protection of the right to be free from fear, might offer greater protection against U.S. cybersurveillance operations, and might have altered the result in the *Clapper* case. In other word, the plaintiffs in that case might have been able to establish standing to challenge the NSA's cybersurveillance program.

Professor Jon Mills and J.D. Jill Guidera Brown, in their article, *Privacy in the Culture of Intrusion*, suggests that the legal system has not kept pace with advances in technology. While technological advancements have affected and intruded upon virtually every aspect of our lives, they note that "the legal sys-

---

2. 4 HARV. L. REV. (1890).
3. 568 U.S. 398 (2013).

tem has offered an "unpredictable and sometimes inefficient patchwork of privacy protections." Indeed, "since many foundational U.S. privacy laws were enacted, society has moved from desktop computers and clunky data processors to sophisticated Internet-connected microcomputers in nearly everyone's pocket, plus GPS, recreational drones, connected home goods, universal CCTV, Facebook, big data, machine learning, government surveillance, and predictive analytics." As a result, individuals, motivated by diverse emotions such as "curiosity, cruelty, gossip, jealousy, revenge, anger, and fear " have the ability to penetrate deeply into other people's lives. However, not only individuals, but also businesses and the government, have used modern technologies to usher "in a global culture of intrusion that only continues to expand as we depend more on mobile devices, peer-to-peer networks, and the sharing economy for daily tasks. " They conclude that, while "the Internet has a history of rugged individualism that preserved free speech at all costs," that individualism must now be tempered against the "varied privacy and security interests," and they argue that this "is best done by considering the multitude of cultural and individual triggers that compel us to act in our digital lives."

Professor Mark D. Cole, and PhD candidate Teresa Quintel, LL.M., submitted a paper entitled *"Is There Anybody Out There?" Retention of Communications Data: An Analysis of the Status Quo in Light of the Jurisprudence of the Court of Justice of the European Union (CJEU) and the European Court of Human Rights (ECtHR)*. In their paper, they argue that citizens are subjected to manifold forms of surveillance of their communications. This routine of—often covert measures by national intelligence services, but frequently also by obligation on private parties to retain data of their customers—regular collection and processing of communications data has an impact on the fundamental rights of individuals. Consequently, in a number of cases, European courts have concluded that various surveillance and collection techniques involve unjustified intrusions on privacy or a violation of data protection laws. In their paper, Professor Cole and Ms. Quintel analyze decisions of the CJEU and ECtHR, including the CJEU's very recent *Tele2/Watson* as well as *Digital Rights Ireland* case, and ECtHR's judgments in the *Zakharov/Russia* and *Szabó & Vissy/Hungary* cases. The article suggests that the two courts are elegantly working with each other in an effort to protect the privacy rights of European citizens.

Professor Jane Reichel and PhD candidate Joanna Chamberlain in their article, *The Swedish Understanding of Privacy as a Fundamental Right in a Comparative Perspective—Overview and Possibilities*, examine the history and development of the right to privacy in Sweden. In their article, they note that Sweden's foray into privacy protections began with the creation of the right to personal integrity. However, it was difficult for Sweden to expand the right of personal integrity for a variety of reasons. For one thing, Swedish jurisprudence, including the school of thought referred to as Scandinavian Legal Realism, suggested that nothing could exist outside of the natural context of time and space, and therefore that immaterial things such as rights could not exist. In addition, freedom of speech and of the press were accorded a higher status than the right of personal integrity, as were the principles of openness and transparency, and therefore privacy rights were subordinated. All of this began to change as new technologies began to infringe on the privacy rights of individuals, and Sweden decided to enact its Data Act. Change was also prompted by Sweden's accession to the European Union, and its decision to become a party to the European Convention on Human Rights, as well as because of the European Union's adoption of its Data Protection Directive. Chamberlain and Reichel use these recent changes to discuss developments regarding the right of privacy in Europe and in the United States, and make suggestions regarding how Sweden can learn from U.S. and European efforts, and bring about change either through constitutional amendment or through case law.

Professor András Koltay's article, *Internet Gatekeepers as Editors—The Case of Online Comments*, examines privacy in the context of the internet, and the posting of online comments. He notes the potential tension between Article 10 and Article 8 of the EctHR, which protect freedom of expression and privacy, respectively, in regard to online comments. He then analyzes European Court of Human Rights decisions regarding the liability of internet participants for such comments. He notes the distinction between "moderated" and "unmoderated" comments, and "active" and "passive" control of websites. Ultimately, he suggests the need for greater clarification and elaboration regarding the rules governing internet service providers. He argues that the need for such rules is apparent given that online comments may be directly related to the public interest, but can also involve hate speech, defamatory material, etc.

Senior Lecturer Mariette Jones's article, *Privilege, Power and the Perversion of Privacy Protection*, examines the tension between individual privacy and the societal need for protection against terrorists, as well as the tradeoffs that societies contemplate in order to protect themselves. She notes that privacy protections run the risk of becoming a tool of the powerful, analogous to the (alleged) abuse of pre-reform libel laws. She also notes that the nature of modern life has led to a *de facto* surrender of privacy rights. Indeed, quoting from the famous Warren and Brandeis article, she argues that a "true understanding of life lived fully in a modern state reveals that the average person is almost *never* 'left alone.' " While she acknowledges that, when privacy interests are weighed against security interests, the balance will usually favor security, she questions whether it can "be proven that giving up more privacy rights would necessarily improve the security situation?" Indeed, even though security agencies routinely claim that they were able to thwart terrorist incidents, it is difficult to know whether their claims are true. Everything is conducted in secret. As a result, it is difficult to know whether further intrusions on privacy interests would "have a positive effect on preventing future atrocities when it seems that many of those that do happen seemingly could have been prevented without much intrusion on privacy. For example, questions are raised about the authorities' failure to take repeated alerts about the Manchester bomber seriously."

Professors Ellen Podgor and Louis Virelli's contribution is entitled *"Accountability in Criminal Discovery."* In their article, they examine recent litigation against the U.S. Department of Justice (DOJ), referred to as the "Blue Book Litigation," which deals with the tension between the DOJ's discovery authority in criminal prosecutions and the public's right to know what its institutions (in that case, DOJ's exercise of its prosecutorial powers) are doing. The Blue Book, which plaintiffs wished to see, contained information and advice for criminal prosecutors regarding the conduct of discovery in criminal cases. DOJ refused to divulge the contents of the Blue Book on the theory that it involved protected work product and was therefore privileged. Professors Podgor and Virelli take issue with the DOJ's position, noting that "secrecy outside the confines of a specific case, and more importantly as to policies regarding such procedures, remains questionable" because it directly contradicts the prosecutorial role of being a "minister of justice" and puts prosecutors in the uncomfortable position of seemingly being engaged in what is effectively a "sporting event." In addition, they argue that the DOJ's secrecy "flies in the face of key administrative law principles of legitimacy: expertise, accountability, and efficiency."

Finally, Professor Russell Weaver's contribution, *Privacy and Free Expression*, examines the tension between the right to free speech and the right to privacy. He notes that, in the U.S., freedom of expression is generally treated as a "preferred right" in the sense that it often prevails over other competing rights. As a result, in competition with the right to be free from defamatory comment, the intentional infliction of mental and emotional distress, or even the right to be free from offensive words, the right to freedom of expression is generally given precedence. The privacy area is a bit unique. While the right to free speech will generally prevail over the right to privacy as well, there are situations when the right to privacy will prevail. Nevertheless, he concludes that there is a significant gulf between the U.S. and Europe with regard to the handling of both free speech and privacy interests. Whereas the U.S. is often very protective of speech interests, treating freedom of expression as an interest that is entitled to special or preferred protection, European countries are generally more protective of privacy interests. As a result, in many types of privacy cases (e.g., false light privacy and intrusion on seclusion), it can sometimes be difficult for U.S. plaintiffs to prevail against free speech claims. However, in one area, cases involving appropriation of plaintiff's name or likeness for business or commercial purposes, U.S. plaintiffs have been more successful.

Comparative Perspectives on Privacy in an Internet Era

Luke Milligan*

Freedom from Fear

Introduction

In 1890, Samuel Warren and Louis Brandeis authored "The Right to Privacy."[1] Perhaps the most influential law review article ever written,[2] "The Right to Privacy" begins with a survey of the gradual expansion of the common law.[3] In the "very early times," wrote Warren and Brandeis, the law provided a "remedy only for physical interferences with life and property; for trespasses *vi et armis*."[4] Once it became clear that "only a part of the pain, pleasure, and profit of life lay in physical things," then the "right to life" came to mean the "right to enjoy life — the right to be let alone."[5]

Warren and Brandeis's idea of the "right to be let alone" was multidimensional. One dimension involved the *breadth* of harm. Harm, they explained, could occur by physical or non-physical means. They wrote that "[i]nstantaneous photographs and newspaper enterprise have invaded the sacred precincts of private and domestic life; and numerous mechanical devices threaten to make good the prediction that 'what is whispered in the closet shall be proclaimed from the housetops.'"[6] Later on, Justice Brandeis would elaborate on this idea in *Olmstead v. United States*,[7] arguing that the Fourth Amend-

---

* Professor of Law, University of Louisville Brandeis School of Law.

1. Samuel D. Warren & Louis D. Brandeis, *The Right to Privacy*, 5 Harv. L. Rev. 194 (1890).

2. Neil Richards, *The Puzzle of Brandeis, Privacy, and Speech*, 63 Wash. L. Rev. 1295 (2010) ("Two short texts by Louis D. Brandeis are the foundation of American privacy law."); Melville B. Zimmer, *The Right of Publicity*, Law & Contemp. Probs. 203, 203 (1954) (describing "The Right to Privacy" as "perhaps the most famous and certainly the most influential law review article ever written").

3. Warren & Brandeis, *supra* note 1, at 194.

4. *Id.*

5. *Id.* ("Political, social, and economic changes entail the recognition of new rights, and the common law, in its eternal youth, grows to meet the demands of society.").

6. *Id.* at 195.

7. Olmstead v. United States, 277 U.S. 438, 471 (1928) (Brandeis, J., dissenting).

ment of the U.S. Constitution prohibited not only physical trespasses, but, more generally, "unjustifiable intrusions by the Government upon the privacy of the individual."[8] Brandeis wrote:

> The makers of our Constitution … conferred, as against the Government, the right to be let alone—the most comprehensive of rights, and the right most valued by civilized men. To protect that right, every *unjustifiable intrusion by the Government upon the privacy of the individual,* whatever the means employed, must be deemed a violation of the Fourth Amendment.[9]

In addition to its breadth dimension, Warren and Brandeis's "right to be let alone" also featured a *depth* dimension: harm can be caused by incomplete actions, such as attempts or threats. In its survey of the common law, Warren and Brandeis explained that liberty once meant nothing more than "freedom from *actual* restraint," and the right to life served only to "protect the subject from battery in its various forms."[10] But with "recognition of man's spiritual nature, of his feelings and his intellect," the "protection against actual bodily injury was extended to prohibit mere attempts to do such injury; that is, *the putting another in fear of such injury.*"[11] For Warren and Brandeis, the "freedom from fear" was an important aspect of the "right to be let alone."

One hundred and twenty-seven years after the publication of "The Right to Privacy," Warren and Brandeis's "right to be let alone" has been only partially incorporated into Fourth Amendment regulations of searches and seizures. Citing "The Right to Privacy," the Supreme Court in the 1960s broadened the scope of Fourth Amendment harm to include non-physical invasions of privacy.[12] This is good law today.[13]

---

8. *Id.*

9. *Id.* (empahsis added).

10. Warren & Brandeis, *supra* note 1, at 193.

11. *Id.* (emphasis added); *see* also Jerome Hall, *Criminal Attempt—A Study of Foundations of Criminal Liability,* 49 Yale L.J. 789 (1940).

12. Berger v. New York, 388 U.S. 41 (1967); Katz v. United States, 389 U.S. 347, 350 n.6 (1967) (citing Warren & Brandeis, *supra* note 1); *Id.* at 360 (1967) (Harlan, J., concurring); United States v. White, 401 U.S. 745, 779 (Harlan, J., dissenting) (describing *Berger* as "following a path opened by Mr. Justice Brandeis' dissent in *Olmstead*").

13. Florida v. Jardines, 569 U.S. 1, 5 (2013) ("By reason of our decision in *Katz v. United States,* 389 U. S. 347 (1967), property rights are not the sole measure of Fourth Amendment violations.") (citations omitted).

But the *depth* dimension of the "right to be let alone"—the "freedom from fear"—remains undeveloped in the Fourth Amendment case law. The case of *Clapper v. Amnesty International USA* is instructive.[14] In 2013, the Supreme Court explained that surveillance programs—no matter how extensive and unreasonable—cannot cause Fourth Amendment injury to an individual until the government succeeds in actually "intercepting" or "acquiring" that individual's communications.[15] The *Clapper* Court reaffirmed that the Fourth Amendment is not violated by mere threats or attempts to conduct unreasonable searches or seizures. Nor is it violated by a vast surveillance scheme which just happens to spare the individual claimant. As currently interpreted, the Fourth Amendment guarantees not the right to be "free from fear," but merely the right to be "spared."

In the hopes of encouraging a fuller incorporation of the "right to be let alone" into Fourth Amendment doctrine, this article sets forth a brief, originalist analysis of the "freedom from fear."[16] As it turns out, the idea of "freedom from fear" was very much on the minds of the founding generation. Moreover, it seems that a corresponding "right" to be "free from fear" can be gleaned from the original meaning of the Fourth Amendment's text.[17]

---

14. 568 U.S. 398 (2013).

15. *Id.* at 417 (explaining that to establish a Fourth Amendment injury, plaintiffs must prove that their communications were actually intercepted or otherwise acquired); *Id.* at 422 (Breyer, J., dissenting) ("Thus, the basic [standing] question is whether *the injury, i.e., the interception,* is "actual or imminent.") (emphasis added). A Fourth Amendment "injury" requires an "actual" intrusion. Litigants, however, have standing to sue to prevent a *future* injury if they can show that the "injury" (i.e., actual intrusion) is "certainly impending." *Id.* at 417. The *Clapper* Court emphasized the strictness of this standard. *Id.*

16. Wilson v. Arkansas, 514 U.S. 927 (1995) (observing that "our effort to give content to this term may be guided by the meaning ascribed to it by the Framers of the Amendment").

17. *See* Luke M. Milligan, *The Forgotten Right to Be Secure*, 50 HASTINGS L.J. 713 (2014); *see also* THOMAS CLANCY, THE FOURTH AMENDMENT: ITS HISTORY AND INTERPRETATION, sec. 3.4.4. n.218 (3d Ed. 2017) ("My views are consistent with Professor Milligan's in that 'secure' includes freedom from fear. There is ample historical basis for that claim. However, I did not contemplate that usage to permit individuals to make pre-search or pre-seizure claims to prevent those intrusions or to prevent regulations that would permit them. I just never contemplated that application—but I agree that it can be so construed.... Professor Milligan's insights should not be overlooked: the framers valued security and that concept included freedom from fear. Otis, after all, in the Writs litigation sought to prevent certain procedures—suspicionless, general searches—not to litigate them after the fact."); DAVID GRAY, FOURTH AMENDMENT IN AN AGE OF SURVEILLANCE (2017) ("Americans who read the Fourth Amendment in 1791 would have understood that it sought to secure a basic set of protections against threats to them, their homes, their

I. To Be Secure

Borrowing heavily from Article XIV of the Massachusetts Constitution, the Fourth Amendment provides:

> The right of the people *to be secure* in their persons, houses, papers, and effects, against unreasonable searches and seizures, shall not be violated; and no Warrants shall issue, but upon probable cause, supported by Oath or affirmation, and particularly describing the place to be searched, and the persons or things to be seized.[18]

Compared with its textual counterparts (i.e., "search," "seizure," and "unreasonable"), the "to be secure" language has been largely ignored over the centuries.[19] No court has defined it.[20] Commentators have paid it little attention.[21]

---

writings, and their property that would leave them as 'well-guarded as a prince in [their] castle[s].'") (citing Milligan, *supra* note 17, at 713).

18. U.S. CONST. amend. IV (emphasis added).

19. Thomas K. Clancy, *The Framers' Intent: John Adams, His Era, and the Fourth Amendment*, 86 IND. L.J. 979, 1047 (2011) ("The congressional history concerning the evolution of the final form of the amendment's language is sparse and somewhat disputed. The provision generated very little recorded debate."); *see also id.* at 1028 (stating that John Adams, the author of the Massachusetts template, "never seems to have commented on the Massachusetts search and seizure provision").

20. Jed Rubenfeld, *The End of Privacy*, 61 STAN. L. REV. 101, 119 (2008) (observing that the "to be secure" text "play[s] little role in current doctrine."). While the Court has not interpreted "to be secure," it has on occasion made reference to the value of "security." In *Hoffa v. United States*, the Court wrote that "the Fourth Amendment protects the security a man relies upon when he places himself or his property within a constitutionally protected area...." 385 U.S. 293 (1966); *see also* Soldal v. Cook County, 506 U.S. 56 (1992) ("What matters is the intrusion on the people's security from governmental interference."); Johnson v. United States, 333 U.S. 10, 14 (1948) ("The right of officers to thrust themselves into a home is also a grave concern, not only to the individual but to a society which chooses to dwell in reasonable security and freedom from surveillance.").

21. *See* Larry Rosenthal, *Seven Theses in Grudging Defense of the Exclusionary Rule*, 10 OHIO ST. J. CRIM. L. 523, 536 (2013) ("The term 'secure' is often ignored in discussions of the Fourth Amendment."). One of the notable exceptions is Thomas Clancy. Clancy has written extensively on the meaning of "to be secure." Thomas K. Clancy, *What Does the Fourth Amendment Protect: Property, Privacy, or Security?*, 33 WAKE FOREST L. REV. 307 (1998); Thomas K. Clancy, *The Fourth Amendment as a Collective Right*, 43 TEXAS TECH L. REV. 255 (2010); Thomas K. Clancy, *The Importance of James Otis*, 82 MISS. L.J. 487 (2012). *See also* GRAY, *supra* note 17 (discussing the "to be secure" text).

The leading dictionaries of the founding era defined "secure" as "free from fear," and, alternatively "protected from danger."[22] When read in the context of the Fourth Amendment, both meanings suggest that the Court's prevailing "spared" interpretation is probably too narrow.[23] After all, one may be actually "spared" a search or seizure, yet nonetheless not be "free from fear" or "protected from danger." The differences among these concepts were not lost on 18th Century thinkers. In 1746, William Warburton wrote: "For by the Equity of our Civil Constitution the Consciences of Men are not only left in Freedom, but *protected* in it.... [24] Warburton's passage highlights the difference between being "left" (i.e., spared) and "protected" in freedom. The Oxford English Dictionary offers a good example: "A very safe road, *secured* from all winds."[25] Was the road "secured" from wind because it was "spared" wind, or because the road was "protected" from wind? The latter makes far more sense.[26] *Titus Andronicus* further illustrates: "Repose here in rest, *Secure* from worldly chaunces and mishaps."[27] The "readiest champions" of Rome were "secure," not because they would happen by pure luck to be "spared," but because, upon death, their spirits were "protected" or "free from fear."[28]

The broader understandings of "secure" ("free from fear" and "protected") are further substantiated by pre-ratification writings concerning general war-

---

22. IX Oxford English Dictionary 367 (1970) (defining "secure" as: "safe, free from danger"; "protected from or not exposed to danger"; or "being free from fear or anxiety"); Johnson's Dictionary of the English Language (1st Am. ed. 1819) (defining "secure" as: "free from danger, that is safe"; "to protect"; "to insure"; "free from fear"; or "sure, not doubting"); *see also* 2013 Executive Summary of the President's Review Group on Intelligence and Communications Technologies at *76 ("In Latin, the word "securus" offers the core meanings, which include "free from care, quiet, easy," and also "tranquil; free from danger, safe."); Id. at *75 ("In a free society, one that is genuinely committed to self-government, people are secure in the sense that they need not *fear* that their conversations and activities are being watched, monitored, questioned, interrogated, or scrutinized. Citizens are free from this kind of *fear*.") (emphases added).

23. *See* Clapper v. Amnesty Int'l USA, 568 U.S. 398 (2013) (stating that injury from communications surveillance does not occur prior to "interception" or "acquisition").

24. William Warburton, A Sermon Occasioned By the Present Unnatural Rebellion (Knapton 1746).

25. IX Oxford English Dictionary, *supra* note 22 at 367 (emphasis added).

26. If the road had been exposed to winds that for some natural reason never came, it would seem strange to provide that the road was "secure."

27. William Shakespeare, Titus Andronicus, act I, sc I 152 (1588) (emphasis added).

28. Imagine instead soldiers who were stranded, but by pure luck never suffered "worldly mishap." It would have made little sense to refer to them as "secure."

rants.[29] After James Otis's famous attack on the writs of assistance,[30] it was written that

> *every housholder* [sic] in this province, will necessarily become *less secure* than he was before this writ had any existence among us.... [31]

The author's emphases on the terms "less secure" and "every housholder" are instructive. By writing that "every housholder ... will necessarily become less secure," he is not warning that everyone will *actually* experience more *actual* unreasonable searches. Rather the term "less secure" most likely conveyed that everyone will be left more fearful (or less protected).[32] Moreover, the author writes that one is "less secure" once the "writ ha[s] any existence among us." Had the term "less secure" been used to mean "less spared" (i.e., actually subjected to more searches), the author would have identified the execution of the writ—not its mere "existence"—as the point it imposed costs on citizens.

---

29. *But see* Clancy (*Property, Privacy, Security?*), *supra* note 21, at 351 (stating that "[t]he term 'secure'" has been "associated with being safe or free of danger in a *non*-Fourth Amendment context") (emphasis added).

30. There is no report of the case. The Supreme Court has since described Otis's argument as "perhaps the most prominent event which inaugurated the resistance of the colonies to the oppressions of the mother country." *Boyd v. United States*, 116 U.S. 616 (1886) ("'Then and there,' said John Adams, 'was the first scene of the first act of opposition to the arbitrary claims of Great Britain. Then and there, the child independence was born.'"); WILLIAM J. CUDDIHY, THE FOURTH AMENDMENT: ORIGINS AND ORIGINAL MEANINGS: 602–1791 (Oxford 2009) ("His proclamation that only specific writs were legal was the first recorded declaration of the central idea to the specific warrant clause.").

31. *See, e.g.,* MAURICE HENRY SMITH, THE WRITS ASSISTANCE CASE (1978) (designating Boston Gazette article as "Article, probably by James Otis, in the Boston Gazette for 4 January 1762") (emphasis added); Thomas Y. Davies, *Recovering the Original Fourth Amendment*, 98 MICH. L. REV. 547, 685 n.305 (1999) (claiming that the article was "probably authored by James Otis"); Rubenfeld, *supra* note 20, at 121 (stating that the article was "probably written by Otis himself").

32. The use of the word "secure" is attributed to Otis in additional contexts. He wrote that "[a] man is accountable to no person for his doings. Every man may reign *secure* in his petty tyranny, and spread terror and desolation around him, until the trump of the Archangel shall excite different emotions in his soul." JOSIAH QUINCY, JR., REPORTS OF CASES ARGUED AND ADJUDGED IN THE SUPERIOR COURT OF JUDICATURE OF THE PROVINCE OF MASSACHUSETTS BAY BETWEEN 1791 AND 1772 488 (1865) (quoting Boston Gazette, Jan. 4, 1762)). Examining this usage: if a man is not accountable, then he is "protected" (and likely confident) in his "tyranny." It would be strange to think of one to be "reigning" in "tyranny" if he had only been "spared" accountability. It seems reasonable to infer Otis used the word "secure" in this context to mean "protected" or "free from fear."

Here it's also worth examining the usage of "secure" by John Adams. Adams was the author of Article XIV of the Massachusetts Constitution (which in turn served as the model for the Fourth Amendment).[33] Young Adams, in the gallery transcribing Otis's summation in *Paxton's Case*, attributed to Otis the following: "A Man, who is quiet, is as *secure* in his House, as a Prince in his Castle."[34] Some fifty years later, Adams converted his original notes,[35] substituting the word "secure" for "well-guarded": "A man's house is his castle; and whilst he is quiet, he is as *well-guarded* as a prince in his castle."[36] Because one can be "spared" without being "well-guarded," it seems that Adams's usage of "secure" was intended to convey the meaning of "freedom from fear" or "protected."

II. Structure of the Fourth Amendment

Additional support for the broader reading of "to be secure" can be found in the structure of the Fourth Amendment. The amendment is cast in collective terminology, providing for the right of "the people" to be secure.[37] It's hard to square the amendment's collective terminology with the prevailing "spared" interpretation of "to be secure."[38] After all, at what point are "the people" no

---

33. Clancy, *supra* note 19, at 1047.

34. PETITION OF LECHMERE, ADAMS' MINUTES OF THE ARGUMENT, *in* 2 LEGAL PAPERS OF JOHN ADAMS 125 (L. Kinvin Wroth & Hiller B. Zobel eds., 1965) (emphasis added).

35. Clancy (*Property, Privacy, Security?*), *supra* note 21, at 353 (explaining the discrepancy).

36. 10 THE WORKS OF JOHN ADAMS, app. A at 524–25 (Charles F. Adams ed., 1856) (emphasis added). The discrepancy, according to Clancy, results from the two sources of the speech. Clancy (*Property, Privacy, Security?*), *supra* note 21, at 353.

37. U.S. CONST. amend. IV (emphasis added). Most courts today treat the Fourth Amendment as safeguarding only an individual right. *See District of Columbia v. Heller*, 554 U.S. 570 (2008) (stating that the Fourth Amendment "unambiguously refer[s] to individual rights, not 'collective' rights, or rights that may be exercised only through participation in some corporate body"); Donald L. Doernberg, *Reconciling Collective and Individual Interests under the Fourth Amendment*, 58 N.Y.U. L. REV. 259, 270 (1983) ("These cases clearly contemplate that the rights secured by the fourth amendment are individual rather than a 'right of the people' collectively held."); Anthony Amsterdam, *Perspectives on the Fourth Amendment*, 58 MINN. L. REV. 349, 367 (1974) ("Plainly, the Supreme Court is operating on the atomistic view."). *But see* Johnson v. United States, 333 U.S. 10, 14 (1948) ("The right of officers to thrust themselves into a home is also a grave concern, not only to the individual but to a society which chooses to dwell in reasonable security and freedom from surveillance.").

38. I do not argue that the Amendment should be interpreted as a collective right. Rather I'm simply pointing out that the drafting of the Fourth Amendment in terms of a

longer "spared" unreasonable searches and seizures? It can't be the moment of the first illegal search or seizure. One actual illegal search or seizure does not cause the people *as a whole* to have been "un-spared" (i.e., actually searched or seized). If, on the other hand, "the people" are no longer "spared" once a significant percentage of individuals (say, a majority) have been illegally searched or seized, then the right "to be secure" would have served no practical purpose at the time of the framing—due to limited state resources, a majority of the people would not have been "un-spared" under any imaginable scenario. But this interpretive dilemma can be avoided by reading "secure" to mean "free from fear" (or "protected"). As a practical matter, many types of state action can leave the people "fearful" of (or "unprotected" against) unreasonable searches and seizures. The writs of assistance come to mind. Accordingly, the framers' decision to cast the amendment in collective terminology seems to substantiate a broader reading of "to be secure."

Further support for the "free from fear" and "protected" readings is found in the Warrant Clause. The framers believed the very *issuance* of a general warrant violated the right "to be secure."[39] An important point is that the mere issuance of a general warrant does not always lead to actual searches or seizures.[40] Because issuance necessarily violates the right "to be secure," but only occasionally subjects persons to actual unreasonable searches or seizures, logic dictates that the right "to be secure" conferred more than a right to be "spared."[41] It makes far better sense to read "secure" more broadly, to mean "free from fear" (or "protected"). The mere issuance of a general warrant, after

---

collective right strongly suggests that "secure" was understood to mean either "protected" or "free from fear."

39. U.S. Const. amend. IV (stating that "no warrants shall *issue* without probable cause...."); Nelson B. Lasson, The History and Development of the Fourth Amendment of the United States Constitution 103 (1937) ("The general principle of freedom from unreasonable search and seizure seems to have been stated only by way of premise, and the positive inhibition upon action by the Federal Government limited consequently to issuance of warrants without probable cause."). For a history of the writs of assistance, *see* Thomas Clancy, *The Importance of James Otis*, 82 Miss. L. J. 487, 492–93 (2013).

40. A general warrant could issue but never be exercised.

41. *See* Lasson, *supra* note 39 at 103 ("The general right to security from unreasonable searches and seizures was given a sanction of its own and the amendment thus intentionally given a broader scope."); Davies, *supra* note 31, at 568 (stating that the framers ensured "the *protection* of the person and house by prohibiting legislative approval of general warrants") (emphasis added); Rubenfeld, *supra* note 20 at 126 (stating that a right to not be subjected to unreasonable searches and seizures "doesn't grasp the harm that general warrants actually inflict").

all, left each of the framers more "fearful" (and less "protected") against unreasonable searches and seizures.

Lastly, the prevailing reading of "secure"—to mean "spared"—would render the "to be secure" text gratuitous. If the drafters sought to protect a mere right to be "spared," they could have altogether omitted the language of "to be secure," instead drafting the amendment to provide a "right against unreasonable searches and seizures."[42] If, on the other hand, the drafters sought to confer a right to be "free from fear" (or "protected"), then the inclusion of the "to be secure" text would have been essential.[43]

III. Public Discourse

At the time of the framing, public discourse about the harms from general warrants centered on a popular metaphor: a man in his home is the king of his castle.[44] In the landmark *Semayne's Case*, Chief Justice Coke wrote:[45]

> [T]he house of every one is to him as his … castle and fortress, as well for his defence against injury and violence, as for his repose; and although the life of man is a thing precious and favoured in law … if thieves come to a man's … house to rob him, or murder, and the owner or his servants kill any of the thieves in defence of himself and his house, it is not a felony, and he shall lose nothing…. every one may assemble his friends and neighbours … to defend his house against violence.[46]

The castle metaphor was also utilized by William Pitt in his influential 1763 address to Parliament:

> The poorest man may in his cottage bid defiance to all the forces of the crown. It may be frail—its roof may shake—the wind may blow through it—the storm may enter—the rain may enter—but the

---

42. *See* Rosenthal, *supra* note 21, at 536 ("If the word 'secure' were simply understood as a synonym for a 'right' to be free from unreasonable search and seizure, it would be redundant of the 'right' found earlier in the same clause.").

43. *See* Marbury v. Madison, 1 Cranch 137, 174 (1803) ("It cannot be presumed that any clause in the constitution is intended to be without effect.").

44. *See generally* Clancy, *supra* note 19, at 1021–25.

45. Semayne's Case, 77 Eng. Rep. 194, 194 (K.B. 1604).

46. *Id.* at 195.

King of England cannot enter!—all his force dares not cross the threshold of the ruined tenement![47]

Back in the colonies, James Otis relied on castle imagery in his criticism of the writs of assistance: "A man's house is his castle; and while he is quiet, he is as well guarded as a prince in his castle."[48]

The widespread usage of the castle metaphor offers insight into the original meaning of "to be secure." A "castle" is a place "fortified for defense against an enemy."[49] As a result, allusions to "castles" almost certainly evoked the idea of a place where inhabitants were not simply "spared" intrusions, but enjoyed "freedom from fear" or "protection." The original author of the "to be secure" language,[50] John Adams, seemed to have realized this, writing that the home provides "as compleat a security, safety and Peace and Tranquility as if it was surrounded with Walls of Brass, with Ramparts and Palisadoes and defended with a Garrison and Artillery."[51] Finally, it's worth noting that the archetypical inhabitant of a castle (the Crown) enjoyed special legal protections from threats and attempted harms.[52]

Public discourse at the time of the founding moreover emphasized a connection between the Fourth Amendment and the exercise of speech and religious rights. Coke's papers, for example, had been seized pursuant to a general warrant.[53] *Entick v. Carrington* involved a warrant to search for "the author, or one concerned in the writing of several weekly very seditious papers."[54] In his attack on the writs of assistance, Otis expressly referred to searches relating to the "breach of Sabbath-day acts."[55] The connection between the Fourth

---

47. Henry Peter Brougham, Historical Sketches of Statesmen Who Flourished in the Time of George III, vol. 1 at 41–42 (1839).

48. Clancy, *The Fourth Amendment as a Collective Right*, 43 Texas Tech. L. Rev. 255, 258 (2009) (quoting 2 The Works of John Adams *supra* note 36, 142–44).

49. IX Oxford English Dictionary 956 (1970) Oxford English Dictionary, *supra* note 33, at 956.

50. *See generally* Clancy, *supra* note 19, at 1021–25.

51. L. Kinvin Wroth & Hiller B. Zobel eds., Legal Papers of John Adams, vol. 1 at 137 (1965).

52. For a summary of the relationship between the Crown and attempt laws, *see generally* Hall, *supra* note 11, at 789 (explaining that "compassing" the death of the King constituted treason even without an overt act).

53. Cuddihy, *supra* note 30, at 140–42.

54. *See* Entick v. Carrington, 95 Eng. Rep. 807, 807 (K.B. 1765); *see also* Wilkes v. Wood, 19 Howell St. Trials 1153 (K.B. 1763).

55. 2 The Works of John Adams, *supra* note 36, at 524–25.

Amendment and expressive rights has not been lost on the U.S. Supreme Court. The Court stated in 1961 that "[t]he Bill of Rights was fashioned against the background of knowledge that unrestricted power of search and seizure could also be an instrument for stifling liberty of expression."[56] More recently, in *United States v. Jones*, Justice Sotomayor explained that "[a]wareness that the Government may be watching chills associational and expressive freedoms."[57]

This makes sense. An individual decision whether to exercise speech or religion turns, as practical matter, on a weighing of expected benefits and expected costs. And one of the expected costs is uninvited exposure through an unreasonable government search or seizure. The critical point is that it's the fear of an unreasonable search or seizure—not simply its actuality—that affects a decision whether to express oneself. Because the Fourth Amendment was drafted and ratified in the hope of protecting expressive freedoms, it seems likely that the "to be secure" text was understood to mean not simply "spared" but rather "free from fear" (or "protected").

Conclusion

An essential feature of Warren and Brandeis's "right to be let alone" is the "freedom from fear." While overlooked by U.S. courts, a right to be "free from fear" can nonetheless be found in the original meaning of the Fourth Amendment. A study of dictionary definitions, constitutional structure, and public discourse suggests that the amendment's "to be secure" text conferred on individuals the right to be "free from fear" (or "protected"). Going forward, U.S.

---

56. Marcus v. Search Warrant 367 U.S. 717, 729 (1961); *see also* Frank v. Maryland, 359 U.S. 360, 376 (1959) (Douglas, J., dissenting) ("The commands of our First Amendment (as well as the prohibitions of the Fourth and the Fifth) reflect the teachings of *Entick v. Carrington*. These three amendments are indeed closely related, safeguarding not only privacy and protection against self-incrimination but 'conscience and human dignity and freedom of expression as well.'" (citation omitted*)*); Brinegar v. United States 338 U.S. 160, 180–81 (1949) (Jackson, J., dissenting) ("Among deprivations of rights, none is so effective in cowing a population, crushing the spirit of the individual and putting terror in every heart.... And one need only briefly to have dwelt and worked among a people possessed of many admirable qualities but deprived of these rights to know that the human personality deteriorates and dignity and self-reliance disappear where homes, persons and possessions are *subject at any hour* to unheralded search and seizure by the police." (emphasis added)).

57. 565 U.S. 400, 416 (2012) (Sotomayor, J., concurring).

courts should begin to consider incorporating, albeit selectively, the right to be "free from fear" into Fourth Amendment doctrine.

Although beyond the scope of this article, a deeper appreciation of Fourth Amendment harm could affect the regulation of surveillance programs in the U.S. As it stands, individuals do not suffer Fourth Amendment harm from surveillance programs before they are *actually* surveilled.[58] In turn, strategic state actors evade judicial review of new surveillance programs by simply concealing the use of new programs from their targets.[59] But if the guarantees of the Fourth Amendment were understood to run deeper, to include a reasonable fear of illegal surveillance, plaintiffs unable to prove they had been surveilled could nonetheless challenge new surveillance programs—their reasonable fear of surveillance would be enough.[60] This deeper understanding of Fourth Amendment harm would, in effect, provide earlier standing to plaintiffs looking to challenge surveillance programs—an important counter to government's increasingly strategic concealment of such programs from public scrutiny.[61]

---

58. Clapper v. Amnesty International USA, 568 U.S. 398 (2014).

59. *See* Milligan, *supra* note 17, at 722–27; *see Clapper*, 568 U.S. at 411 (2013) (stating that "respondents have no actual knowledge of the Government's § 1881a targeting practices").

60. Should "freedom from fear" be incorporated into Fourth Amendment doctrine, then state action causing such fear could constitute the Fourth Amendment "injury." This would have the benefit of expediting standing for challenges to new forms of surveillance.

61. *See*, e.g., Kate Zernike, *New Jersey Supreme Court Restricts Police Searches of Phone Data*, N.Y. Times, July 19, 2013, at A1 ("Some departments had manuals advising officers not to reveal the practice to the public."); Scott Shane, *New Leaked Documents Outline U.S. Spending on Intelligence Agencies*, N.Y. Times, Aug. 30, 2013, at A13 ("For decades, administrations from both parties have hidden spy spending in what is popularly known as the 'black budget.'").

Jon L. Mills* and Jill Guidera Brown**

Privacy in the Culture of Intrusion

Introduction: Human Instincts, Technology, and Culture

We live in a culture of intrusion, where deep-rooted human instincts are enhanced by modern technology. While basic human needs and impulses largely inform the technological advancements that shape our current society, these old instincts can also interact with new technology to dramatic and unpredictable ends. Technology touches nearly every aspect of our lives, but slow moving legal systems weave an unpredictable and sometimes inefficient patchwork of privacy protections. In the time since many foundational U.S. privacy laws were enacted, society has moved from desktop computers and clunky data processors to sophisticated internet-connected computers in nearly everyone's pocket, plus GPS, recreational drones, connected devices, universal CCTV, Facebook, big data, machine learning, government surveillance, and predictive analytics.

Oceans of data are created, collected, and analyzed every day. For example, the emerging practice of people analytics uses hardware and software to track movement, vocal patterns, email correspondence, and even health and wellness data, such as heartrate, to improve workplace efficiency and productivity. Companies collect, share, and in some instances sell, our consumer information to third party advertisers, and State and Federal law enforcement agencies surveille online and telecommunications activity. However, it is not just the government and corporations playing the role of Big Brother, it is our friends (and foes) on social media.

* Jon L. Mills, Dean Emeritus, Professor of Law, and Director of Center for Governmental Responsibility, University of Florida Fredric G. Levin College of Law.

** Jill Guidera Brown, J.D. Lead Research Assistant at University of Florida Fredric G. Levin College of Law Center for Governmental Responsibility.

This article was drafted in Summer 2016. The authors would like to thank Sophie Hayashi, Marie Moyle, and Joshua Rieger for their assistance in preparation of this paper.

Against this technical backdrop, a catalogue of human instincts and impulses inform both the desire to protect one's own personal privacy, and the impulse to expose others. Hardwired human instincts such as curiosity, cruelty, gossip, jealousy, revenge, anger, and fear are as old as civilization itself, yet have new life and new impact in the digital realm. While intrusions are not new to society, modern technology facilitates a greater number of potential privacy invasions that can penetrate deeper into people's lives. This fact prompts the question: Have basic human motivations, when combined with or enabled by creative, beneficial, and sometimes unanticipated technology, created a culture of intrusion? This paper will use examples from the law and society to address this query through the lens of four overlapping categories of human instincts and impulses: connection, curiosity, convenience, and security. While this paper focuses primarily on U.S. law, it is important to identify that in many ways, the Internet has facilitated a global culture and a global data privacy regulatory scheme. However, distinct cultural mores and political priorities lead countries to assign varying degrees of privacy protections to its citizens' data.[1] While both human nature and technology may be similar across geographic boundaries, a jurisdiction's unique privacy laws may provide different data protections and varied legal outcomes.

I. Connection

The desire to connect with others is essential to the human condition. In recent years, the methods of connection have been rapidly transformed by technologies. Humans share secrets with others to foster intimacy and solidify social bonds. Now through social media platforms, users share personal details online with friends and strangers alike. While for many, this helps overcome the hurdle of social anxiety leading to greater connections both online and off,[2] for others, social media platforms create a detailed mechanism to snoop, troll, and intrude. Mobile devices give most Americans the ability publish anything instantaneously, without filters or delays, perhaps feeding narcissistic tendencies.[3] While widespread sharing on social media may indicate that users have forfeited their right

---

1. For example, the EU's General Data Protection Regulation ("GDPR") provides for information deletion and disclosures that may be contradictory to American free speech rights (EU 2016/679).

2. 64% of teenagers have met at least one new friend online, and 72% feel closer to their friends because of online interaction. Amanda Lenhart, *Teens, Technology, and Friendships,* PEW RESEARCH CENTER (Aug 6., 2015).

3. Julie Beck, *How to Spot a Narcissist Online,* THE ATLANTIC (Jan. 6, 2014).

to privacy, this is not necessarily the case. A clear majority of young adults report taking some form of affirmative act such as opting-out cookies or choosing products that offer encryption to protect their online privacy.[4]

A. Media and Communications

The First Amendment rights to freedom of speech and the press have evolved rapidly in the new media age. The rise of digital media has expanded the press corps beyond those beholden to traditional journalistic ethics, blurring the lines between citizen and reporter, truth and fiction. Websites quote or create Orwellian "alternative facts,"[5] and sometimes the media repeats these absolute falsehoods.[6] In 2017, U.S. government officials referenced alternative facts[7] and bogus websites.[8]

This phenomenon predates the Trump administration. In 2010, U.S. Department of Agriculture official Shirley Sherrod was defamed by both the old and new media. The conservative blog Breitbart published an edited clip of Sherrod at an NAACP fundraiser, which when taken out of context, gave the impression that Sherrod systematically discriminated against white farmers. The edited video was not fact checked, yet was widely republished by blogs, social media, as well as mainstream news, inciting a racist web-fueled mob. Within twenty-four hours, outrage over the clip led to Sherrod's forced resignation and public condemnation from the NAACP. One day after that, the entire un-edited video surfaced. Government officials retracted its hasty firing and the NAACP offered an apology. Sherrod sued Breitbart for libel[9] and settled with his estate for an undisclosed amount, but her career and public profile suffered irreparable damage.

---

4. Lee Raine, *The State of Privacy in Post-Snowden America*, PEW RESEARCH CENTER (Sept. 21, 2016) available at http://www.pewresearch.org/fact-tank/2016/09/21/the-state-of-privacy-in-america/. (For the purpose of this survey, young adults are those aged 18–29.)

5. Marc Fisher et all, *Pizzagate: From rumor, to hashtag, to gunfire in D.C.* WASHINGTON POST (Dec. 6 2017).

6. See Sheryl Gay Stolberg et all, *With Apology Fired Official is Offered New Job*, NEW YORK TIMES (July 21, 2017).

7. White House advisor Kellyanne Conway claims Press Secretary Sean Spicer used "alternative facts" when addressing the press corps. Meet the Press with Chuck Todd, NBC NEWS (Aired Jan. 22, 2017).

8. Sapna Maheshwari, *10 Times Trump Spread Fake News*, NEW YORK TIMES (Updated Jan. 18, 2017).

9. Josh Gerstein, *Breitbart, Sherrod Near Libel Settlement*, POLITICO (July 1, 2015) *available at* http://www.politico.com/blogs/under-the-radar/2015/07/breitbart-sherrod-near-libel-settlement-209824.

The ease of posting via digital media raises the pressing issue of republication of intrusive information, for example, when a hacker illegally obtains an image or video, which is later posted or republished on the web by a third party.[10] Current law raises two barriers to liability for third-party publishers. First, the Computer Decency Act (CDA) immunizes websites and internet service providers that provide a platform for intrusive material posted by third-parties.[11] Second, a third-party publisher may be protected because he or she is not the originator of the intrusion or the intrusive information. Publishing illegally obtained information may be an exercise of free speech that should be balanced against the newsworthiness of the content, and the nature of the intrusion itself. In *Bartnicki v. Vopper* the United States Supreme Court sets forth a three-part balancing test that weighs the conduct of the defendant, the public importance of the disclosure, and the nature of the disclosure.[12] The high profile invasion of privacy case, *Bollea v. Gawker,* used the *Bartnicki* balancing test to determine whether publishing a video obtained from an anonymous source of a professional wrestler engaging in a sexual act was of high enough public importance to justify the intrusion. A jury found it was not and delivered a $150 million verdict against Gawker,[13] bankrupting the media company.

New media has also updated the process of whistleblowing. Like Daniel Ellsberg[14] before him, Edward Snowden went to journalists to share government documents, in part because he trusted the journalists' judgment to disclose potential instances of government misconduct without threatening national security.[15] As the *New York Times* did with the Pentagon Papers, the *Guardian* fact-checked Snowden's story, but technological advancements allowed them to go to press in days rather than months. Disclosures made by Chelsea Manning

---

10. *See* Kim Zetter, *Ashley Madison Hackers Release an Even Bigger Batch of Data,* Wired (Aug. 20, 2015), *available at* http://www.wired.com/2015/08/ashley-madison-hackers-release-even-bigger-batch-data/; *See also In re Sony Gaming Networks and Customer Data Breach Litigation,* 996 F. Supp. 2d 942, 966-73 (S.D. Cal. 2014).

11. Section §230 of the CDA states that "no provider or user of an interactive computer service shall be treated as the publisher or speaker of any information provided by another information content provider." 47 U.S.C. §230.

12. *Bartnicki v. Vopper,* 532 U.S. 514, 517 (U.S. 2001).

13. Nick Madigan and Ravi Somaiya, *Hulk Hogan Awarded $115 Million in Privacy Suit Against Gawker,* NEW YORK TIMES (March 18, 2016).

14. *See New York Times Co. v. United States,* 403 U.S. 713 (1971).

15. Peter Maass, *How Laura Poitras Helped Snowden Spill His Secrets,* NEW YORK TIMES (Aug. 13, 2013).

were published on WikiLeaks.[16] While Manning's disclosure of military misconduct was very likely newsworthy, the leak was controversial because WikiLeaks does not have the same source and fact checking as traditional journalism. Manning went to WikiLeaks only after contacting the *New York Times* and the *Washington Post*, which were both slow to respond.[17] WikiLeaks provided a direct and efficient route to whistleblowing.

B. Connection to Others

Online platforms create expansive opportunities to connect with others. Facebook is nearly ubiquitous,[18] and Twitter is the president's new bully pulpit. With more of our communication occurring through social media platforms, digital privacy has become a valuable commodity that some companies are offering as valuable product enhancements.[19] WhatsApp, an application once celebrated by its one billion users for its end-to-end encryption, faced criticism when weak spots were discovered in its encryption protocol.[20] This secure (and free) communications system provided a crucial private line for dissidents, activists, and many immigrant communities. The practice of companies leaving intentional weaknesses in encryption protocols has elevated the so-called backdoor debate. This technical issue became a household name in 2016 when Apple resisted the FBI's order to create software to hack into the iPhone of the San Bernardino shooter. The company was weary that the government's broad interpretation of the All Writs Act would create a risky precedent that would leave the privacy and security of millions of users' data in limbo.[21]

---

16. In his final days in office, President Obama truncated Manning's sentence after she served 6 years in military prison. Snowden, having fled the country and never facing trial, has very slim chance of pardon under the Trump administration.

17. Amanda Holpuch, *Chelsea Manning: I leaked reports after seeing how Americans ignored wars*, THE GUARDIAN (June 12, 2017) *available at* https://www.theguardian.com/us-news/2017/jun/12/chelsea-manning-interview-leaked-documents.

18. 79% of online Americans use Facebook. See Shannon Greenwood, Andrew Perrin, and Maeve Duggan, *Social Media Update 2016*, PEW RESEARCH CENTER (Nov. 11, 2016).

19. Perhaps today's most private messaging app is Signal, developed by Open Whisper Systems, (last visited May 28, 2017) available at https://whispersystems.org/.

20. Manisha Ganguly, *WhatsApp vulnerability allows snooping on encrypted messages*, THE GUARDIAN (Jan. 13, 2017) *available at* https://www.theguardian.com/technology/2017/jan/13/whatsapp-backdoor-allows-snooping-on-encrypted-messages.

21. *See* Apple Inc.'s Reply to Government's Opposition to Apple Inc.'s Motion to Vacate Order Compelling Apple Inc. to Assist Agents in Search at 2,5, *In The Matter Of The Search*

Despite the privacy risks, social media has given many the opportunity to find meaningful relationships. Sharing information online can aid those looking for love[22] or long lost relatives.[23] Attempting to connect with others online can also have disastrous effects, as was the case for those exposed by the Ashley Madison data breach[24] and involved in increasingly numerous revenge porn cases.

Beginning in 2011, the nonconsensual intimate media website ugotposted.com hosted over ten-thousand images depicting explicit material, all without consent of the subjects. The website also posted personal identifying information along-side most of the images—such as phone numbers, email, workplace contact information, home addresses, and social media handles, as well as information about employers or family members. Victims of the site received a flood of digital and physical threats. Many became scared for their lives, lost their employment, and suffered damage to their family relationships, identity, and reputation.[25] When asked to remove the information, the victims were instead directed to a second website where ugotposted.com's creator posed as an attorney willing to help remove the information for a $250 fee. The site made more than $10,000 in this operation.[26]

Through its newly formed eCrime Unit, then California Attorney General, now Senator Kamala Harris, launched an investigation leading to the ugotposted.com creator's arrest.[27] Though the prosecution came in the wake of a newly-passed California nonconsensual pornography bill, and is celebrated as the first criminal prosecution of a "revenge porn" website operator, the State's

---

Of An Apple iPhone Seized During The Execution Of A Search Warrant On A Black Lexus IS300, California License Plate 35KGD203 (C.D. Cal. Mar. 15, 2016) (No. CM 16-10 (SP)).

22. Online dating is on the rise in all age groups. 22% of those ages 18–24 use online dating apps, and 12% of older adults aged 55–64 report using an online dating site. Aaron Smith and Monica Anderson, *5 Facts About Online Dating*, PEW RESEARCH CENTER (Feb. 9, 2016) *available at* http://www.pewresearch.org/fact-tank/2016/02/29/5-facts-about-online-dating/.

23. Identical twins adopted to different families identified each other 25 years later on YouTube and Facebook. *See* Anaïs Bordier and Samantha Futerma, *Separated @ Birth: A True Love Story of Twin Sisters Reunited*, Berkley; Reprint edition (Sept. 1, 2015).

24. Kim Zetter, *Hackers Finally Post Stolen Ashley Madison Data*, WIRED (Aug. 18, 2015).

25. Veronica Rocha and Tony Perry, *Kamala Harris: Lives Ruined, Women Terrified in Revenge Porn Case*, LA TIMES (Feb. 3, 2015).

26. *People v. Bollaert*, 248 Cal. App. 699 (4th D.C.A. 2016)

27. *Attorney General Kamala D. Harris Announces Creation of eCrime Unit Targeting Technology Crimes*, Press Release CA DOJ (Dec. 13, 2011) *available at* https://oag.ca.gov/news/press-releases/attorney-general-kamala-d-harris-announces-creation-ecrime-unit-targeting.

legal strategy relied on more traditional tools for prosecuting criminals such as extortion and identity theft.[28]

State legislatures often attempt to fill the holes in the "patchwork"[29] of federal privacy laws. Cyberbullying laws, for example, usually seek to implicate two sets of criminals: the traditional cyberbully and revenge porn publishers. All fifty states have enacted anti-cyberbullying statutes to combat online harassment.[30] Forty states plus D.C. currently have some form of nonconsensual intimate media sharing statutes in place, and eleven more have pending legislation.[31] The best statutes are narrowly tailored and target the real harm done to victims of revenge porn while leaving intact adequate free speech provisions. However, the multi-jurisdictional nature of internet communications makes it difficult to regulate conduct that occurs across state lines or internationally.

* * *

In many ways, new media and social media platforms have facilitated global connectivity. However, there is no universal solution for addressing privacy issues raised by these technologies. International regulatory frameworks for protecting privacy sometimes require coordination with American companies, including the newly enacted General Data Privacy Protection (GDPR),[32] and with respect to cross border transfer EU-U.S. Privacy Shield framework,[33] as well as the implementation of concepts such as the right to be forgotten,[34] and

---

28. *Id.* In April 2015, a California jury convicted Bollaert on twenty-one felony counts of identity theft and six felony counts of extortion. Bollaert was sentenced to eighteen years in prison. His sentence later reduced to eight years, plus ten years' probation. Only one of his victims received compensation for her harm—$143 for work missed and travel to the courthouse.

29. *See* Daniel J. Solove & Chris J. Hoofnagle, *A Model Regime of Privacy Protection*, 2006 U. ILL. L. REV. 357, 357, 401 (2006).

30. *See* Cyberbullying Research Center, *Bullying Laws Across America* (Accessed Aug. 27, 2018) *available at* http://cyberbullying.org/bullying-laws.

31. Adrienne N. Kitchen. *The Need to Criminalize Revenge Porn: How A Law Protecting Victims Can Avoid Running Afoul Of The First Amendment.* Chicago-Kent L. Rev. (2015).

32. GPDR Article 75 (While there will be many issues related to jurisdiction, the GPDR permits EU residents to pursue legal action against any data processor or controller, including those located in the United States, alleged to be in violation of the GPDR).

33. The Privacy Shield Framework's seven privacy principles are fairness, specific purposes, restrictions, accuracy, destruction when obsolete, security, and automated processing. *Privacy Shield Framework Principals*, UNITED STATES DEPARTMENT OF COMMERCE, (Accessed Aug. 1, 2016) *available at* http://ec.europa.eu/justice/data-protection/files/privacy-shield-adequacy-decision-annex-2_en.pdf

34. *Google Spain SL, Google Inc. v Agencia Española de Protección de Datos, Mario Costeja González* (2014).

cross-border data storage.[35] As online platforms continue to facilitate greater global connection, legal standards must consider cross-border implications.

II. Curiosity

Human survival, evolution, and the vibrancy of our culture has long depended on curious, innovative minds. Internet connectivity has accelerated innovation by granting people access to a universe of information and the ability to share ideas worldwide.[36] But curiosity manifests itself in ways that can sometimes lead to unethical conduct, such as an employer conducting research on the personal life of a potential employee, or internet vigilantes engaging in potentially harmful video voyeurism. While curiosity is key to the pursuit of knowledge, internet searches conducted in the name of that pursuit can be compiled by law enforcement or by private corporations to draw conclusions about the searcher that can be used in unethical ways.

A. Pursuit of Knowledge

Internet search histories create a detailed profile of the searcher, whether it's accurate or not. While these searches may seem private, they are often captured by others. The NSA's far-reaching surveillance program XKeyscore collected data from internet searches.[37] Internet search histories are also routinely brought into the courtroom as evidence, as was the case when search queries for temperature and length of time required to kill a child in a vehicle were used to convict a man who deliberately left his child in the backseat of his car.[38] Internet searches are revealing of both cultural norms and individual impulses. Social scientists use this data to more accurately depict racism in the U.S.,[39]

---

35. *Schrems v. Data Protection Comm'r*, CJEU Case C-362/14 (Oct. 6, 2015). (finding that American companies' mere compliance with the U.S.'s Safe Harbor provisions is not, by itself, adequate protection in Europe and may still leave these companies exposed to liability).

36. While the internet provides unfettered access to information for many, that access is not always equitable. Tech deserts (places that lack adequate connectivity or hardware) leave many without reliable internet access, even in developed areas.

37. Glen Greenwald, *XKeyscore: NSA Tool Collects Nearly Everything a User Does on the Internet*, THE GUARDIAN (July 31, 2013) *available at* https://www.theguardian.com/world/2013/jul/31/nsa-top-secret-program-online-data.

38. Alan Blinder, *Georgia Father Is Convicted of Murder in Toddler's Death in Hot Car*, NEW YORK TIMES (Nov. 14, 2016).

39. Christopher Ingraham, *The Most Racist Places in America, According to Google*, THE WASHINGTON POST (April 18, 2015) *available at* https://www.washingtonpost.com/

and to paint intimate portraits of the human condition through searches related to marriage, love, and sex.[40]

This data also highlights a cultural trend of using internet searches to informally learn. Conversely, some online learning practices more directly resemble formal academic pursuits. Online learning platforms, digital courses, and Massive Open Online Courses (MOOCs) are augmenting traditional education systems. For example, Florida public K–12 schools now allow certain categories of MOOCs to be taken for school credit.[41] When integrating digital learning into traditional classroom settings, administrators must determine when to protect user data using FERPA[42] education record protections, or COPPA guidelines for data collected from users younger than 13.[43]

B. Morbid Curiosity

The right to privacy is often balanced against the right to access information. This balance is often muddled by a human curiosity to understand tragic,

---

news/wonk/wp/2015/04/28/the-most-racist-places-in-america-according-to-google/?utm_term=.5d55e6584474.

40. Larry Getlen, *Google Data Reveals Your Most Perverted Secrets*, THE NEW YORK POST (May 13, 2017) *available at* http://nypost.com/2017/05/13/google-data-reveals-your-most-perverted-secrets/

41. § 1004.0961, Fla. Stat, (2014) (Beginning in the 2015–2016 school year, students can earn academic credit for online courses, including MOOCs, before initial enrollment at a postsecondary institution. The rules of the State Board of Education and regulations of the Board of Governors must include procedures for credential evaluation and the award of credit, including, but not limited to, recommendations for credit by the American Council on Education; equivalency and alignment of coursework with appropriate courses; course descriptions; type and amount of credit that may be awarded; and transfer of credit.; courses must be taught by Florida accredited teachers, have final exams, and be in biology, algebra, or geometry); See also Kathleen McGory, *Florida Lawmakers get Schooled on MOOCs*, TAMPA BAY TIMES (Nov. 7, 2016) (describing Florida the goal of the Florida MOOC statute is to allow students the opportunity to take college-level courses to better prepare for advanced testing or college admissions.)

42. The Family Educational Rights and Privacy Act (FERPA) regulates how education records may be accessed, stored, and shared. FERPA requires educational agencies and institutions to provide parents, or qualifying students, access to their own records, as well as restricts how an educational agency or institution may share student data with third parties. 20 U.S.C. § 1232g.

43. The Children's Online Privacy Protection Act (COPPA) makes it unlawful for an operator of a commercial website that is either targeted at children under the age of thirteen or that knowingly collects, uses, or discloses personal information from a minor child, to do so without notice and in some cases consent from a parent or guardian. 15 U.S.C. § 6501—6505.

traumatic events. In 2011, Dawn Brancheau, a senior trainer at SeaWorld, was killed while interacting with one of the park's orcas. There was tremendous public interest in the attack, for various reasons, such as a sentimental connection to the amusement park and its well-known whales. Some sought to profit from it, feeding a depraved market for death videos. Others wished to engage in internet-enabled citizen investigations[44] to determine if the whale's mistreatment lead to the attack. Ultimately, the video could not provide answers beyond the formal investigation, and a Florida court granted Brancheau's family's request to keep the graphic video of their daughter's death private.

While disclosing horrible images or videos may fulfill some individuals' curiosity, publication of these images or videos is deeply scarring to the families of the deceased. The level of intrusiveness is often dictated by the medium of the intrusion. For example, a federal judge ruled that audio from the tragic Challenger space shuttle explosion could be withheld from Freedom of Information Act ("FOIA") requests because to release the tapes would invade the surviving family's privacy interests: "[e]xposure to the voice of a beloved family member immediately prior to that family member's death … would cause the Challenger families pain."[45] However, newspapers were permitted to publish transcripts of the audio. In Brancheau's case, if the underwater video footage were made available to some, there is no doubt it would be shared across the Internet. The Brancheau family did not seek the spotlight and were attempting to find the space to mourn. The family's privacy interests prevailed over the public's curiosity to see the videos.

C. Innovation

While self-driving cars may seem like a futuristic goal, major tech and auto companies are already testing and refining autonomous vehicles (AV). Semi-autonomous features such as adaptive cruise control are in use on public roads today.[46] Thirteen states have passed legislation allowing AV testing.[47] Three locations (New York, Tampa, Wyoming) are running federally-backed pilot programs for intelligent transportation systems.[48] Connected infrastructure, as

---

44. See also Reddit Boston Bombing example—where users identified the wrong suspects & were convinced they had solved the case.

45. *NY Times v. NASA*, 782 F.Supp. 628, 631 (D.D.C. 1991).

46. Paul Lewis, Gregory Rogers, Stanford Turner, *Beyond Speculation: Automated Vehicles and Public Policy*, ENO CENTER FOR TRANSPORTATION (May 2017) *available at* https://www.enotrans.org/wp-content/uploads/2017/04/AV_FINAL.pdf.

47. *Id.*

48. The pilot program uses signals sent from the cars to public infrastructure, such as stoplights, streetlamps, or even pedestrian's mobile phone. *See* Connected Vehicle Pilot De-

well as internal and external computing processes, facilitate autonomous and connected vehicles to collect droves of data.[49]

A unique issue of data ownership arises from the use of AV. Many stakeholders lay claim to the data. Consumer data is valuable to businesses; data on travel and traffic patterns is of interest to urban planners and municipalities; and crash data could be used against the driver in litigation. To the driver, ownership of the data is critical to privacy concerns because this data often contains sensitive information such as real time geolocation, voice recognition, and other personally identifiable information. A vehicle has long been considered private domain[50] and Florida's Fourth DCA has held that GPS information in the car's black box could only be accessed by police with a valid warrant.[51] However, even in states that have legislation declaring that the vehicle's human operator owns the data, the operator may still need a court order to access it.[52]

AV technology also presents fascinating cybersecurity concerns. Driving software can be hacked causing catastrophic crashes, damage to property, personal injury, or even death. Whether emotional pain or personal injury, as more aspects of daily life become internet-enabled, the stakes for data privacy rise. The human impulse of curiosity can drive us toward heightened understanding, or increased harm to others.

III. Convenience

The Internet fosters a global culture of convenience, largely focused on home entertainment and rapid delivery of consumer goods.[53] Online shopping has driven the way many companies collect, sort, store, and analyze data. Shoppers in turn willingly provide their personal information, consumer histories, and location data with online vendors to improve their consumer expe-

---

ployment Program, United States Department of Transportation (Last Updated Mar. 30, 2017) available at https://www.its.dot.gov/pilots/.

49. Dorothy J. Glancy, *Privacy in Autonomous Vehicles*, 52 Santa Clara L. Rev. 1171 (2012).

50. *Katz v. United States*, 389 U.S. 347 (1967).

51. *State v. Abbey*, 28 So.3d 208, 211-12 (Fla. 4th D.C.A. 2010).

52. *See* Lewis, infra footnote 49.

53. Media consumption through online streaming services such as Netflix, Hulu, or Amazon Prime. Amazon is building and testing 30-minute drone delivery for small packages under five pounds. *See* Amazon Prime Air (Last Visited May 20, 2017) *available at* https://www.amazon.com/Amazon-Prime-Air/b?node=8037720011.

rience. Because of our robust digital lives, Americans have come to expect less privacy. In 2015, Pew Research found that 91% of American adults felt that they have lost control over how personal information is collected and used by companies.[54]

Beyond the consumer realm, health professionals use the efficiency of digital records to manage patient information and allow patients the convenience of accessing health records through online portals. Management of health records is regulated by the Health Insurance Portability and Accountability Act (HIPAA),[55] yet even HIPAA compliant practices may be susceptible to modern cyberattacks, as demonstrated by the global WannaCry ransomware attack which held digital data hostage, forcing several UK hospitals to temporarily halt patient care.[56]

A. Predictive Analytics

While the industrial revolution ushered in the efficient mass manufacturing of consumer goods, the internet revolution offers convenience and direct access to consumers. Feeding the industry, consumers share information such as email addresses and location data in exchange for deals or special offers. Data brokers and marketers create detailed consumer profiles using shopping patterns, internet search history, time spent on webpages, navigation pathways to reach websites, and cursor and keystroke movement. Targeted advertisements guide the modern consumer experience and confer benefits to both consumers and businesses, as well as third parties that buy and sell enormous amounts of data. Though 51% of all shopping is now done online,[57] brick and mortars also benefit from data analytics. Location-based marketers can track location data using GPS in mobile devices and then use algorithms that can predict consumer behavior to entice spending at strategic nearby storefronts.

---

54. Lee Raine, *The State of Privacy in Post-Snowden America*, PEW RESEARCH CENTER (Sept. 21, 2016) available at http://www.pewresearch.org/fact-tank/2016/09/21/the-state-of-privacy-in-america/.

55. Health Insurance Portability and Accountability Act of 1996, Pub. L. No. 104-191, §110 Stat. (1936).

56. Denis Campbell and Haroon Siddique, *Operations Cancelled as Hunt Accused Of Ignoring Cyber-Attack Warnings*, THE GUARDIAN (May 15, 2017), *available at* https://www.theguardian.com/technology/2017/may/15/warning-of-nhs-cyber-attack-was-not-acted-on-cybersecurity.

57. Madeline Farber, *Consumers Are Now Doing Most of their Shopping Online*, FORTUNE (June 8, 2016) *available at* http://fortune.com/2016/06/08/online-shopping-increases/.

As Target's Director of Guest Data Management said, "We want to know everything we can."[58] But being all-knowing has caused Target trouble in recent years. In 2012, Target received criticism for their data collection policies after sending coupons for maternity goods to a teenage girl whom had not yet informed her family of her pregnancy.[59] Target had tracked her purchase history and used algorithms to determine that her purchases were consistent with an expectant mother. The analytics were correct, but intrusive. In 2013, Target's negligence in contracting with a third-party vendor resulted in a hack that revealed the financial data for nearly 40 million accounts. Whether consumer information is at risk of being exposed to one's family or the entire world, the sensitive information we share with business is vulnerable to exposure.

Predictive analytics can also be used for the greater good and has been used to predict when individuals were experiencing symptoms of depression, prevent disease outbreaks, and assist counterterrorism efforts. With the vast amount of information available through big data, public records, online activity, and social media, data analytics systems have plenty of material to work with to predict individuals' behavior.

B. Internet-Connected Technologies

The impulse for convenience has driven innovations in home and wearable technologies. The Internet of Things (IoT) creates unique vulnerabilities to personal privacy in the most private spheres of our lives, our homes and bodies. Nest systems deploy sensors that know when you are home and offers the convenience of adjusting one's thermostat remotely. The convenience of this application results in the creation and storage of data that can easily reveal patterns of when a homeowner is away or hosting guests. Nest can also connect to Amazon Echo's Alexa, which has an embedded microphone that, although it can be deactivated, is by default recording audio from the home at all times.[60] Further, Internet-connected smart TV's allow seamless browsing and content streaming between devices but may be sharing consumer viewing data

---

58. Charles Duhigg, *How Companies Learn Your Secrets*, NEW YORK TIMES (Feb. 16, 2012).

59. *Id.*

60. *See Alexa and Alexa Device FAQ*, AMAZON (Last Accessed Jan 28, 2016) *available at* https://www.amazon.com/gp/help/customer/display.html?nodeId=201602230; *See also* Christopher Melee, *Bid for Access to Amazon Echo Audio in Murder Case Raises Privacy Concerns*, NEW YORK TIMES (Dec. 28, 2016) (Police seized an Amazon Echo device as evidence in a homicide investigation, and requested that Amazon provide the recorded data from the device. Amazon refused the request).

with advertisers, as was highlighted in the FTC's $2.2 million settlement with Vizio.[61]

Wearable technologies, like Apple watches and Fit Bits, are combined with technologies like GPS, cloud computing, biometric data, and image and voice capture. Uploading our health data to social platforms helps us track and incentivize our fitness goals, but may trigger HIPAA or other data privacy protections. Further, the information collected by corporations become vulnerable to breach or hack. For many consumers, a hypothetical breach of Amazon data would reveal a comprehensive mosaic of their life—shopping and browsing habits, movies watched and books read, home addresses, precise times away from the home, everyday inquires, and recorded intimate conversations.

The IoT is not limited to consumer goods. Workplaces are increasingly adopting "people analytics" which use RFID devices fitted with GPS and microphones to track employees to gauge workplace efficiency.[62] Although the workplace data is usually anonymized or pseudonymized, an employee's entire day may be monitored, including phone calls to home, instant messaging content, pace of movement, tone of voice, and number of trips to the restroom.[63]

IV. Security

One of the best documented trade-offs for personal privacy is for security. Fear is a valuable survival mechanism and can help rationalize the exchange of privacy for security. Post-September 11, many Americans were willing to submit to increased communications monitoring, full body scans at the airport, and police checkpoints in mass transportation systems all in the name of national security. Sixteen years later, a Fourth Amendment loophole allows Cus-

---

61. *VIZIO to Pay $2.2 Million to FTC, State of New Jersey to Settle Charges It Collected Viewing Histories on 11 Million Smart Televisions without Users' Consent*, Federal Trade Commission press release (Feb. 6, 2017) *available at* https://www.ftc.gov/news-events/press-releases/2017/02/vizio-pay-22-million-ftc-state-new-jersey-settle-charges-it.

62. *People Analytics: Using Social Sensing Technology to Transform Organizations* MIT MEDIA LAB (May 24, 2013) *available at* http://blog.media.mit.edu/2013/05/people-analytics-using-social-sensing.html.

63. Developers claim bathroom breaks are not monitored, but the author holds breaks can be conferred by combining location data and lack of activity at computer station.

toms and Border Control agents to conduct mobile phone searches at border crossings.[64]

A. Government Surveillance

Traditionally, the eye of Big Brother is perceived as government surveillance on its civilians. The Edward Snowden disclosures confirmed that the U.S. government was engaged in the ongoing mass surveillance of U.S. citizens. While Section 702 of the FISA Act currently authorizes massive intelligence gathering of American citizens under the banner of foreign surveillance,[65] advocates challenge the efficacy and morality of legal government surveillance.[66]

The Fifth Amendment right against self-incrimination has also evolved to cover modern realities. Recently, the Florida Fourth District Court of Appeals (DCA) held that the state may compel a defendant to provide the combination of numbers that constitutes his or her cell phone password, if the state had a valid search warrant, because the password was not considered testimony.[67] Likewise, the Minnesota Fifth DCA ruled that a defendant may be compelled to provide biometric data, such as a thumbprint, to unlock a mobile device without violating the Fifth Amendment privilege against self-incrimination.[68]

Much of the technology now considered part of everyday civilian life was originally developed for government programs. For example, GPS (Global Positioning System) was created by the United States Naval Research Academy to track the Sputnik satellite at the height of the Cold War. This sophisticated military tool, once found to be too dangerous for civilian use, is now embedded into the applications found on our phones, watches, and cars. In 1991, after four decades of development in government agencies and MIT computer science labs, the World Wide Web as we know it was formed.[69] At that time, few beyond the most computer savvy were logged on—non-technical lines of

---

64. Cynthia McFadden, E.D. Cauchi, William M. Arkin and Kevin Monahan, *American Citizens: U.S. Border Agents Can Search Your Cellphone*, NBC NEWS (Mar. 13, 2017) *available at* http://www.nbcnews.com/news/us-news/american-citizens-u-s-border-agents-can-search-your-cellphone-n732746.

65. Foreign Intelligence Surveillance Act (FISA) 50 U.S.C. § 1881a.

66. Alex Abdo, *How the NSA's Surveillance Procedures Threaten Americans' Privacy*, ACLU (June 21, 2013).

67. *State v. Stahl*, Case No. 2D14-4283 (Fla. Dist. Ct. App. Dec. 7, 2016).

68. *State v. Diamond*, 2017 WL 163710 (Minn. Dist. Ct. App. Filed Jan. 17, 2017).

69. In 1958 the United States Government created the Advanced Research Projects Agency (ARPA) to address technology-based national security concerns. In 1986, an early version of the internet we know today was formed. The network, named ARPANET became

communications opened up but were confined to the topics of science fiction, sports, and cars.[70] Today, Internet access is so intertwined with the fabric of our society, and access to the Internet is akin to a basic human right.[71]

Aerial surveillance has been used since World War I. Modern drones are precision and multi-purpose machines that can perform both acute reconnaissance and war strikes and deliver Amazon Prime orders straight to one's doorstep. In 2016, the Federal Aviation Administration (FAA) set forth guidelines for the civilian operation of drones.[72] The guidelines only regulate commercial drones weighing more than half a pound and outline who can operate a drone, how high they can fly, and where.[73] The FAA guidance does not address critical privacy issues such as what images drones may capture, at what locations, and from what distances. The purpose behind drone image capturing may trigger different legal standards. For example, law enforcement drones conducting aerial surveillance could run afoul of the Fourth Amendment, while paparazzi drones taking video of celebrities may be protected by the First Amendment.

B. Local Law Enforcement

Local law enforcement agencies justify intrusive practices, using advanced surveillance through technologies such as stingrays and software to analyze civilian social media use, and can do so by tapping into the fear-driven desire for security. Various data points can be fed into algorithms for predictive policing, a law enforcement technique that may help prevent crime in dangerous neighborhoods but is highly criticized for reinforcing racial prejudices and biases.[74] Police use internet surveillance to combat crimes such as accessing or sharing indecent depictions of minors. However, in 2011, a typo in an IP ad-

---

more sophisticated through the early 1970's. In 1983, ARPANET transitioned to the more user-friendly TC/IP protocol, but was used little beyond technical communications.

70. Helen McLure, *The Wild, Wild Web: The Mythic American West and the Electronic Frontier*, Western Historical Quarterly, Vol. 31, No. 4, 457 (Winter 2000).

71. Tim Sandle, *UN thinks internet access is human right*, Business Insider (July 22, 2016) *available at* http://www.businessinsider.com/un-says-internet-access-is-a-human-right-2016-7.

72. Summary of Unmanned Aircraft Rule, Federal Aviation Authority (Updated June 21, 2016) *available at* https://www.faa.gov/uas/media/Part_107_Summary.pdf.

73. *Id.*

74. Rachel Ehrenberg, *Data-driven Crime Prediction Fails to Erase Human Bias*, SCIENCE NEWS (Mar. 8, 2017) *available at* https://www.sciencenews.org/blog/science-public/data-driven-crime-prediction-fails-erase-human-bias.

dress led police to charge an innocent social worker in the United Kingdom of the heinous crime.[75]

In the aftermath of a tragic string of shootings by police officers, many precincts across the country invested in body-mounted cameras to increase accountability among officers. The desire to prevent police brutality or misconduct often outweighs privacy concerns, however interesting questions arise when civilians are filmed by the devices:[76] Who owns the data, and for how long should it be stored? Is such data a public record and if so, who should have access to it? What if it contains sensitive information such as a minor or a victim of violent crime? These are just a few questions raised by the technologies designed to further police practices and to keep society safe.

C. Public Safety

One component of security is personal safety. In New York City, transportation advocates are organizing for traffic enforcement technologies such as speeding cameras and red light cameras.[77] These technologies can curb dangerous driving, and pilot programs have shown a decrease in traffic injuries and fatalities, particularly for more vulnerable street users like children and older adults. However, some privacy advocates are skeptical and fear the cameras are collecting more data than necessary and for purposes other than traffic enforcement.[78]

Conclusion: Privacy in the Culture of Intrusion

The modern technologies of the internet era have ushered in a global culture of intrusion that only continues to expand as we depend more on mobile devices, peer-to-peer networks, and the sharing economy for daily tasks. Even

---

75. Adam Eley and Jo Adnitt, *My Life Was Ruined by a Typo*, BBC NEWS (Mar. 21, 2017) *available at* http://www.bbc.com/news/uk-39328853.

76. Kami Chavis Simmons, *Body-mounted Police Cameras: A Primer on Police Accountability vs. Privacy*, 58 How. L.J. 881 (Spring 2015).

77. David Meyer, *TA and Families for Safe Streets Call for Speed Cameras at #EverySchool*, STREETSBLOG (Mar. 10, 2015) available at http://nyc.streetsblog.org/2016/03/10/ta-and-families-for-safe-streets-call-for-speed-cameras-at-everyschool/.

78. Emmarie Huetteman, *Traffic Cameras Draw More Scrutiny by States*, NEW YORK TIMES (April 1, 2013); *ACLU Responds to Plan to Use Surveillance Cameras to Track Drivers Who Run Red Lights*, ACLU Press Release (July 13, 2000) *available at* https://www.aclu.org/news/aclu-responds-plan-use-surveillance-cameras-track-drivers-who-run-red-lights.

in countries where access to information is limited, the desire to connect, seek information, and consume are driving people to connected solutions. In America, the Internet has a history of rugged individualism that preserved free speech at all costs, which must now be balanced against varied privacy and security interests. This balance is best done by considering the multitude of cultural and individual triggers that compel us to act in our digital lives.

The most successful approaches to cybersecurity involve a multi-factored approach to mitigating risk at both the high-tech and human points[79] of the life-cycle of data management.[80] Likewise, approaches to privacy protection must be holistic, and as creative as the new technology that facilitates such privacy risks. Additionally, successful privacy protections should consider the human impulse to share information and instincts to protect individual privacy. A multi-disciplinary understanding of the human condition can create more precise and effective legal solutions that get to the heart of the problem, rather than treating symptoms of data intrusions, breaches, or security incidents.

---

79. Mahmood Sher-Jan, *Data indicate human error prevailing cause of breaches, incidents,* IAPP (June 26, 2018) *available at* https://iapp.org/news/a/data-indicates-human-error-prevailing-cause-of-breaches-incidents.

80. *See Start with Security: A Guide for Business,* FTC (June 2015) *available at* https://www.ftc.gov/system/files/documents/plain-language/pdf0205-startwithsecurity.pdf.

Mark D. Cole and Teresa Quintel[1]

"Is there anybody out there?" — Retention of Communications Data: Analysis of the status quo in light of the jurisprudence of the Court of Justice of the European Union (CJEU) and the European Court of Human Rights (ECtHR)

I. Introduction

When communicating electronically today, one should routinely ask the question in the title coined after a famous track in Pink Floyd's epochal "The Wall": "Is there anybody out there?".[2] Although in actual fact this might be quite superfluous as with current knowledge we can routinely expect some body or someone listening/reading or at least registering the data created by the electronic communication one has set up. In a time of increased fear and demand for public security combined with ever-growing technological abilities, it seems nearly inevitable that citizens are becoming more transparent and surveillance of their (communications) activities routine. However, this is in stark contrast to the legal evaluation of the situation: just as frequently as measures are adopted and introduced it seems that courts on the occasion of analyzing the instruments

---

1. *Mark D. Cole* is Professor for Media and Telecommunication Law at the Faculty of Law, Economics and Finance of the University of Luxembourg and Director for Academic Affairs at the Institute of European Media Law (EMR) in Saarbrücken. *Teresa Quintel*, LL.M. is an FNR-funded Ph.D. student at the University of Luxembourg under supervision of Prof. Cole.
2. *Pink Floyd*, The Wall, released 1979, Track 2 on CD / Record 2, cf. http://www.pinkfloyd.com/music/albums.php. All URLs in this contribution were accessed on 10 October 2017 except where otherwise mentioned.

with fundamental rights standards conclude that there is an unjustified intrusion of privacy or violation of data protection rights. The more general, all-encompassing and wide the collection and retention of data, the less targeted and limited, the more likely it is that courts strike down the measure.

This paper aims at presenting on a European level the status quo concerning data retention measures for law enforcement purposes in the light of important case law by the Court of Justice of the European Union ("CJEU"). Most recently in December 2016, the CJEU has handed down a very important judgment concerning national data retention measures in *Tele2*[3], thereby continuing on its previous groundbreaking judgment of April 2014 in *Digital Rights Ireland*.[4] One of the authors of this paper previously co-authored an extensive study on the consequences of the *Digital Rights Ireland* decision for national data retention measures, which were at that time not subject of the judgment.[5] Developing this further in light of the more recent case law is one aspect that will be addressed in this article, but combining it with the consequences of two major decisions by the European Court of Human Rights ("ECtHR") (*Zakharov*[6] and *Szabó/Vissy*[7]) will widen the perspective. Also on these two mentioned cases, one of the authors has co-authored an extensive case analysis, which will be the basis for one of the sections of the present contribution.[8] Combining these two perspectives will allow to identify a whole set of requirements that States in Europe have to fulfill in order to be able to introduce legally and without fundamental rights violations communications data collection and retention schemes. Each of the elements seem like stones

---

3. Joined Cases C-203/15 and C-698/15, *Tele2 Sverige AB* (C-203/15) and *Watson* (C-698/15) (CJEU, 21 December 2016) ECLI:EU:C:2016:970. Cf. *Teresa Quintel*, 'Hello! Is It Me You're Looking for? Not after Tele2 Anymore…,' (case comment) *RSIEAblog*, 2 August 2017, http://RSIblog.blogactiv.eu/2017/08/02/hello-is-it-me-youre-looking-for-not-after-tele2-anymore/.

4. Joined Cases C-293/12 and C-594/12, *Digital Rights Ireland Ltd* (C-293/12) and *Seitlinger* (C-594/12) (CJEU, 8 April 2014) ECLI:EU:C:2014:238.

5. Franziska Boehm and Mark D. Cole, 'Data Retention after the Judgement of the Court of Justice of the European Union', study for the Greens/EFA Group in the European Parliament. Münster/Luxembourg, 30 June 2014, available at http://www.janalbrecht.eu/fileadmin/material/Dokumente/Boehm-Cole-data_retention-study-print-layout.pdf.

6. *Roman Zakharov v Russia* App no 47143/06 (ECtHR, 4 December 2015).

7. *Szabó and Vissy v Hungary* App no 37138/14 (ECtHR, 12 January 2016).

8. Mark D. Cole and Annelies Vandendriessche, 'Case Note: From Digital Rights Ireland and Schrems in Luxembourg to Zakharov and Szabó/Vissy in Strasbourg: What the ECtHR Made of the Deep Pass by the CJEU in the Recent Cases on Mass Surveillance Roman Zakharov v Russia (App no 47143/06) and Szabó and Vissy v Hungary (App no.37138/14)', (2016) 2(1) *European Data Protection Law Review* (EDPL), p. 103–107.

in a wall that is getting higher and wider and which needs to be overcome before communications data retention is possible. To add to this, a brief look at
neighboring data retention schemes—namely in the financial data sector, the
use of PNR data—and a forward-looking view at the draft e-Privacy-Regula-
tion[9] will complement the analysis.

From a theoretical perspective, the outcome of the overall analysis will be that
the CJEU (in Luxembourg) and the ECtHR (in Strasbourg) are on this very matter playing elegantly the ball forth and back and as a result the scrutiny of data
retention schemes gets more intense. This respective referencing of the case law
of the two courts is exemplary for the cooperation that will be necessary in future
when the EU will join the European Convention on Human Rights ("ECHR").[10]
At the same time it underlines how strongly national margins for creating legislation even in fields which are not in an extensive manner within EU competence
are limited by the corresponding case law of the two Courts. This applies also for
the new EU framework for data protection[11] which will be applied in parts from
May 2018 at least for the EU General Data Protection Regulation ("GDPR")[12]
and is not only directly binding but also contains strong data subject rights.
More specifically the so-called e-Privacy Directive[13]—for which according to a
current legislative proposal by the Commission a replacement also in form of a

---

9. Proposal for a Regulation of the European Parliament and of the Council concerning the respect for private life and the protection of personal data in electronic communications and repealing Directive 2002/58/EC (Regulation on Privacy and Electronic Communications), COM(2017) 10 final, Brussels, 10 January 2017.

10. Cf. Art. 6 of the Treaty on European Union (TEU); on the problems of preparing
the ratification see Opinion 2/13 (CJEU, 18 December 2014) ECLI:EU:C:2014:2454.

11. 'Reform of EU Data Protection Rules', *European Commission*, http://ec.europa.eu/
justice/data-protection/reform/index_en.htm. The EU Data Protection Reform includes the
General Data Protection Regulation, Regulation (EU) 2016/679 (GDPR) and Directive (EU)
2016/680, which will be applicable for data processing in the area of law enforcement. The
European Commission put forward its EU Data Protection Reform in January 2012 and on
4 May 2016 the official texts of the Regulation and the Directive were published in the EU
Official Journal (see infra). While the Regulation entered into force on 24 May 2016 but will
only apply from 25 May 2018, the Directive entered into force on 5 May 2016 and EU Member States have to transpose it into their national law by 6 May 2018.

12. Regulation (EU) 2016/679 of the European Parliament and of the Council of 27 April
2016 on the protection of natural persons with regard to the processing of personal data and
on the free movement of such data, and repealing Directive 95/46/EC [2016] OJ L 119/1.

13. Directive 2002/58/EC of the European Parliament and of the Council of 12 July
2002 concerning the processing of personal data and the protection of privacy in the electronic communications sector (Directive on privacy and electronic communications) Official Journal L 201/37, as amended by Directive 2009/136 [2009] OJ L 337/11.

Regulation is coming[14]—is especially significant for the electronic communications sector.

II. Data Protection in Europe—An overview

This is not the place for an extensive overview of data protection law as provided for on the European level. However, a brief recap of the most important legal bases is necessary to better understand the combining of standards emanating from two different international organizations simultaneously. An obvious reason is that all EU Member States are also Members of the Council of Europe and thereby parties to the most relevant of its conventions, the European Human Rights Convention.[15] But there are also substantive reasons: specific legislative acts of the European Union dealing with data protection issues exist just as well as a Convention of the Council of Europe on the topic; on a more elevated level, treaty law of the EU mentions data protection; but finally and foremost, in both organizations the starting point is the protection of privacy and personal data as a fundamental right.

A. The fundamental rights dimension

In the ECHR, Article 8 protects private and family life and the jurisprudence of the ECtHR has developed an extensive understanding of this provision as a privacy right protecting e.g. against defamation, as much as a right against invasions into "data privacy", i.e. a data protection right.[16] On EU level, the Charter of Fundamental Rights of the European Union[17] ("EU Charter") introduced this right in an equivalent way in Article 7, whilst Article 8 added an explicit data protection right. Without having to discuss whether there is a distinction in practice between the main scope of protection of the two rights,

---

14. European Commission: Proposal for a Regulation of the European Parliament and of the Council concerning the respect for private life and the protection of personal data in electronic communications and repealing Directive 2002/58/EC (Regulation on Privacy and Electronic Communications). COM(2017) 10 final, Brussels, 10 January 2017.

15. Convention for the Protection of Human Rights and Fundamental Freedoms (European Convention on Human Rights, as amended), ETS No. 5.

16. Cf. e.g. *S. and Marper v. the United Kingdom* App nos 30562/04 and 30566/04 (ECtHR, 4 December 2008) at 67. Overview of relevant cases e.g. European Court of Human Rights, Factsheet—Personal Data Protection, September 2017, www.echr.coe.int/Documents/FS_Data_ENG.pdf.

17. See Articles 7 and 8 of the Charter of Fundamental Rights of the European Union.

it is certain that both the right to privacy and the right to data protection are recognized as fundamental rights. For Member States of the two organizations this means that they cannot enact national law or measures that violate the standards of Article 8 ECHR, otherwise they risk being condemned by the ECtHR, and they also have to respect the framework set by the EU Charter when adopting national laws if these have the goal of implementing EU law or concern the scope of application of the EU Treaties. In that case, according to Art. 52 (1) EU Charter, any restriction of the rights enshrined in the Charter must be provided for by law, be proportionate, strictly necessary and meet objectives of general interest recognized by the European Union as well as respect the essence of the rights enshrined in the Charter.[18] Moreover, individuals whose rights are potentially violated must have the possibility to seek legal remedy before national courts, even if such violation did not occur concretely or did not affect the individual directly, and the national court may then involve the CJEU in a preliminary reference procedure to clarify the interpretation of applicable EU law prior to using the answer to resolve the (national) dispute before it. Particularly in the area of data retention, access to personal data by law enforcement authorities ("LEAs") and the issue of mass surveillance by intelligence agencies, there have been important cases especially during the last couple of years.[19]

On EU level, the CJEU has progressively strengthened data subjects' rights through its case law[20], in particular, since the Lisbon Treaty of 2009 converted the

---

18. Art. 52 (1) of the Charter of Fundamental Rights of the European Union.

19. See for instance Joined Cases C-293/12 and C-594/12, *Digital Rights Ireland Ltd* (C-293/12) and *Seitlinger* (C-594/12) (CJEU, 8 April 2014) ECLI:EU:C:2014:238; Joined Cases C-203/15 and C-698/15 *Tele2 Sverige AB* (C-203/15) and *Watson* (C-698/15) (CJEU, 21 December 2016) ECLI:EU:C:2016:970 and with regard to ECtHR cases *Roman Zakharov v Russia* App no 47143/06 (ECtHR, 4 December 2015) and *Szabó and Vissy v Hungary* App no 37138/14 (ECtHR, 12 January 2016) as well as earlier *Kennedy v. the United Kingdom* App no 26839/05 (ECtHR, 18 May 2010).

20. Cases concerned with data retention and mass surveillance, see: Case C-301/06 *Ireland v European Parliament and Council*, (CJEU, 10 February 2009) ECLI:EU:C:2009:68; Joined Cases C-293/12 and C-594/12, *Digital Rights Ireland Ltd* (C 293/12) and *Seitlinger* (C 594/12) (CJEU, 8 April 2014) ECLI:EU:C:2014:238; Case C 362/14, *Schrems* (CJEU, 6 October 2015) ECLI:EU:C:2015:650; Joined Cases C-203/15 and C-698/15 *Tele2 Sverige AB* (C-203/15) and *Watson* (C-698/15) (CJEU, 21 December 2016) ECLI:EU:C:2016:970; C-212/13 *Rynes* (CJEU, 11 December 2014) ECLI:EU:C:2014:2428; C-419/14 WebMindLicenses Kft (CJEU, 17 December 2015) ECLI:EU:C:2015:832. Cf. case comments on these cases: Tijmen Wisman, 'Privacy: Alive and Kicking—Digital Rights Ireland: Joined Cases C-293/12 and C-594/12', (2015) 1(1) EDPL, p. 80–84; Hielke Hijmans, 'On Private Persons Monitoring the Public Space—Case C-212/13, Rynes', (2015) 1(2) EDPL, p. 149–152; Neal Cohen, 'The Privacy Follies: A Look Back at the CJEU's Invalidation of the EU/US Safe Harbor

EU Charter into a legally binding instrument of EU primary law, progressively serving as basis for the CJEU's interpretation of fundamental rights, whereas previously the Court had been dependent on referring to fundamental rights as general principles of EU law and thereby being able to include the substance of Article 8 ECHR in its jurisprudence.[21] Particularly in the area of privacy and data protection the CJEU has positioned itself as a "fundamental rights / EU Charter rights Court". Although in EU secondary law provisions concerning these rights exist since more than two decades—see below—the CJEU regularly used the much broader interpretable text of the EU Charter as a basis for its decisions and expanded the understanding of rights related to the protection of personal data.[22] The Court thus utilized the Charter as "gap-filling instrument" instead of referring to EU secondary law provisions, which raises questions also for national legislators about the practical implementation of the judgments for laws of the Member States.[23]

Because of the equivalence of the protection in Article 8 ECHR and Article 7 Charter, another interesting and very relevant trend has come to the fore concerning data protection cases: the CJEU extensively refers to the case law of the ECtHR even in the interpretation of secondary law concerning data protection and the ECtHR in turn has begun to include references to the CJEU judgments in its own data protection-related cases (especially in the area of

---

Framework—Case C-362/14, Schrems', (2015) 1(3) EDPL, p. 240–244; Stephanie Mihail, 'Interception of Telecommunications and Emails Seizure: What are the EU Charter's Limitations?—WebMindLicenses Kft v Nemzeti Ado-es Vamhivatal, CJEU', (2016) 2(2) EDPL, p. 258–261; Caroline Calomme, 'Strict Safeguards to Restrict General Data Retention Obligations Imposed by the Member States—Case Tele2 AG Opinion', (2016) 2(4) EDPL, p. 590–595; Will R Mbioh, 'Post-och Telestyrelsen and Watson and the Investigatory Powers Act 2016', (2017) 3(2) EDPL, p. 273–282, and *Opinion 1/15* on the background of the envisaged agreement concerning the transfer and processing of PNR data between the EU and Canada, ECLI:EU:C:2017:592, 26 July 2017.

21. Cf. e.g. Case C-465/00 and C-138/01 *Rechnungshof v ORF* (CJEU, 20 May 2003) ECLI:EU:C:2003:294, para. 70 et seq.

22. For instance the "right to be forgotten" (or, more precisely, to be delisted from search engine results) that the CJEU established in Case C-131/12 *Google Spain and Google Inc.*(CJEU; 13. May 2014) EU:C:2014:217.

23. One of the results being the *Tele2* judgment, which mainly clarifies the meaning of the previous *Digital Rights Ireland* case (that concerned the EU Directive itself) for national laws such as those that had originally implemented the Directive that was struck down in the previous judgment. On this aspect Franziska Boehm and Mark D. Cole, 'Data Retention after the Judgement of the Court of Justice of the European Union', study for the Greens/EFA Group in the European Parliament. Münster/Luxembourg, 30 June 2014, available at http://www.janalbrecht.eu/fileadmin/material/Dokumente/Boehm-Cole-data_retention-study-print-layout.pdf.

data retention and surveillance measures). This fruitful "ping-pong", which will be discussed more in detail below is happening even though the EU — irrespective of the obligation under Article 6 Treaty on European Union ("TEU") since the Treaty of Lisbon to accede the Convention — is not a ratifying party to the ECHR. With the EU Charter stipulating in its Article 52 (3) that Charter rights corresponding with those rights enshrined in the ECHR shall be the same in both meaning and scope (as a minimum level of protection that can be extended), the view to Strasbourg from Luxembourg — talking in terms of the courts' seats — was already essential. With Strasbourg now also integrating comparative insights from Luxembourg even without the case necessarily concerning an EU law related matter in the national context, this is an indispensable must. As the issue of data retention and mass surveillance by national authorities has been looked at intensively by both the CJEU and the ECtHR on numerous occasions, it is a good example to show this connection.

B. The relevant legal texts

For the EU it is noteworthy that beyond having a fundamental rights basis and several secondary law texts on data protection, there is also a separate mention of data protection as a fundamental right ("Everyone has the right ...") in Article 16 Treaty on the Functioning of the European Union ("TFEU"), which serves as legal basis for secondary EU rules on data protection.[24] Already in 1995, the then European Community enacted the Data Protection Directive 95/46/EC.[25] This general framework for data processing was based on the relevant Convention No. 108 of the Council of Europe — see below — and was later amended and supplemented by other legislative acts. Most relevant, for the sector of electronic communications networks and services a specific privacy-related Directive was added in 2002: the so-called e-Privacy Directive 2002/58/EC, which was significantly amended in 2009.[26] Specific legislation followed for the area of communications data retention, as will be shown below, and there

---

24. Cf. on this also Hielke Hijmans, *The European Union as Guardian of Internet Privacy: The Story of Art 16 TFEU*, Dordrecht 2016.

25. Directive 95/46/EC on the protection of individuals with regard to processing of personal data and on the free movement of such data (Data Protection Directive) [1995] OJ L281/31.

26. Directive 2002/58/EC of the European Parliament and of the Council of 12 July 2002 concerning the processing of personal data and the protection of privacy in the electronic communications sector (Directive on privacy and electronic communications) Official Journal L 201/37, as amended by Directive 2009/136/EC, [2009] OJ L 337/11.

were additional acts such as in the field of judicial and police cooperation.[27] More recently, as is widely known, the EU managed to reform its main data protection framework completely and replace the Directive by a Regulation, which is already in force and will be applicable as of 25 May 2018 in all Member States: the General Data Protection Regulation[28], which is complemented by a Directive for processing by authorities concerned with combatting crimes ("Law Enforcement Directive").[29] Beyond these two major elements of the reform, the third legislative act passed in parallel, Directive 2016/681[30], which regulates the collection and processing of PNR ("Passenger Name Records") data in the EU as well as the effective exchange of this information between the Member States, must be transposed into national law by 25 May 2018. Also, the e-Privacy Directive is subject to be replaced by a Regulation, which has been proposed by the European Commission in January 2017.[31] In that regard, it is worth highlighting that the CJEU issued an Opinion[32] on 26 July 2017 concerning the EU-Canada-PNR agreement, which will be further discussed below.

---

27. E.g. Council Framework Decision 2008/977/JHA of 27 November 2008 on the protection of personal data processed in the framework of police and judicial cooperation in criminal matters, [2008] OJ L 350/60 currently covers cross-border data that are being processed by Law Enforcement Authorities. But see also Regulation 2001/45/EC of the European Parliament and of the Council of 18 December 2000 on the protection of individuals with regard to the processing of personal data by the Community institutions and bodies and on the free movement of such data, [2001] OJ L 8/1 applied to data processing by (several but not all) EU institutions.

28. Regulation 2016/679 of the European Parliament and of the Council of 27 April 2016 on the protection of natural persons with regard to the processing of personal data and on the free movement of such data, and repealing Directive 95/46/EC (General Data Protection Regulation), [2016] OJ L119/1.

29. Directive (EU) 2016/680 of the European Parliament and of the Council of 27 April 2016 on the protection of natural persons with regard to the processing of personal data by competent authorities for the purposes of the prevention, investigation, detection or prosecution of criminal offences or the execution of criminal penalties, and on the free movement of such data, and repealing Council Framework Decision 2008/977/JHA, [2016] OJ L 119/89.

30. Directive (EU) 2016/681 of the European Parliament and of the Council of 27 April 2016 on the use of passenger name record (PNR) data for the prevention, detection, investigation and prosecution of terrorist offences and serious crime [2016] OJ L 119/132.

31. As *lex specialis* of Regulation 2016/679. European Commission: Proposal for a Regulation of the European Parliament and of the Council concerning the respect for private life and the protection of personal data in electronic communications and repealing Directive 2002/58/EC (Regulation on Privacy and Electronic Communications). COM(2017) 10 final, Brussels, 10 January.2017.

32. *Opinion 1/15* (CJEU, 26 July 2017) ECLI:EU:C:2017:592.

For the Council of Europe it needs to be underlined that the first major international binding treaty (for the ratifying States) concerning data protection was actually its Convention No. 108 for the protection of Individuals with regard to Automatic Processing of Personal Data of 1981.[33]

III. Framework for Communications Data Retention in the EU

A. The specific legislative acts

Under the general single market harmonization Article 114 TFEU as well as the above mentioned authorization in Article 16 of the TFEU[34] the EU has harmonized the laws of its Member States in the field of data protection in order to promote the establishment and the functioning of its internal market, which was used not only in general data protection terms with Directive 95/46/EC, but also specifically for the question of data retention: In 2006 the EU enacted Directive 2006/24/EC[35] ("Data Retention Directive"), which was later quashed by the CJEU in *Digital Rights Ireland*. It is worth noting that the original Data Protection Directive of 1995 permitted Member States to adopt derogating measures necessary to safeguard fundamental state interests such as "*national security*"[36], but there was no common data retention framework on EU level even after the e-Privacy Directive had been transposed by the Member States.[37] That Directive also contained a derogation provision for national schemes. Against the background of very diverse national situations concerning retention of communications data[38],

---

33. Convention 108 covers data processing by the judiciary and law enforcement authorities. (Convention for the Protection of Individuals with regard to Automatic Processing of Personal Data, Council of Europe, CETS No. 108, 1981). A modernized version of Convention 108 is supposed to be adopted in October 2018 (Convention 108+). In addition, Council of Europe Committee of Ministers Recommendation No. R (87)15 suggests a framework for the use of Personal Data in the Police Sector to the Member States.

34. See Art 114(1) TFEU.

35. Directive 2006/24 on the retention of data generated or processed in connection with the provision of publicly available electronic communications services or of public communications networks and amending Directive 2002/58, [2006] OJ L 105/54.

36. Article 13(1) Directive 95/46/EC.

37. Article 14(1) Directive 97/66/EC of the European Parliament and of the Council of 15 December 1997 concerning the processing of personal data and the protection of privacy in the telecommunications sector ([1998] OJ L 24/1) was the first explicit mention of data retention rules possible for the Member States. This was replaced by Article 15 of the e-Privacy Directive.

38. In 2004, 15 Member States did not have laws requiring data retention. Where such laws existed, in half of the cases, there were no implementing measures. In the other half, the scope

the Commission sought to harmonize this patchwork of data retention laws across the EU[39] and in 2005, submitted the proposal for a Data Retention Directive.[40] In consideration of the Madrid and London terrorist attacks[41], many governments of EU Member States seemed keen to intensify their surveillance structures[42] and therefore, the Commission sought to establish a European framework in order to avoid further disparity among the data retention schemes in the Member States and to use these schemes as preventive tool to fight serious crime and terrorism more effectively.[43] So although the motivation behind the proposal—which was adopted in the until then fastest legislative procedure for a Directive in the EU—was clearly linked to combatting terrorism, the legal basis chosen was to counteract obstacles to the functioning of the internal market.[44]

---

and periods of retention were highly disparate. See European Commission, Data Retention Directive, MEMO/05/328, europa.eu/rapid/press-release_MEMO-05-328_en.htm?locale=en.

39. The Commission initially followed the submission of the UK, France, Sweden and Ireland of a draft Framework Decision on data retention. See 'Statewatch News Online: EU: Data Retention Proposal Partly Illegal, Say Council and Commission Lawyers', http://www.statewatch.org/news/2005/apr/02eu-data-retention.htm.

40. Proposal for a Directive of the European Parliament and of the Council on the retention of data processed in connection with the provision of public electronic communication services and amending Directive 2002/58/EC, COD 2005/0182. The Commission submitted the Proposal albeit the Legal Service of both the EU Council and the Commission had previously indicated that former Article 95 (Article 114 TFEU) was the wrong legal basis and data retention not a First Pillar issue regulating the activities of service providers in the single market, but would effectively fall within the scope of former Third Pillar issues (Justice and Home Affairs), see: Conseil de L'Union Européenne: Avis du Service Juridique, LIMITE 7688/05, Brussels, 5 April 2005.

41. See for instance: 'Spain Train Bombings Fast Facts—CNN.com', http://edition.cnn.com/2013/11/04/world/europe/spain-train-bombings-fast-facts/index.html and '7 July London Bombings: What Happened That Day?—BBC News', http://www.bbc.com/news/uk-33253598.

42. At a time referred to as "heightened alert of imminent terrorist attacks", Directive 2006/24 was adopted shortly after the bombings in Madrid in 2004 and the attacks in the London in July 2005, see http://database.statewatch.org/article.asp?aid=6458. After the Madrid train bombings in March 2004, the "EU Declaration on combating terrorism" advocated the mandatory data retention across the EU. See: Council of the European Union 'EU Plan of Action on Combating Terrorism', LIMITE 10586/04, Brussels, 15 June 2004.

43. See The Hague Program on strengthening freedom, security and justice in the European Union [2005] OJ C53/1; European Council Declaration on combating terrorism, 7906/04 JAI, 100; European Council Presidency Conclusions of 16 and 17 June 2005, 10255/1/05 REV and Steve Peers, 'Background to the EU Data Retention Directive', http://eulawanalysis.blogspot.com/2014/04/background-to-eu-data-retention.html.

44. Case C-301/06, *Ireland v European Parliament and Council* (CJEU, 10 February 2009) ECLI:EU:C:2009:68.

Besides disagreements regarding the legal basis of the Data Retention Directive and whether an intergovernmental Framework Decision would have not been more appropriate to deal with this topic, there had been concerns regarding the interpretation of the term *"serious crime"* within the Member States' national laws[45], prior to the entry into force of the Data Retention Directive[46] and shortly after its implementation. These concerns turned out to be justified, when the Commission in its first evaluation report concerning the Directive had to admit that *"[m]ost transposing Member States, in accordance with their legislation, allow the access and use of retained data for purposes going beyond those covered by the Directive, including preventing and combating crime generally [...]"*.[47] The dissent concerning a definition of *"serious crime"* seems to have remained prevalent until today, even after the invalidation of the Data Retention Directive by the CJEU in 2014.[48] After that judgment several Member States repealed or changed their national data retention laws, in some cases they were annulled by national constitutional courts and in other States the laws were maintained or even newly introduced.[49] On the level of the EU, since the striking down of the Data Retention Directive, no new proposal in this direction has been made, which is why in the current situation the question is whether Member States' approaches to communications data retention is in line with applicable EU law.

---

45. Article 1 (1) states that "[...] *retention of certain data* [...] *for the purpose of the investigation, detection and prosecution of serious crime, as defined by each Member State in its national law"*.

46. Article 29 Working Party stated that *"The data should only be retained for specific purposes of fighting terrorism and organized crime, rather than with regard to any other undetermined "serious crime". This limited purpose should be also referred to in the title of the proposed Directive."* Opinion 4/2005, p. 8.

47. European Commission: Report from the Commission to the Council and the European Parliament: Evaluation report on the Data Retention Directive (Directive 2006/24/EC); COM(2011) 225 final. Brussels, 18.4.2011, p. 8.

48. Joined Cases C-293/12 and C-594/12, *Digital Rights Ireland Ltd* (C-293/12) and *Seitlinger* (C-594/12) (CJEU, 8 April 2014) ECLI:EU:C:2014:238.

49. For an overview of this development see e.g. *Reports section*, (2015) 1(3) EDPL 206 et seq..The UK, Sweden or France kept their national laws or increased additional obligations, while judgments of the Constitutional Courts in Austria, Czech Republic or German declared the national laws transposing the Data Retention Directive to be unconstitutional. Cf. Franziska Boehm and Mark D. Cole, 'EU Data Retention—Finally Abolished? Eight Years in the Light of Article 8', in: *CritQ, Critical Quarterly for Legislation and Law*, Volume 1, 2014, 1-78.

B. The CJEU on the Data Retention Directive

The CJEU has had several opportunities to decide on the retention of communications data, not only in the *Digital Rights Ireland* judgment when it struck down the Data Retention Directive. This legislative act had already been challenged before and even after its invalidity before the CJEU.

1) Ireland v EP *(2009)*

In 2006, Ireland's attempt to challenge the Data Retention Directive in case C-301/06, *Ireland v European Parliament*[50], in which the Irish Government held the underlying purpose of the directive to be a law enforcement purposes and not internal market matters, failed.[51] The Court solely scrutinized the legal basis of the Data Retention Directive and rejected the request for its annulment without any further assessment concerning the Directive's proportionality in relation to the alleged interference with the fundamental rights enshrined in Article 8 ECHR.[52]

2) Digital Rights Ireland *(2014)*

With the 2014 *Digital Rights Ireland* judgment[53], the issue of privacy and data protection became closely associated to citizens' fundamental rights within the Union's legal order.[54] The judgment followed the critical opinion by Advocate General Cruz Villalón from December 2013, in which he had already suggested to invalidate the Data Retention Directive on grounds of its incompatibility with the EU Charter[55], although opinion and judgment differ

---

50. Case C-301/06, *Ireland v European Parliament and Council* (CJEU, 10 February 2009) ECLI:EU:C:2009:68.

51. Case C-301/06, *Ireland v European Parliament and Council* (CJEU, 10 February 2009) ECLI:EU:C:2009:68, para. 83. See Elspeth Guild and Sergio Carrera, '*The Political and Judicial Life of Metadata: Digital Rights Ireland and the Trail of the Data Retention Directive*', 2014, https://papers.ssrn.com/sol3/papers.cfm?abstract_id=2445901, p. 4.

52. See Case C-301/06, *Ireland v European Parliament and Council*, AG's Opinion para. 81–86. See also para. 34 of the Court's Judgment.

53. Joined Cases C-293/12 and C-594/12, *Digital Rights Ireland Ltd* (C-293/12) and *Seitlinger* (C-594/12) (CJEU, 8 April 2014) ECLI:EU:C:2014:238.

54. For a detailed assessment of the judgment cf. Franziska Boehm and Mark D. Cole, 'Das EuGH-Urteil zur Vorratsdatenspeicherung und seine Folgen—Auswirkungen des Urteils auf Mitgliedstaaten, EU-Rechtsakte und internationale Abkommen', in: *Zeitschrift für Datenschutz*, 11/2014, p. 545–596.

55. Joined Cases C-293/12 and C-594/12, *Digital Rights Ireland Ltd* (C-293/12) and *Seitlinger* (C-594/12), Opinion of Advocate General Cruz Villalon (12 December 2013) ECLI:EU:C:2013:845.

somewhat in the reasoning. The CJEU explicitly held that "*Directive 2006/24 entails a wide-ranging and particularly serious interference with fundamental rights*"[56] and found that the "*general absence of limits in Directive 2006/24* […] *by which to determine the limits of the access of the competent national authorities*" was insufficient in view of the requirements of the Charter. In particular, the Court criticized that "*Directive 2006/24 simply refers,* […] *in a general manner to serious crime, as defined by each Member State in its national law*" and therefore lacked objective criteria to determine the limits of access to retained data.[57]

3) Tele2 *(2016)*

In the more recent *Tele2* case[58], the CJEU was asked to what extent national data retention laws were (still) practicable in light of the previous judgment. The court clearly uses this opportunity to remind that the findings in *Digital Rights Ireland* were meant to be of general nature and not only concerning the (invalidated) Data Retention Directive. Unsurprisingly, the verdict remains the same: the general retention of metadata from all subscribers of electronic communication services (i.e. bulk data retention) is a serious interference with data subjects' fundamental rights and not compatible with Articles 7 and 8 of the EU Charter. If national laws disrespect this standard by not fulfilling the list of conditions set by the CJEU on a narrow possibility of foreseeing communications data retention rules, then they are in conflict with EU law.

The CJEU found that only the fight against *serious crime* would allow for *targeted* retention and thereby set limits for national data retention obligations. According to the Court, such limits could be determined along a distinct geographical area where the commission or perpetration of *serious crime* would be probable. Moreover, the collection of data must be preceded by objective evidence in order to reveal a link to such crime and follow precise procedural standards. While the Court in *Digital Rights Ireland* had suggested potential criteria to permit retention of and access to retained data (therefore leaving some space for interpretation by the national legislators), after *Tele2* only *serious crime* may be a valid ground to grant access by competent authorities to

---

56. Joined Cases C-293/12 and C-594/12, *Digital Rights Ireland Ltd* (C-293/12) and *Seitlinger* (C-594/12) (CJEU, 8 April 2014) ECLI:EU:C:2014:238.

57. ibid., para 60.

58. Joined Cases C-203/15 and C-698/15, *Tele2 Sverige* AB (C-203/15) and *Watson* (C-698/15) (CJEU, 21 December 2016) ECLI:EU:C:2016:970.

data retained solely in an amount limited to what is strictly necessary for the purpose of crime prevention.[59] However, as previously in its *Digital Rights Ireland* judgment, the Court could not, due to its limited competence (in light of the lack of competency of the EU) to rule in the area of criminal law, clearly define the term *serious crime*.

4) The development in the Court's approach

While the CJEU avoided the discussion concerning fundamental rights issues in *Ireland v European Parliament*, not least because it did not need to rely on this aspect in that case, it used the opportunity when finally presented with another preliminary reference request by two Member State Courts to apply privacy and data protection rights in scrutinizing the validity of the Data Retention Directive. The main change between 2009 and 2014 was surely the entry into force of the Lisbon Treaty and with it the EU Charter becoming legally binding. Moreover, albeit not submitting requests for preliminary rulings before the CJEU on that issue, there had been several Member States' constitutional courts giving critical judgments concerning the national implementation acts of the Data Retention Directive.[60] Maybe not to be underestimated, the interest for privacy and data protection rights was fed globally by the Snowden revelations in 2013, which were incidentally, also mentioned in the *Zakharov* case of the ECtHR.[61] Therefore, although unexpected in its weight and fundamental position initially, when reflecting, it is not surprising that the cases in *Digital Rights Ireland* and *Tele 2* were decided by the Grand Chamber and that the latter took the opportunity to clarify the relevance of data protection rights in a digitalized communication environment. On a side note, however, one may want to point out that the judge rapporteur in both cases (as well as in the related *Schrems* judgment[62]) was the same judge originating from Germany where the fundamental right to data protection (or, as it is mentioned in the German context of automated processing, to "informational self-determination") has a very specific position.[63]

---

59. Joined Cases C-203/15 and C-698/15, *Tele2 Sverige* AB (C-203/15) and *Watson* (C-698/15) (CJEU, 21 December 2016) ECLI:EU:C:2016: para 115 and 125.

60. Elspeth Guild and Sergio Carrera, '*The Political and Judicial Life of Metadata: Digital Rights Ireland and the Trail of the Data Retention Directive*', 2014, https://papers.ssrn.com/sol3/papers.cfm?abstract_id=2445901, p. 5.

61. *Szabó and Vissy v Hungary* App no 37138/14 (ECtHR, 12 January 2016), separate opinions: 2. Legislature and judiciary: the Court should respect difference, p. 85.

62. Case C-362/14, *Maximilian Schrems*, (CJEU, 6 October 2015) ECLI:EU:C:2015:650.

63. Prof. Dr. Dr. Thomas von Danwitz is a judge at the CJEU since 2006 and president of the fifth chamber of the Court since 2012. The fundamental case of the Federal Consti-

In *Digital Rights Ireland* and *Tele2*, the CJEU specifically referred to numerous ECtHR cases, the most recent ones being *Roman Zakharov v Russia*[64] and *Szabó and Vissy v Hungary*[65]. This makes it worthwhile taking a closer look at these two cases, particularly, because the ECtHR in return made explicit reference to *Digital Rights Ireland* with regard to data retention for law enforcement purposes. Although both cases before the ECtHR dealt with mass surveillance and not data retention *per se*, the link established between the ECtHR cases and those before the CJEU is evident: "*The fact that the data is retained without the subscriber or registered user being informed is likely to cause the persons concerned to feel that their private lives are the subject of constant surveillance*".[66] The element of mass surveillance, oversight mechanisms as well as access requirements and notification of or remedies for individuals play a crucial role in all of these cases.

IV. Relevant Case law by the ECtHR on Mass Surveillance

The ECtHR is competent to hear applications of individuals in the Council of Europe Member States claiming that a State party to the Convention — by a legislative, executive or judicial measure — violated their rights as laid down in the ECHR. In the past two years, the ECtHR had the opportunity to continue its already existing case law on data retention and surveillance measures concerning communications of individuals.[67] The Court decided two major cases concerning issues of national mass surveillance measures shortly after each

---

tutional Court on the right to self-determination is the Census decision: BVerfGE 65, 1 (15 December 1983), p. 41 et seq., available at http://www.servat.unibe.ch/dfr/bv065001.html; unofficial English translation in Jürgen Bröhmer, Clauspeter Hill and Marc Spitzkatz (Eds.), '60 Years German Basic Law: The German Constitution and its Court. Landmark Decisions of the Federal Constitutional Court of Germany in the Area of Fundamental Rights', 2nd ed., Konrad-Adenauer-Stiftung Berlin 2012 / Ampang, Malaysia, available at www.kas.de/wf/doc/kas_32858-1522-1-30.pdf?121123115540.

    64. *Roman Zakharov v Russia* App no 47143/06 (ECtHR, 4 December 2015).

    65. *Szabó and Vissy v Hungary* App no 37138/14 (ECtHR, 12 January 2016).

    66. Joined Cases C-203/15 and C-698/15, *Tele2 Sverige* AB (C-203/15) and *Watson* (C-698/15) (CJEU, 21 December 2016) ECLI:EU:C:2016:970 para. 100.

    67. Franziska Boehm and Mark D. Cole, 'Data Retention after the Judgement of the Court of Justice of the European Union', study for the Greens/EFA Group in the European Parliament. Münster/Luxembourg, 30 June 2014, available at http://www.janalbrecht.eu/fileadmin/material/Dokumente/Boehm-Cole-data_retention-study-print-layout.pdf, p. 21–27.

other: In *Roman Zakharov v Russia* of December 2015 the Grand Chamber, and in *Szabó and Vissy v Hungary* of January 2016 the Fourth Section of the Strasbourg Court, responded to individual applications made under Article 34 of the Convention regarding violations of the right to respect for private life and correspondence according to Article 8 of the Convention.[68] Beyond the significant findings concerning these types of surveillance measures, the cases are noteworthy in view of the interplay between the ECtHR and the CJEU in relation to the right to privacy.

A. *Zakharov v Russia* (2015)

In *Roman Zakharov v Russia,* the applicant lodged a claim with the ECtHR alleging the Russian system of mobile telephone communication interception to be in violation of Article 8 ECHR and that, contrary to Article 13, the laws did not provide for effective remedies.

In its judgment, the Court first assessed the admissibility of the application by evaluating whether or not the applicant could claim to have been a victim of an Article 8 ECHR violation. The Court held that, although it was ordinarily not its task to review laws of Member States *in abstracto,*[69] in the field of secret surveillance this was exceptionally necessary and important to guarantee an effective control and supervision of secret surveillance measures.[70] Referring to its verdict in *Kennedy*[71], the ECtHR affirmed that the mere existence of a law allowing secret surveillance might cause an interference with a person's rights under Article 8 ECHR, depending on whether he or she would belong to a group that could possibly be targeted by such surveillance measures. Secondly, an interference with Article 8 rights would exist if there was no effective remedy available at domestic level for an individual suspecting that he or she was subject to secret surveillance.[72]

Furthermore, the Court assessed at length the proportionality test: whether or not the interference with the right to privacy of communications pursued a le-

---

68. This section of the paper is based on an extensive case note of both cases: Mark D. Cole and Annelies Vandendriessche, 'Case Note: From Digital Rights Ireland and Schrems in Luxembourg to Zakharov and Szabó/Vissy in Strasbourg: What the ECtHR Made of the Deep Pass by the CJEU in the Recent Cases on Mass Surveillance Roman Zakharov v Russia (App no 47143/06) and Szabó and Vissy v Hungary (App no.37138/14)', (2016) 2(1) EDPL, p. 103–107.

69. *Zakharov v Russia* App no 47143/06 (ECtHR, 4 December 2015), para 164.

70. *Klass and Others v Germany* App no 5029/71 (ECtHR, 6 September 1978) para 34.

71. *Kennedy v the United Kingdom* App no 26839/05 (ECtHR, 18 May 2010) para 124.

72. *Zakharov v Russia* App no 47143/06 (ECtHR, 4 December 2015), para 171.

gitimate aim and was necessary in a democratic society in accordance with Article 8(2). The Court acknowledged that national security is a legitimate aim, which can also be pursued by secret surveillance measures, but that laws foreseeing such measures must balance the interests of national security with rights of individuals, in particular, they must allow for sufficient review as a guarantee against abuse.

The Court found that all parties to the dispute agreed that the secret surveillance measures were provided in domestic law, and pursued the legitimate aim of protecting national security, public safety, and the economic well-being of the State, and of preventing crime.[73] However, the Court emphasised that the concept of *"foreseeability"* interpreted in the context of secret surveillance should mean that the law must clearly stipulate under which conditions secret surveillance measures may take place[74] and that the scope of discretion awarded to authorities carrying out surveillance measures must be provided by law in a clear manner.[75]

The Court proceeded by verifying the necessity of such a law in a democratic society along six aspects:

(1) accessibility,

(2) its scope of application,

(3) procedures for the examination, use, storage, communication, erasure and destruction of recordings,

(4) procedures for authorisation,

(5) rules on supervision of the carrying out of the measures and finally,

(6) procedures for notification and the availability of remedies under domestic law.

The Court found that according to these criteria, the framework of the Russian law did neither sufficiently protect individual rights, nor offer adequate safeguards against arbitrariness. Both the procedures for destruction[76] and the lack of clarity concerning the wide discretion granted to the trial judge for storage and erasure[77] were not justifiable under Article 8 ECHR. Moreover, the Court found that although interceptions must be authorised

---

73. ibid., para 237.

74. ibid., para 229.

75. ibid., para 230.

76. Allowing recordings to be stored for six months before being erased even if the person they concern was never charged with a crime.

77. *Zakharov v Russia* App no 47143/06 (ECtHR, 4 December 2015), paras 254–256.

by a court,[78] the scope of review by the Russian judges was very limited in practice.[79]

The Court further found the Russian surveillance regime to be particularly conducive to abuse, since it technically enabled the authorities to circumvent judicial authorisation and to directly access all communications data without needing to show mobile network providers an authorisation for interception.[80] In addition, supervision was not of a judicial nature but entrusted to supervisory bodies,[81] which lacked either independence[82] or the necessary powers and competences to supervise surveillance measures in the field of counterintelligence.[83] Even more, the Court found supervision under Russian legislation to be a particularly opaque process, far removed from public scrutiny.[84] Finally, under the Russian law no notification of the individuals subject to the surveillance measures was foreseen at any point in time.[85] The ECtHR emphasised that remedies are only available to those individuals having obtained information about the actual interception of their communications, after having been charged with a crime and did not consider these to be effective remedies.[86] The Court therefore found that Russian legislation concerning mass surveillance did not sufficiently protect individuals against arbitrariness and abuse,[87] went beyond what is necessary in a democratic society and thus, was in violation with the rights enshrined in Article 8 ECHR.

B. *Szabó and Vissy v Hungary* (2016)

In *Szabó and Vissy v Hungary*, two Hungarian nationals, staff members of an NGO critical of the Hungarian Government, lodged a claim with the ECtHR that surveillance measures conducted within the framework of antiterrorism under the Hungarian Police Act[88] violated Article 8 and lacked judicial control, also leading to a violation of Articles 6 and 13 of the Convention.

---

78. ibid., para 259.
79. ibid., para 263
80. ibid., para 270.
81. ibid., para 277.
82. ibid., para 279.
83. ibid., para 281.
84. ibid., para 283.
85. ibid., para 291.
86. ibid., para 298.
87. ibid., para 302.
88. Act no. XXXIV of 1994 on the Police, as amended by Act no. CCVII of 2011.

Such surveillance is conducted in accordance with the National Security Act[89] with two goals: the prevention of terrorist acts and the protection of national security on the one hand, and the rescue of Hungarian nationals captured abroad in the context of war or terrorism on the other. Surveillance measures have to be authorised by the Minister of Justice and can only be resorted to when the required intelligence cannot be gathered by other means. No particular rules indicate the circumstances under which this surveillance can be conducted. Its timeframe is 90 days, with the possibility of prolongation for the same period by the Minister, who is not informed of the results of the on-going surveillance when making this decision. Further, the authorities are under no particular duty to delete any irrelevant intelligence procured.

When the ECtHR in *Szabó and Vissy v Hungary* examined the admissibility of the application it based its assessment on the approach developed in *Zakharov v Russia*.[90] Since Hungarian law does not offer the option for individuals concerned by interceptions of their communications to lodge a complaint with an independent body, the Court deemed the application to be admissible. As far as an interference is concerned, the Court stated that these measure entail *"a menace of surveillance"*, necessarily threatening *"freedom of communication between users of the postal and telecommunication services"*.[91] The Court also recognised that the interference in the case at hand pursued a legitimate aim within the meaning of Article 8(2) ECHR by seeking to safeguard national security and preventing disorder.[92]

The Court then applied the six criteria used in *Zakharov* to assess whether the law in question meets the requirement of *"foreseeability"* by providing sufficient safeguards and being considered necessary in a democratic society. The Court reemphasised that foreseeability should not be interpreted as meaning that an individual must be able to know exactly when the authorities may intercept his communications since this would allow him to adjust his behaviour.[93] However, legislation must give an adequate indication to citizens of the conditions under which authorities may exercise their powers in the field of secret surveillance.[94] The Court found that the Hungarian legal framework inadequately protected individual rights and did not offer sufficient safeguards against arbitrariness, particularly with regard to the following aspects:

---

89. Act no. CXXV of 1995 on the National Security Services.
90. *Szabó and Vissy v Hungary* App no 37138/14 (ECtHR, 12 January 2016), para 36.
91. ibid., para 53.
92. ibid., para 55.
93. ibid., para 62.
94. ibid.

The Court was concerned by the wide range of persons which could be included in interception authorisations without a specific need to prove a relation between each person and the prevention of a terrorist threat.[95] This is potentially a blanket authorisation and suggests that such authorisations may go beyond what is *strictly* necessary in a democratic society and may lead to the unlimited interception of communications of *all* citizens.[96] Moreover, the broadly formulated provisions in Hungarian legislation were problematic since the ECtHR found that they would facilitate indiscriminate interception of private communications.[97] The fact that governments could establish detailed profiles of citizens' private lives based on the acquired data, further compounds this issue.[98] The lack of an *ex ante* judicial authorisation for interception was further considered to be problematic.[99] Given the technological capabilities of the authorities, proportionality in the framework of mass surveillance must therefore be limited to what is *"strictly necessary"*. At this point, the Court referred to the approach adopted by the CJEU in *Digital Rights Ireland*.[100] Strict necessity must be understood in this context as containing two elements: first, secret surveillance must be necessary for the protection of democratic institutions, and second, it must be necessary for the acquiring of *"vital intelligence in an individual operation"*.[101]

The Court held that Hungarian legislation did not foresee any notification to the individuals concerned by secret surveillance, preventing them from lodging a complaint if they were completely unaware of the measures[102] and rendering the complaint procedure irrelevant.[103] Moreover, the Court noted a lack of judicial control during the process of authorisation and application of the surveillance measures.[104] Supervision of surveillance measures is predominantly political, by the Ministry of Justice, which the Court believed not to be suited for assessing whether or not surveillance measures complied with the criterion

---

95. ibid., para 67.
96. ibid., para 67.
97. ibid., para 69.
98. ibid., para 70.
99. ibid., para 73.
100. Joined Cases C-293/12 and C-594/12, *Digital Rights Ireland Ltd* (C-293/12) and *Seitlinger* (C-594/12) (CJEU, 8 April 2014) ECLI:EU:C:2014:238 para 62. Cf. on this case comment by Tijmen Wisman, 'Privacy: Alive and Kicking' (2015) 1, *European Data Protection Law Review* (EDPL), p. 80.
101. *Szabó and Vissy v Hungary* App no 37138/14 (ECtHR, 12 January 2016), para 73.
102. ibid., para 86.
103. ibid., para 83.
104. ibid., para 75.

of *"strict necessity"* prior to granting authorisation, and not to be appropriate for verifying whether the means of secret surveillance engaged are in accordance with the aims pursued.[105] The Court emphasised that it was not necessary for *ex post* and *ex ante* control to be exercised by the judiciary, but at least one of the two to be a prerequisite for guaranteeing the rule of law.[106] In the case at hand, both *ex post* and *ex ante* control were attributed to the executive, more precisely the Ministry of Justice, and therefore could not offer sufficient guarantees for the protection of individual rights.[107] As a result, the ECtHR concluded that Hungarian legislation did not provide sufficient safeguards to protect individual rights and therefore violated Article 8 of the Convention.[108]

C. Consequences for Secret Surveillance Measures

In both *Zakharov v Russia* and *Szabó and Vissy v Hungary*, the Strasbourg Court acknowledged that the safeguarding of national security and public order as well as the prevention of crime[109] and even the protection of the economic well-being of a country[110], pursued through a system of secret surveillance measures, constituted legitimate aims of that legislation within the meaning of Article 8(2) ECHR. Laws foreseeing these measures must nevertheless balance individual rights, and must, in particular, provide for review and effective procedural safeguards. The Court emphasised that the secret nature of surveillance measures should not stand in the way of an effective review, remedies must be *"practical and effective"*, rather than *"theoretical and illusory"*.[111] To know about such interference would be an even greater challenge considering the lack of notification requirements in both the Russian and the Hungarian legislations.

The manner in which the ECtHR dealt with the question of victim status in both these cases also demonstrates the Court's willingness to evaluate the mere existence of secret surveillance legislation as an interference with the rights protected under Article 8. In *Szabó and Vissy v Hungary* the Court referred to the current-day situation where many democratic States find their national security threatened by terrorism, and emphasised that situations of emergency

---

105. ibid., para 75–76.
106. ibid., para 77.
107. ibid., para 77.
108. ibid., para para 89.
109. ibid., para 55; *Zakharov v Russia* App no 47143/06 (ECtHR, 4 December 2015), para 237.
110. ibid., para 237.
111. ibid., para 288.

may render prior judicial authorisation of secret surveillance measures unviable due to the required urgency to act.[112] The ECtHR, however, also stressed that it is only willing to accept that such legislation may be necessary in a democratic society to protect national security *"under exceptional circumstances".*[113] The Court thus showed a very low tolerance for such legislation and has demonstrated in *Szabó and Vissy v Hungary* that it will evaluate its necessity strictly, leaving a very narrow margin of discretion for Member States party to the ECtHR. Moreover, generally justifying secret surveillance measures with the aim of combating terrorist threats is not possible and measures carried out according to urgency provisions should nevertheless be subject to *ex post factum* judicial review.[114] In other words, the Court stressed that an absence of judicial review for secret surveillance activities is unacceptable.

D. "Playing Ping-Pong" with the CJEU

In both cases, the European Court of Human Rights referred to the Court of Justice of the European Union and its judgement in *Digital Rights Ireland.*[115] Most directly, it did so in *Szabó and Vissy v Hungary* since the case concerned a Member State of the European Union. In the said case, the ECtHR held that mass surveillance with its potential for acquiring *"a detailed profile of the most intimate aspects of citizens' lives"* must be subject to enhanced requirements in order to guarantee the rights protected under Article 8 ECHR.[116] Although not all communications are automatically stored, as was the case under the EU Data Retention Directive, the fact that authorities have the technical means to plug into any conversation at any time makes it possible to refer to this type of surveillance as factually *"mass"* surveillance.

Yet, mass surveillance in the two ECtHR cases is of another category than the data retention considered in *Digital Rights Ireland,* since it concerns actual interception of the content of communications.[117] The assertion that the interception of content would possibly lead to a more serious infringement of the right to pri-

---

112. *Szabó and Vissy v Hungary* App no 37138/14 (ECtHR, 12 January 2016), para 80.

113. ibid.

114. ibid., para 81.

115. Joined Cases C-293/12 and C-594/12, *Digital Rights Ireland Ltd* (C-293/12) and *Seitlinger* (C-594/12) (CJEU, 8 April 2014) ECLI:EU:C:2014:238 para 62.

116. *Szabó and Vissy v Hungary* App no 37138/14 (ECtHR, 12 January 2016), para 70.

117. Franziska Boehm and Mark D. Cole, 'Data Retention after the Judgement of the Court of Justice of the European Union', study for the Greens/EFA Group in the European Parliament. Münster/Luxembourg, 30 June 2014, available at http://www.janalbrecht.eu/fileadmin/material/Dokumente/Boehm-Cole-data_retention-study-print-layout.pdf.

vacy was, however, weakened by the CJEU in *Tele2*[118] (see below in detail). In that case, the Court found that "*[e]ven if such legislation does not permit retention of the content of a communication and is not, therefore, such as to affect adversely the essence of those rights, the retention of traffic and location data could nonetheless have an effect on the use of means of electronic communication* […]".[119]

Another way in which the two ECtHR cases are similar to case law of the CJEU is that in *Zakharov v Russia*, just as in *Digital Rights Ireland*, *Schrems* and *Tele2*, private companies are used as instruments for State authorities to intercept communications. With *Zakharov v Russia*, the ECtHR laid down the standards secret surveillance legislation should live up to for an adequate protection of individual rights compliant with Article 8 ECHR. Although *Zakharov* did not constitute a precedent, the Court established a harmonized approach for introducing victim status in secret surveillance cases. The ECtHR developed a set of criteria for assessing the necessity in a democratic society of legislation foreseeing secret surveillance measures, which was developed into a more general rule in *Szabó and Vissy v Hungary*. From that, it can be deduced that the scope of action of Member States is significantly reduced when it comes to enacting mass surveillance legislation. In *Szabó and Vissy v Hungary*, the Court hinted that it will scrutinize mass surveillance legislation along even stricter standards of protection of individual rights in the future.[120] The Court therefore indicated the course it will be embarking upon, and implied the principles developed in *Zakharov v Russia* and in *Szabó and Vissy v Hungary* to be its starting point.

V. What's new in the EU? From the CJEU's *Digital Rights Ireland* to *Tele2*

On 21 December 2016, the Grand Chamber of the Court of Justice in Luxembourg handed down its eagerly anticipated *Post-och Telestyrelsen and Watson* judgment[121], a joined case following the request for a preliminary ruling from Sweden (*Post-och Telestyrelsen*, C-203/15) and the United Kingdom (*Watson*, C-698/15). In its judgment, the CJEU clearly rejected obligations im-

---

118. Joined Cases C-203/15 and C-698/15, *Tele2 Sverige* AB (C-203/15) and *Watson* (C-698/15), (CJEU, 21 December 2016) ECLI:EU:C:2016:970.

119. ibid., para 101.

120. *Szabó and Vissy v Hungary* App no 37138/14 (ECtHR, 12 January 2016), para 70.

121. Short title used hereinafter by the name of the provider that challenged the obligation imposed on it by the Swedish Telecom Regulatory Authority.

posing general data retention regimes on national telecommunication providers in order to allow access by LEAs for the purpose of crime prevention. The Court thereby went much further than Advocate General ("AG") Saugmandsgaard Øe in his opinion, in which the AG had established a list of requirements to be fulfilled for retaining data in a generalized manner.[122] The judgment should, however, not have come as a surprise: citing *Digital Rights Ireland* overall sixteen times in its *Tele2* judgment[123], the CJEU reiterated whole passages concerning the risk implied by the retention of and access to communications data for fundamental rights.

A. The application of Article 15(1) e-Privacy Directive as exception clause

With *Tele2*, the Court set clear limits for the derogations under Article 15(1) of the e-Privacy Directive, which had, after the invalidation of the Data Retention Directive, been used by some Member States as exception clause to introduce national laws governing data retention, in the assumption that those data retention schemes would fall outside the scope of the e-Privacy Directive. The said article allowed Member States to restrict the right to confidentiality of subscribers' communications for the purpose of national security, defense, public security, and the prevention, investigation, detection and prosecution of criminal offences, and permitted the adoption of legislative measures for data retention during a limited period.[124] Claiming that their national data retention schemes were for national security purposes and therefore *allegedly* not within the scope of either EU Law or the e-Privacy Directive, several Member States maintained the retention frameworks that they had introduced under the Data Retention Directive.

The laws in question before the Court obliged telecommunications providers to retain metadata of all subscribers that were transmitted through publicly available networks in a generalized and indiscriminate manner. Mak-

---

122. Opinion of Advocate General Saugmandsgaard Øe delivered on 19 July 2016 in Joined Cases C-203/15 and C-698/15, *Tele2 Sverige* AB (C-203/15) and *Watson* (C-698/15) ECLI:EU:C:2016:572.

123. Joined Cases C-203/15 and C-698/15, *Tele2 Sverige* AB (C-203/15) and *Watson* (C-698/15), (CJEU, 21 December 2016) ECLI:EU:C:2016:970, paras 92, 96, 98, 99, 100, 101, 102, 105, 106, 109, 118, 120, 122, 123.

124. Article 15 of Directive 2002/58/EC of the European Parliament and of the Council of 12 July 2002 concerning the processing of personal data and the protection of privacy in the electronic communications sector [2002] OJ L201.

ing no differentiation between criminals, suspects and those individuals that had never been suspected or convicted for a crime, the stored data were to be retained by the network providers in order to make them available for LEAs. The data to be stored by the telecommunications providers would be filtered by search engines and subsequently serve as basis for warrants and to gain access to the content of electronic communications.[125] Although the actual content of the communications was not to be retained at that stage, information concerning when, where, in what form, and to which contacts a communication took place was stored. So-called metadata, according to the Court, is therefore "*liable to allow very precise conclusions to be drawn concerning the private lives of the persons whose data has been retained*".[126]

The questions referred to the Court sought to clarify whether the derogations under Article 15(1) of the e-Privacy Directive, read in the light of the Charter, would allow for the general and indiscriminate retention of metadata for the purpose of fighting crime.[127] Furthermore, the UK Court of Appeal sought to ascertain whether the *Digital Rights Ireland* judgment would lay down mandatory requirements of EU law applicable to a Member State's domestic regime governing law enforcement access to retained data.[128] While the AG found that general data retention "*may be compatible with EU law* [if it is] *subject to compliance with strict requirements*"[129], the CJEU held that EU Law, and in particular the EU Charter, precludes the general and indiscriminate retention of traffic and location data from all subscribers of telecommunications services.[130]

B. Relationship between Article 1(3) and Article 15(1) e-Privacy Directive

In its answer to the first question in case C-203/15, the CJEU, other than the AG, provided a throughout analysis of the e-Privacy Directive's structure in order to assess whether general data retention obligations imposed on

---

125. 'Report of the Bulk Powers' *UK Independent Reviewer of Terrorism Legislation*,' (Review by David Anderson Q.C., Cm 9326 August 2016).

126. Joined Cases C-203/15 and C-698/15, *Tele2 Sverige* AB (C-203/15) and *Watson* (C-698/15), (CJEU, 21 December 2016) ECLI:EU:C:2016:970, para. 99.

127. ibid., para 62.

128. ibid., para 59.

129. Opinion of Advocate General Saugmandsgaard Øe delivered on 19 July 2016 in Joined Cases C-203/15 and C-698/15, *Tele2 Sverige* AB (C-203/15) and *Watson* (C-698/15) ECLI:EU:C:2016:572, para 116.

130. Joined Cases C-203/15 and C-698/15, *Tele2 Sverige* AB (C-203/15) and *Watson* (C-698/15) (CJEU, 21 December 2016) ECLI:EU:C:2016:970, para 125.

telecommunications providers would fall within the scope of EU Law. The Court, to examine the applicability of EU Law for general data retention obligations, first looked at the architecture of the e-Privacy Directive and distinguished between Article 1(3), activities that fall outside the scope of the directive and Article 15, derogations from data subjects' rights.

The CJEU admitted that the objectives pursued in those two articles would overlap substantially[131], but that Article 15 would presuppose the applicability of EU Law, as otherwise that article would be deprived of any purpose.[132] The·CJEU emphasized that the laws introduced under Article 15(1) of that Directive would therefore *not* fall outside the scope of EU data protection law (as some Member States had supposed), but were covered by the e-Privacy Directive. The Court further held that access to retained data by competent authorities would fall within the scope of that directive too[133], and that consequently both retention and access to data, would only be acceptable on the basis that they are *"appropriate"*, *"limited to what is strictly necessary"* and *"proportionate within a democratic society"*[134]. If the exception in Article 15 e-Privacy Directive would become a general rule, then Article 5 of that directive (right to confidentiality of communications) would become meaningless.[135]

Like in *Digital Rights Ireland*, the Court made clear that *"the retention of traffic and location data could [...] have an effect on the use of means of electronic communications"*[136], as it might give the users of electronic communication services the impression of constant surveillance, and could affect their way of communication and therefore, their rights enshrined in Article 11 of the Charter.[137] The interference entailed by the legislation in question with the rights enshrined in Articles 7 and 8 of the Charter must, according to the Court, be considered to be particularly serious and far-reaching.[138]

---

131. Joined Cases C-203/15 and C-698/15, *Tele2 Sverige* AB (C-203/15) and *Watson* (C-698/15) (CJEU, 21 December 2016) ECLI:EU:C:2016:970, para 72.

132. ibid., para 73.

133. ibid., para. 77.

134. See for instance para 95 of that judgment, Cases C-293/12 and C-594/12.

135. Joined Cases C-203/15 and C-698/15, *Tele2 Sverige* AB (C-203/15) and *Watson* (C-698/15), (CJEU, 21 December 2016) ECLI:EU:C:2016:970 para 89.

136. ibid., para 101.

137. ibid., paras 100, 101, 107 (see, by analogy, in relation to Directive 2006/24, Joined Cases C-293/12 and C-594/12, *Digital Rights Ireland Ltd* (C-293/12) and *Seitlinger* (C-594/12) (CJEU, 8 April 2014) ECLI:EU:C:2014:238, para 37).

138. ibid., para 100.

C. Requirements for Member States when implementing targeted data retention measures

The CJEU in *Tele2* confirmed that even in times of terrorist threats, Charter rights would not be subject to negotiation and that even *targeted* retention required objective evidence of *"serious crime"* in order to allow access by law enforcement authorities. It accepted, however, that there might be a need for having certain data available, such as in respect of *"a public whose data is likely to reveal a link [...] with serious criminal offenses, and to contribute [...] to fighting serious crime or to preventing a serious risk to public security."*[139]

Further, national laws providing for targeted retention would have to comply with EU data protection standards, lay down clear and precise rules, would have to be subject to minimum procedural safeguards and in any case *"meet objective criteria, that establish a connection between the data to be retained and the objective pursued".*[140] The CJEU unequivocally held that access to retained data by competent national authorities would presuppose prior review by either a court or an independent authority and that, for the sake of review and data security, data must be stored within the territory of the European Union.[141]

The Court therefore confirmed the line that it had provided in *Digital Rights Ireland* and went further by requiring objective evidence to allow both targeted retention and access to retained data. Furthermore, competent national authorities to whom access to retained data had been granted, were obliged to notify the data subjects concerned of the interference with their rights (as soon as such notification would no longer jeopardize the investigations) and to retain the data within the territory of the EU.

The Court reaffirmed that, because of the intrusiveness of traffic and location data, general and indiscriminate retention or access to retained data was contrary to EU Law. However, if Member States were to introduce provisions for *targeted* data retention, national legislation would have to provide the following safeguards:

(1) The purpose for retention would have to be limited to the fight against serious crime,

(2) Retention would have to be targeted to what is "strictly necessary" for the purpose of fighting serious crime,

---

139. ibid., para 111.
140. ibid., para 110.
141. ibid., para 114.

(3) Access to retained data would have to be subject to prior review by a court or an independent administrative authority,

(4) Data subjects would have to be informed of the interference with their rights as soon as possible, and

(5) Retained data would have to be stored within the European Union in order to guarantee the security of the data.

National legislation such as the one at issue would therefore exceed the limits of what is strictly necessary and could not be justified within a democratic society read in the light of Articles 7, 8, 11 and 52(1) of the Charter.[142]

With *Tele2,* the CJEU thus, continued the data protection and privacy friendly case-law that it had established in previous judgments and excluded the possibility for Member States to derogate from the principle of confidentiality of communications for national security purposes.[143]

VI. Comparing Standards: Strasbourg and Luxembourg

The patterns of all judgments from Strasbourg and Luxembourg as discussed above are reoccurring, although the cases before the ECtHR dealt with mass surveillance measures, whereas the CJEU decided on data retention legislation. Both Courts found the possibility for Governments to establish detailed profiles of citizens' private lives, or even just a potential for this, to be problematic where legislation did not provide for sufficient procedural safeguards to protect individual rights. Particularly the principle of proportionality in the framework of data retention and mass surveillance plays a crucial role in all of the Courts' judgments. Moreover, the Courts are critical about lacking *ex ante* authorization procedures and missing judicial control. Both the CJEU and the ECtHR require the notification of individuals concerned—even though obviously in the aftermath of a surveillance measure—in order to allow data subjects to make use of remedies and seek judicial review.

---

142. ibid., para 107.

143. 'CJEU Opposes General Data Retention Regime (Case Tele 2 Sverige)', in: *eucrim, The European Criminal Law Associations* Forum, 2016/04. p. 164.

A. The main points found by the ECtHR

Where the CJEU has, with the *Tele2* and *Digital Rights Ireland* cases, and connected to these the *Schrems* decision, narrowly limited data collection and storing activities based on EU law and in doing so used previous case law from Strasbourg to substantiate its interpretation of Articles 7 and 8 of the Charter, the Strasbourg Court explicitly (*Szabó and Vissy*) or implicitly (*Zakharov*) referred to the judgements of the CJEU when declaring national laws on mass surveillance incompatible with Article 8 ECHR. In coming to the conclusion that both the Russian and Hungarian legal framework constitute a violation of Article 8 ECHR, the ECtHR held several very important points:

Firstly, it tackled the problem of *"secrecy"* of laws when contemplating whether or not to accept the victim status of the applicant. Deviating from the general rule that the ECtHR does not examine legislation *in abstracto*, the Court accepted the applicant's claim since it considered it to be unacceptable that the secret nature of surveillance measures would deprive individuals of access to effective review. The Court therefore sees the mere existence of surveillance laws as a threat. Secondly, it developed a range of minimum safeguards of individual rights that must be provided by mass surveillance laws in order to ensure compliance with Article 8. It requires the legislature to provide sufficiently clear rules in order to avoid arbitrariness and abuse concerning the categories of people which are likely to have their communications intercepted, the duration of the measures, the procedures for storing, collecting and destroying data, the rules concerning the authorisation and supervision of surveillance, and the notification of surveillance measures connected to the availability of effective remedies.

Finally, the ECtHR took a strong position on the acceptability of mass surveillance in a democratic society, by making the remarkable observation that *"the risk of abuse is inherent in any system of surveillance".*[144] It emphasised that this risk is *"particularly high in a system where the secret services and the police have direct access, by technical means, to all mobile telephone communications".*[145] Some observers regard this as a *"heavy blow"* to the lawfulness of such measures and conclude that the Court showed its intention to contribute through its jurisprudence to the restriction of such regimes.[146]

---

144. *Zakharov v Russia,* para 302.

145. *Zakharov v Russia* App no 47143/06 (ECtHR, 4 December 2015), para 302.

146. Carly Nyst, 'European Human Rights Court Deals a Heavy Blow to the Lawfulness of Bulk Surveillance' (Just Security, 9 December 2015), https://www.justsecurity.org/28216/echr-deals-heavy-blow-lawfulness-bulk-surveillance/.

B. The CJEU's focus in the *Tele2* judgment

A similar approach was taken by the CJEU in both its *Digital Rights Ireland* and the *Tele2* judgments, where the Court held that the mere existence of general data retention schemes that did not differentiate between individuals who had committed a crime and those that were unsuspected, would be likely to cause the persons concerned "*to feel that their private lives are the subject of constant surveillance*".[147] In that line the Court also alludes to the (U.S. inspired) *chilling effects* doctrine in free speech law according to which already the knowledge of potential consequences will have a cooling effect on the willingness to utter e.g. critical statements of Government. Recent activities in some European States that are member to the Council of Europe make this fear seem very real.

The CJEU in *Tele2* followed the approach of the Strasbourg Court and required similar prerequisites to safeguard data subject rights, arguing that "[n]*ational data retention schemes imply the existence of provisions relating to access by competent national authorities, as the data is retained only for that purpose*".[148] Moreover, the Court found that the "*national legislation concerned must be based on objective criteria in order to define the circumstances and conditions under which the competent national authorities are to be granted access to the data of subscribers or registered users*".[149] The CJEU declared the only purpose for data retention to be the fight against *serious* crime, found *ex ante* authorization by a Court or independent authority indispensable for granting LEAs access to retained data, insisted on *ex post* notification provisions and remedies for individuals, and required retained data to be stored within the territory of the European Union.

These judgments demonstrate an aligning of standards between Luxembourg and Strasbourg irrespective of the current muteness between the two Courts on political level after the CJEU handed down its opinion on accession of the EU to the ECHR.[150] The ECtHR continued on the path traced by the

---

147. Joined Cases C-293/12 and C-594/12, *Digital Rights Ireland Ltd* (C-293/12) and *Seitlinger* (C-594/12) (CJEU, 8 April 2014) ECLI:EU:C:2014:238, para 37 and Joined Cases C-203/15 and C-698/15, *Tele2 Sverige* AB (C-203/15) and *Watson* (C-698/15) (CJEU, 21 December 2016) ECLI:EU:C:2016:970, para 100.

148. Joined Cases C-203/15 and C-698/15, *Tele2 Sverige* AB (C-203/15) and *Watson* (C-698/15) (CJEU, 21 December 2016) ECLI:EU:C:2016:970, para 79.

149. ibid., para 119.

150. Opinion 2/13, (CJEU, 18 December 2014) ECLI:EU:C:2014:2454.

CJEU in *Schrems*[151] where the entirety of the surveillance regime of a State was examined and was measured against fundamental rights standards.[152] The same approach was chosen by the CJEU, citing both recent cases on mass surveillance that had been handed down by the ECtHR.[153] The strict minimum standards set by both the CJEU and the ECtHR will be difficult for any European mass surveillance law to live up to.[154] Yet, in answering the second question referred by the UK Court in *Tele2*, the CJEU underpins its opinion concerning the EU's accession to the ECHR and even goes one step further by affirming that it is not bound to interpret EU fundamental rights in the light of the Convention, but that instead Charter rights might offer an even higher degree of protection, particularly with regards to the rights enshrined in Article 7 Charter.[155]

Irrespective of this consideration, in a time when, due to increased terrorist threats, the derogations under Article 15 (1) of the e-Privacy Directive and the CJEU's critical assessment concerning the question of establishing a satisfactory level of protection of personal data in *Schrems* are disregarded and when new surveillance measures are being introduced or existing measures more widely applied notwithstanding the CJEU's decision concerning the Data Retention Directive, the most recent judgments leave no room for doubt: (mass) surveillance and generalized data retention are supposed to be *exceptions, not a rule* and therefore laws widely allowing such measures are reversing the principle-exception-relation and are prone to be declared violating the ECHR and the EU Charter. This position has now been maintained in *Tele2*, where the CJEU highlighted that data retention for the purpose of crime prevention is required to be an exception under the e-Privacy Directive.[156] General and indis-

---

151. Case C-362/14 *Maximilian Schrems v Data Protection Commissioner* (CJEU, 6 October 2015) ECLI:EU:C:2015:650.

152. Paul De Hert and Cristobal Bocos , 'Case of Roman Zakharov v. Russia: The Strasbourg Follow up to the Luxembourg Court's Schrems Judgment', *Strasbourg Observers*, December 23, 2015, https://strasbourgobservers.com/2015/12/23/case-of-roman-zakharov-v-russia-the-strasbourg-follow-up-to-the-luxembourg-courts-schrems-judgment/.

153. Joined Cases C-203/15 and C-698/15, *Tele2 Sverige* AB (C-203/15) and *Watson* (C-698/15) (CJEU, 21 December 2016) ECLI:EU:C:2016:970 paras 119 and 120.

154. In the words of two commentators: *"the hunting has started"*, Paul De Hert and Cristobal Bocos , *"Case of Roman Zakharov v. Russia: The Strasbourg Follow up to the Luxembourg Court's Schrems Judgment"*, Strasbourg Observers, December 23, 2015, https://strasbourgobservers.com/2015/12/23/case-of-roman-zakharov-v-russia-the-strasbourg-follow-up-to-the-luxembourg-courts-schrems-judgment/.

155. Joined Cases C-203/15 and C-698/15, *Tele2 Sverige* AB (C-203/15) and *Watson* (C-698/15) (CJEU, 21 December 2016) ECLI:EU:C:2016:970 paras 126–133.

156. ibid. para 104.

criminate data retention of unsuspected individuals for subsequent access and use for law enforcement purposes is contrary to the rights enshrined in Articles 7 and 8 of the Charter, and not in line with the Article 8 ECHR requirements. Both Courts require a solid proof regarding the necessity of data retention and only allow such retention for the prevention of *serious* crime to avoid unnecessary data collection from unsuspicious persons.[157]

C. Comparison of the Courts' parallels in the context of data retention and surveillance

Both the ECtHR and the CJEU have, in their recent case law, irreversibly linked the two legal orders of the Convention and the EU Charter, and have opened the possibility to interpret the fundamental rights to privacy and data protection in a parallel way. This approach permits to derive conclusions made by the CJEU concerning data retention and to link these to comparable findings of the ECtHR. Both Courts established general principles for data retention measures that need to be taken into account when evaluating similar retention measures on national level.[158]

The repercussion from the Courts in Luxembourg and Strasbourg will certainly have an impact on respective legislation in those EU Member States that have introduced measures providing for data retention before the annulment of the Data Retention Directive with *Digital Rights Ireland*. German data retention law[159] for instance provides for shorter retention periods and maintained these laws or enacted new legislation on data retention than British or Swedish law, but also anticipates blanket retention measures without limiting storage to the fight against serious crime.[160] The Russian and Hungarian cases, but also the case of the UK DRIPA and the Swedish laws on data retention are convincing illustrations why these approaches by the

---

157. Franziska Boehm and Mark D. Cole, 'Data Retention after the Judgement of the Court of Justice of the European Union', study for the Greens/EFA Group in the European Parliament. Münster/Luxembourg, 30 June 2014, available at http://www.janalbrecht.eu/fileadmin/material/Dokumente/Boehm-Cole-data_retention-study-print-layout.pdf, p. 118.

158. ibid., p. 112.

159. Only passed at the end of 2015: Gesetz zur Einführung einer Speicherfrist und einer Höchstspeicherfrist für Verkehrsdaten, 10 December 2015. BGBl (Federal Gazette) 2015 pt. I No 51 (17. December 2015, p. 2218), https://www.bgbl.de/xaver/bgbl/start.xav?startbk=Bundesanzeiger_BGBl#__bgbl__%2F%2F*%5B%40attr_id%3D%27bgbl115s2218.pdf%27%5D__1497181933481.

160. 'CJEU Opposes General Data Retention Regime (Case Tele 2 Sverige)' in: *eucrim The European Criminal Law Associations* Forum, 2016/04,p. 164. Cf. also below at VIII.

ECtHR and the CJEU are necessary and it is to be welcomed that the Courts used their competence to clarify the incompatibility of such measures with rights under the ECHR and the EU Charter. Or, to put it in the words of the ECtHR itself: there has to be "a *European supervision*" because of "*the risk that a system of secret surveillance set up to protect national security may undermine or even destroy democracy under the cloak of defending it*".[161]

VII. Retaining other than Communications Data: The case of Financial Data and PNR Data for crime prevention

The above judgments on data retention should not solely be evaluated in relation to the retention of telecommunications data, but may be applied to other data retention regimes on EU level, which are to be assessed concerning their (in)compatibility with the standards set by the CJEU and by the jurisprudence of the ECtHR. Such regimes reach from financial data and PNR schemes to border management systems and immigration databases, all of which provide for mass collection and access by LEAs to data of unsuspected persons.[162]

Two areas, which will be considered as being important for the sake of this analysis—due to the long retention periods and the potential use of personal data for law enforcement purposes—are the fields of financial and PNR data.[163] These data allow to draw very detailed pictures of individuals' (travel) habits, credit worthiness and private lives, and may even include sensitive data. With financial data, it is possible to accurately conclude on the shopping behavior of a purchaser and to determine his or her exact location, as payments are easily traceable. PNR data, by means of automated processing, are being used to create detailed profiles of airline passengers to facilitate the establishment of risk assessments concerning potential perpetrators.

---

161. *Zakharov v Russia* App no 47143/06 (ECtHR, 4 December 2015), para 232.

162. For a detailed analysis of these databases with regard to the *Digital Rights Ireland* judgment, including their purpose, retention period and access requirements, Franziska Boehm and Mark D. Cole, 'Data Retention after the Judgement of the Court of Justice of the European Union', study for the Greens/EFA Group in the European Parliament. Münster/Luxembourg, 30 June 2014, available at http://www.janalbrecht.eu/fileadmin/material/Dokumente/Boehm-Cole-data_retention-study-print-layout.pdf, p. 73 et seq.

163. Cf. also case comment Bart van der Sloot, 'Is Tax Data Sensitive Data?—GSB v Switzerland App no 28601/11, ECtHR, 22 December 2015', (2016) 2(2) EDPL, p. 262–265.

The following section will give a brief overview of EU anti-money-laundering legislation currently under reform and shortly refer to ECtHR case law concerning retention of financial data for subsequent use by LEAs. The significance of PNR data will be discussed along the Opinion of the CJEU concerning the Draft Agreement between the EU and Canada on the transfer of PNR data, which the Court declared to be not compliant with EU data protection standards in July 2017.[164] The implications of the Opinion for the EU PNR data Directive[165]—the Directive concerning the collection and exchange of PNR data within the EU—and for the anticipated Entry-Exit System (EES)[166]—a Regulation that shall give the framework for data collection and use of third country nationals arriving at the EU's external borders—will not be covered by the analysis, as this would go beyond the scope of the discussion in this contribution.

A. The Issue with Financial and Bank Data

1. The significance of the Anti-Money Laundering Directive

Particularly with regard to terrorism financing, money laundering and tax evasion, data retention has become an important tool for LEAs. On EU level, the Fourth Anti-Money Laundering Directive[167] ("AML Directive") has been published in June 2015 and was supposed to be effective in all Member States from June 2017 onwards. In February 2016[168], however, the Commission issued a Communication laying down an Action plan for further strengthening the fight against terrorist financing and, on 21 December 2016, launched a

---

164. Opinion 1/15 on the background of the envisaged agreement concerning the transfer and processing of PNR data between the EU and Canada (CJEU, 26 July 2017) ECLI:EU:C:2017:592.

165. Directive (EU) 2016/681 of the European Parliament and of the Council of 27 April 2016 on the use of passenger name record (PNR) data for the prevention, detection, investigation and prosecution of terrorist offences and serious crime, [2016] OJ L 119/132.

166. Proposal for a Regulation of the European Parliament and of the Council establishing an Entry/Exit System (EES) to register entry and exit data and refusal of entry data of third country nationals crossing the external borders of the Member States of the European Union and determining the conditions for access to the EES for law enforcement purposes and amending Regulation (EC) No 767/2008 and Regulation (EU) No 1077/2011, COM/2016/0194 final—2016/0106 (COD).

167. Directive (EU) 2015/849 of the European Parliament and of the Council of 20 May 2015 on the prevention of the use of the financial system for the purposes of money laundering or terrorist financing, amending Regulation (EU) No 648/2012 of the European Parliament and of the Council, and repealing Directive 2005/60/EC of the European Parliament and of the Council and Commission Directive 2006/70/EC, [2015] OJ L 141/73.

168. COM(2016) 50 final, 2 February 2016.

proposal[169], aiming at complementing the provisions of the (revised) Fourth AML Directive.[170]

The fifth revision to the AML Directive tackles risks of terrorist financing linked to virtual currencies and anonymous pre-paid instruments, antici-pates a higher level of safeguards for financial flows from high-risk third countries, suggests centralized payment account registers[171] and seeks to en-hance the powers of EU financial intelligence units ("FIUs") and facilitating their cooperation with national counterparts.[172] Both the Fourth AML Di-rective and the proposed amendments aim at detecting illegal money laun-dering activities by requiring obliged (financial) entities to identify and verify their customers' identity, to monitor and to report suspicious transactions on money laundering to national FIUs.[173]

The new proposal would enable any person who is able to demonstrate a *"legitimate interest"* with respect to money laundering, terrorist financing, and associated predicate offences to access beneficial ownership registers. [174] The fifth revision to the AML Directive also seeks to extend the Directive's scope insofar as to cover trusts and similar types of legal arrangements, which were previously excluded from the scope. These trusts would then be obliged to meet full transparency requirements, including the need to identify beneficial owners. Moreover, virtual currency platforms would be included within the scope of the Fifth AML Directive, being required to fulfill the same customer identification obligations as banks.[175]

Currently, data processed under the AML Directive is protected under Di-rective 95/46/EC and will, from May 2018 fall within the scope of the GDPR. Access to financial data by competent LEAs for law enforcement purposes and

---

169. COM(2016) 826 final, Proposal for a Directive of the European Parliament and the of the Council on countering money laundering by criminal law, first proposed on 5 July 2016. The proposal is part of a Commission action plan against terrorist financing, announced in February 2016. It also responds to the "Panama Papers revelations" of April 2016.

170. Fifth revision of Directive (EU) 2015/849. The legislative procedure has started, The draft report was presented on 7 November 2016 and adopted by joint committee vote on 28 February 2017.

171. '[…] or central data retrieval systems in all Member States'.

172. 'Legislative Train Schedule', *European Parliament*, http://www.europarl.europa.eu/legislative-train.

173. 'Europe's upcoming Fourth AML/CFT Directive', *ACAMS Today.* December 2014-Februry 2015, p. 56 ff.

174. Recital (35), amendments to Article 31 of Directive (EU) 2015/849.

175. 'Legislative Train Schedule', *European Parliament*, http://www.europarl.europa.eu/legislative-train.

any subsequent processing for such purposes will be governed by Directive (EU) 2016/680; the "twin" of the GDPR.

The Fourth AML Directive pursues a *"risk-based approach"*, meaning that high-risk money transfers justify more privacy intrusive procedures, while less risky operations only permit privacy intrusive measures to a smaller extend.[176] Thus, entities that are subject to reporting obligations are expected to identify, assess and understand the money laundering process as well as terrorist financing risks they are exposed to.[177] This risk-based approach would be partly abandoned where the fifth version of the AML Directive introduces a new strategy, which would allow for emergency measures for the timely detection of illicit transactions. However, while timely detection and access to data would be crucial in the context of the prevention of terrorism, it may be less decisive for other crimes such as tax evasion and might disproportionally interfere with data subject rights.[178] One controversial term that is existent in both texts and not clearly defined is the provision concerning access to information regarding beneficiary ownership, which is, according to Article 30 (5) (c) of both versions, to be *"accessible to any person or organization that can demonstrate a legitimate interest"*.[179]

In his opinion from February 2017, the European Data Protection Supervisor ("EDPS") pointed to both matters, the departure from the risk-based approach and the wider access rights to beneficiary ownership information, acknowledging the imprecise purpose for data processing and expressing serious doubts concerning the Article 52 (1) Charter requirements, in particular the principle of proportionality.[180]

In relation to the proportionality principle, the EDPS further criticized the heterogeneous nature of entities involved in the processing of data, as well as the varying objectives of different data controllers that might jeopardize the

---

176. EDPS, 'Opinion 1/2017 on a Commission Proposal amending Directive (EU) 2015/849 and Directive 2009/101/EC. Access to beneficial ownership information and data protection implications'. EDPS, 2 February 2017, https://edps.europa.eu/sites/edp/files/publication/17-02-02_opinion_aml_en.pdf.

177. Steve Peers, '*The New EU Anti-Money Laundering Legal Framework: The Race Has Started Again* …', http://eulawanalysis.blogspot.com/2015/09/the-new-eu-anti-money-laundering-legal.html.

178. EDPS, 'Opinion 1/2017 on a Commission Proposal amending Directive (EU) 2015/849 and Directive 2009/101/EC. Access to beneficial ownership information and data protection implications'. EDPS, 2 February 2017, https://edps.europa.eu/sites/edp/files/publication/17-02-02_opinion_aml_en.pdf, p. 12.

179. ibid.

180. ibid., p. 11.

principle of purpose limitation.[181] The EDPS further highlighted the drawbacks of strengthened FIU discretion under the proposed amendments to the Fourth AML Directive, which would no longer require FUIs to obtain additional information on suspicious transactions in order to get access to information, but permit access merely based on the FIUs' own analysis and without demonstrating prior reporting on suspicion. According to the EDPS, such methods would be comparable to data mining and turn the investigative-based role of FIUs into an intelligence-based one.[182]

The proposed amendment to the AML Directive follows the path of the previous text but obliges more entities to fight money laundering, expands the category of suspected persons, and adds more offences to the scope of the Fourth AML Directive.[183] Both the Fourth AML Directive, but particularly the amended version therefore raise questions regarding their compatibility with the fundamental rights to privacy and data protection.

2. Relevant Case law of the ECtHR on Financial Data

While on EU level, the CJEU has not yet had the opportunity to review Articles 7 and 8 rights related to financial data, the ECtHR has in three recent judgments[184] ruled on Article 8 ECHR infringements emerging from the disclosure of and access to financial data of individuals not being (directly) linked to criminal offences.

In *M.N. and others v. San Marino*[185] the applicants lodged a complaint alleging that their right to privacy had been violated by a seizure of documents concerning their bank data without a suspicion of criminal offences committed by them.[186] The applicants claimed that the investigating authorities had virtually

---

181. ibid., p. 12, para 49.

182. ibid., p. 12, para 52.

183. Alexandre Met-Domestici, 'The Fight against Money Laundering in the EU. The Framework Set by the Fourth Directive and Its Proposed Enhancements'. In: *eucrim The European Criminal Law Associations* Forum, 2016/04, p. 171.

184. *M.N. and others v. San Marino* App no 28005/12 (ECtHR, 7 October 2015); *Brito Ferrinho Bexiga Villa-Nova v. Portugal* App no 69436/10 (ECtHR, 1 December 2015) and *Sommer v. Germany* App no 73607/13 (ECtHR, 27 April 2017). Cf. also *GSB v Switzerland* App no 28601/11 (ECtHR, 22 December 2015). Also see Bart van der Sloot, 'Is the Human Rights Framework Still Fit for the Big Data Era? A Discussion of the ECtHR's Case Law on Privacy Violations Arising from Surveillance Activities'. In: Gutwirth S., Leenes R., De Hert P. (eds): '*Data Protection on the Move*', Dordrecht 2016.

185. *M.N. and others v. San Marino* App no 28005/12 (ECtHR, 7 October 2015).

186. ibid., para 12.

unlimited discretion in order to identify which documents should be seized[187], that they had not been notified about the measures against them and that the interference had not been proportionate as there was no pressing need of general interest to justify the seizure.[188]

The ECtHR considered that the interference in the case was *"prescribed by law […] which provided for an exception to the right of banking secrecy precisely in the context of measures taken by judicial authorities in criminal proceedings.*[189] However, the Court noted that the applicants only became officially aware of the seizure and its implementation following a notification more than one year after the investigation measure had been ordered.[190] Moreover, the applicants did not have available to them the *"effective control"* to which citizens are entitled under the rule of law and which would have been capable of restricting the interference in question to what was *"necessary in a democratic society"*.[191] According to the Court, the wide nature of the seizure, the delayed notification of the applicants and the lack of effective control led to a violation of Article 8 ECHR.[192]

The ECtHR decided in a similar way in the case *Brito Ferrinho Bexiga Villa-Nova v. Portugal,* when a lawyer claimed that her professional secrecy, and with that her right to privacy, had been violated by access to her bank data due to a suspicion of tax evasion. In that case, the Court held that Mrs Brito Ferrinho Bexiga Villa-Nova had been unable to present her arguments during the national proceedings against her and found that the requirement of *"effective control"* laid down in Article 8 of the Convention had not been ensured. In view of the absence of procedural safeguards and an effective judicial review of the procedure, the Court found that the Portuguese authorities did not strike a fair balance between the requirements of the public interest and the protection of the applicant's right to privacy, and concluded that there had been an Article 8 violation.[193]

In the most recent case concerning access to financial data that was decided before the ECtHR in April 2017[194], *Sommer v. Germany,* the Court had to deal

---

187. ibid., para 58.
188. ibid., para 59.
189. ibid., para 74.
190. ibid., para 79.
191. ibid.
192. ibid., para 85.
193. Press Release Chamber judgments; *Brito Ferrinho Bexiga Villa-Nova v. Portugal* App no 69436/10. ECtHR, Strasbourg, 1 December 2015.
194. *Sommer v. Germany* App no 73607/13 (ECtHR, 27 April 2017).

with an Article 8 violation that concerned the collection and storage of information from the professional bank account of a defense lawyer succeeding a transfer that had been made to his account by one of his clients and which was suspected to have stemmed from illegal activities.[195] The applicant, Mr. Sommer, claimed that the wide range of information processed and the long period during which these measures pertained, allowed to draw a complete picture of his professional activities and provided detailed information of his clients.[196] Moreover, the information collected had been disclosed to an unknown number of people, although there had not been any criminal investigation opened against him.[197] The applicant acknowledged that the basis of the request for the collection of his bank data had been provided for by law, but argued that the interference had been disproportionate and not necessary in a democratic society.[198]

In its judgment, the ECHR stressed the wide scope of the prosecutorial requests for information, which concerned information about all transactions[199], and observed that the German Code of Criminal Procedure allows "*relatively low levels of interference as soon as there is a suspicion of a criminal offence,* […] *that the threshold for interference is relatively low* and *that the provision does not provide particular safeguards*".[200] The Court found the suspicion against the applicant rather vague and unspecific and argued that the only limitation for the information request was the period in question but that it "*otherwise concerned all information concerning the bank account*".[201] In the light of the low threshold for inspecting the applicant's bank account, the wide scope of the requests for information, the subsequent disclosure and continuing storage of the applicant's personal information, and the insufficiency of procedural safeguards, the ECtHR concluded that the interference was not proportionate, therefore not "*necessary in a democratic society*" and that there had accordingly been a violation of Article 8 of the Convention.[202]

---

195. ibid., para 3, 8.
196. ibid., para 37.
197. ibid., paras 38 and 39.
198. ibid., para 39.
199. ibid., para 57.
200. ibid., paras 58 and 60.
201. ibid., para 61.
202. ibid., para 63.

B. The Issue of Flight Passenger Data Transfer to Third Countries from the EU

1. *Passenger Name Records Exchange Agreement with Canada*

After the expiry of the 2006 Passenger Name Records ("PNR") Agreement between the EU and Canada[203] , the European Parliament, in the absence of an updated general framework for transfers of PNR data, adopted a resolution on the launch of negotiations for a renewed PNR agreement with Canada.[204] In 2013, the European Commission adopted the Agreement for Council Decisions on the conclusion and the signature of the agreement for the transfer of PNR data between the EU and Canada, and subsequently submitted the proposals to the EDPS to seek his advice. The proposed PNR Draft Agreement anticipated the systematic and continuous transfer of PNR data of all airline passengers travelling between the EU and Canada, and provided for retention periods of PNR data up to five years after an individual's stay in Canada. In addition, the Canadian authorities were permitted to transfer the stored PNR data to non-EU countries, all for the purpose of combatting terrorism and serious forms of transnational crime.[205]

The EDPS, in his Opinion of September 2013[206], criticized the agreement, questioning the necessity of bulk PNR data schemes and subsequent transfers to third countries. Moreover, the EDPS was skeptical towards the data protection safeguards, the proposed retention periods and the processing of sensitive data foreseen in the agreement.[207]

In 2014, the PNR Draft Agreement, negotiated by representatives of the EU and Canada, was signed (despite the reservations of the EDPS) and submitted to the European Parliament for approval. The latter, in order to ascertain the

---

203. Decision 2006/230/EC on the conclusion of an Agreement between the European Community and the Government of Canada on the processing of API/PNR data, [2006] OJ L 82/14). The agreement expired in 2009.

204. The resolution was adopted in May 2010, [2011] OJ C 81 E/70. See Opinion 1/15 on the background of the envisaged agreement concerning the transfer and processing of PNR data between the EU and Canada (CJEU, 26 July 2017) ECLI:EU:C:2017:592, para 14.

205. See the summary of the content in Court of Justice of the European Union, Press Release No 84/17, Luxembourg, 26 July 2017.

206. EDPS, 'Opinion of the European Data Protection Supervisor on the Proposals for Council Decisions on the conclusion and the signature of the Agreement between Canada and the European Union on the transfer and processing of Passenger Name Record data', EDPS, 30 September 2013, https://edps.europa.eu/sites/edp/files/publication/13-09-30_canada_en.pdf.

207. ibid., p. 10–11.

Draft Agreement compatibility with EU data protection standards, submitted a request for an opinion to the CJEU[208], questioning whether the Draft Agreement was in compliance with the provisions of the TFEU and of the EU Charter, and contesting the Draft Agreement's legal basis.

On 26 July 2017, the Court delivered its opinion, declaring that the EU-Canada PNR Draft Agreement may not be concluded in its current form[209], thereby generally following the line of the opinion of Advocate General Paolo Mengozzi of September 2016.[210]

In its answer to the questions submitted by the European Parliament, the Court identified several shortcomings with regard to the data protection standards envisaged by the Draft Agreement. However, the Court noted that the legal basis of such an agreement needs to be both Article 87 TFEU (judicial cooperation in criminal matters and police cooperation) *and* Article 16 TFEU (protection of personal data), whereas the Parliament had suggested that Article 16 would be the only valid legal basis for agreements of this type.[211]

Although the Court held that the processing of PNR data for the purpose of combatting terrorism and serious transnational crime was appropriate, and the interference with the fundamental rights enshrined in Articles 7 and 8 of the EU Charter justified by meeting an objective of general interest of the EU,[212] several provisions of the foreseen Draft Agreement were declared incompatible with EU data protection law. The CJEU found that the Draft Agreement was not sufficiently precise with regard to the data to be transferred to the Canadian authorities and did not clearly delimit the scope of interference with Articles 7 and 8 Charter.[213] The Court further held that the Draft Agreement was lacking a solid justification concerning the provisions for the processing of sensitive data, and

---

208. European Parliament resolution of 25 November 2014 on seeking an opinion from the Court of Justice on the compatibility with the Treaties of the Agreement between Canada and the European Union on the transfer and processing of Passenger Name Record data (2014/2966(RSP)), [2016] OJ C 289/2.

209. Court of Justice of the European Union, Press Release No 84/17, Luxembourg, 26 July 2017.

210. Opinion 1/15, Opinion of Advocate General Paolo Mengozzi (8 September 2016) ECLI:EU:C:2016:656.

211. Opinion 1/15 on the background of the envisaged agreement concerning the transfer and processing of PNR data between the EU and Canada (CJEU, 26 July 2017) ECLI:EU:C:2017:592, para 118.

212. ibid., paras 151, 153.

213. ibid., para 163.

therefore did not provide for sufficient safeguards concerning such data.[214] Moreover, the fact that data would be analyzed mainly by means of automated processing, thereby risking a high margin of error, required an individual examination by non-automated means in case the result of the processing would adversely affect a data subject.[215]

The Court, however, found that the Draft Agreement would not exceed the limits of what is strictly necessary regarding the transfer of data of *all* passengers to Canada. It argued that the Chicago Convention, to which all EU Member States are signatories, stipulates that all air passengers must comply with the laws of a contracting state and PNR data was processed as part of border controls in any case.[216] Furthermore, the use of data for border checks was acceptable as this would accelerate security checks and identify individuals who may present a risk to public security.[217] Yet, the use of personal data to combat terrorism and serious transnational crime, in order not to exceed the limits of what is strictly necessary, must be subject to prior review by a court or an independent authority.[218] Moreover, the retention of passenger data for up to five years after a stay in Canada was not necessary, except in cases where certain individuals would represent a risk as regards terrorism or serious transnational crime.[219] Only under such circumstances would the retention of PNR data for such a long period be acceptable, provided that independent prior review had taken place[220] and that rules laying down substantive and procedural conditions to protect the data in question against the risk of abuse would be guaranteed.[221]

The Court then referred to the possibility of transfer of PNR data by Canadian authorities to countries outside the EU, and stipulated that such transfers may only take place under the condition that the receiving third country would provide a level of data protection essentially equal to the level in the EU[222] and only

---

214. ibid., para 165.
215. ibid., para 173.
216. ibid., para 188–189.
217. ibid., paras 187, 197 and 199.
218. ibid., paras 201–203.
219. ibid., para 206–211.
220. ibid., para 208.
221. Court of Justice of the European Union Press Release No 84/17, Luxembourg, 26 July 2017, p. 2.
222. Opinion 1/15 on the background of the envisaged agreement concerning the transfer and processing of PNR data between the EU and Canada (CJEU, 26 July 2017) ECLI:EU:C:2017:592, paras 134, 214.

if an international agreement between the EU and that third country, or an adequacy decision[223] by the Commission concerning the respective State existed.[224]

Finally, the Court highlighted the importance of data subject rights to rectification and notification by the controller during their stay in Canada and after their departure.[225] In accordance with Article 47(1) Charter, data subjects must have the right to effective judicial remedy as soon as notification would no longer jeopardize ongoing investigations.[226] Moreover, oversight carried out by an independent authority to ensure compliance with data protection rules was imperative to guarantee data subject rights.[227]

2. Mass profiling but not mass surveillance

The Court relied on the *Digital Rights Ireland, Schrems,* and *Tele2* judgments in numerous passages of the PNR Opinion, thereby leaving no doubt that all decisions (including the most recent one) form part of the Court's strict interpretation of EU data protection rules. Referring to *Tele2,* the Court affirmed that derogations from and limitations to the protection of personal data should apply only in so far as they are strictly necessary[228], in particular, where sensitive data are at stake.[229] As noted in *Tele2,* legislation regarding data retention must establish a connection between the personal data to be retained and the objective pursued.[230] Further, access to stored data must lay down substantive and procedural conditions governing the use of that data.[231] Additionally, the processing of that data for an effective contribution to combating terrorism and serious transnational crime must not

---

223. The Council and the European Parliament have given the Commission the power to determine, on the basis of Article 25(6) of Directive 95/46/EC (Article 45 GDPR and Article 36 of Directive 20167680) whether a third country ensures an adequate level of protection by reason of its domestic law or of the international commitments it has entered into.

224. Opinion 1/15 on the background of the envisaged agreement concerning the transfer and processing of PNR data between the EU and Canada (CJEU, 26 July 2017) ECLI:EU:C:2017:592, para 214.

225. Court of Justice of the European Union Press Release No 84/17, Luxembourg, 26 July 2017, p. 3.

226. Opinion 1/15 on the background of the envisaged agreement concerning the transfer and processing of PNR data between the EU and Canada (CJEU, 26 July 2017) ECLI:EU:C:2017:592, para 220.

227. ibid., para 231.

228. ibid., para 140.

229. ibid., para 141.

230. ibid., para 191 and 207.

231. ibid., para 192.

exceed the limits of what is strictly necessary and requires prior review by a court or an independent authority.[232] Finally, at the end of the retention period, data must be destroyed irreversibly[233] and before that data subjects must be provided with the right to access their data, the right to rectification and the right to effective judicial remedy.[234]

Although the CJEU in the PNR Opinion cites *Tele2* as reference to these requirements, it seems as if the Court waters down the absolute prohibition of the "*general and indiscriminate retention of all* [traffic and location] *data*"[235], by proposing exceptions to that prohibition in cases where derogations may be justified by the objective of fighting terrorism and international crime.[236] For that purpose, the Court accepts data retention periods of five years[237] "*where there is objective evidence from which it may be inferred that the PNR data of one or more air passengers might make an effective contribution to combating terrorist offences and serious transnational crime*".[238]

One could claim that the mass data collection in *Tele2* had different dimensions, as air travelers generally and specifically to Canada are only a small part of the population and can choose not to fly to countries that (will) have PNR agreements with the EU. However, with the same logic, it could be argued that individuals can choose not to enter into a phone contract. The Court, however, did not seem to view PNR data retention and the automatic analysis of passengers' data as form of mass surveillance[239] comparable to the feeling of constant surveillance mentioned in *Digital Rights Ireland* and *Tele2*[240], although the EDPS had ar-

---

232. ibid., paras 202 and 205.

233. ibid., para 210.

234. ibid., para 220.

235. Joined Cases C-203/15 and C-698/15, *Tele2 Sverige* AB (C-203/15) and *Watson* (C-698/15) (CJEU, 21 December 2016) ECLI:EU:C:2016:970, paras 103 and 134.

236. Christopher Kuner, 'Data Protection, Data Transfers, and International Agreements: The CJEU's Opinion 1/15', *Verfassungsblog*, http://verfassungsblog.de/data-protection-data-transfers-and-international-agreements-the-cjeus-opinion-115/.

237. Opinion 1/15 on the background of the envisaged agreement concerning the transfer and processing of PNR data between the EU and Canada (CJEU, 26 July 2017) ECLI:EU:C:2017:592, paras 190–211.

238. ibid., para 201.

239. However, the Court refers to the use of PNR as "*intelligence tool*", see ibid., para 130.

240. Joined Cases C-203/15 and C-698/15 *Tele2 Sverige AB* (C-203/15) and *Watson* (C-698/15) (CJEU, 21 December 2016) ECLI:EU:C:2016:970, para. 100 and Joined Cases C-293/12 and C-594/12, *Digital Rights Ireland Ltd* (C-293/12) and *Seitlinger* (C-594/12) (CJEU, 8 April 2014) ECLI:EU:C:2014:238, para 37.

gued that *"the non-targeted and bulk collection and processing of data of the PNR scheme amount to a measure of general surveillance"*.[241]

With regard to the foregoing considerations, it might not be surprising that the CJEU did not apprehend the Advocate General's suggestion of following the standards adopted by the ECtHR in *Zakharov v. Russia* and in *Szabò and Vissy v. Hungary* regarding the targeting of individuals who might be under a '*reasonable suspicion*' of participating in terrorism or serious transnational crime.[242] In his opinion, the AG had referred to the ECtHR case law, applying the above cases to authorization for access to PNR data[243] , *ex ante* control in the case of disclosure, as well as transfers of data[244] and the control to be carried out by an independent authority pursuant to Article 8(3) Charter.[245] The CJEU in contrast emphasizes the need for PNR data and even accepted the risks emerging from analyzing passengers by means of automated processing, merely recognizing that *"the need for [...] safeguards is all the greater where personal data is subject to automated processing"*.[246]

With the Opinion, the Court missed the occasion to establish guidelines for technology-led techniques of profiling and other forms of automated data processing (for crime prevention). Particularly with regards to the forthcoming new data protection framework, this is unfortunate considering some of the ambiguities regarding the provision on profiling under the GDPR and the Law Enforcement Directive and the likeliness that these issues will therefore need to return to the CJEU for clarification.

Although the CJEU's Opinion is not binding on the European Parliament or the Commission, the Draft Agreement will have to be amended during the

---

241. EDPS, 'Second Opinion 5/2015 on the Proposal for a Directive of the European Parliament and of the Council on the use of Passenger Name Record data for the prevention, detection, investigation and prosecution of terrorist offences and serious crime', 24 September 2015, https://edps.europa.eu/sites/edp/files/publication/15-09-24_pnr_en.pdf, para. 63.

242. Opinion 1/15, Opinion of Advocate General Paolo Mengozzi (8 September 2016) ECLI:EU:C:2016:656, para 256. Cf. on this Maxime Lassalle, 'Opinion 1/15: AG Mengozzi Looking for a New Balance in Data Protection (Part I)', *European Law Blog*, 18 October 2016, 1, http://europeanlawblog.eu/2016/10/18/opinion-115-ag-mengozzi-looking-for-a-new-balance-in-data-protection/.

243. Opinion 1/15, Opinion of Advocate General Paolo Mengozzi (8 September 2016) ECLI:EU:C:2016:656, para 270.

244. ibid., para 302.

245. ibid., para 312.

246. *Opinion 1/15* on the background of the envisaged agreement concerning the transfer and processing of PNR data between the EU and Canada (CJEU, 26 July 2017) ECLI:EU:C:2017:592, para 141.

coming months in order to avoid its annulment after ratification. Moreover, the opinion will certainly have an impact on other PNR agreements currently negotiated and probably lead to the revision of the only recently passed EU PNR Directive.[247] As the EDPS noted prior to the ruling, *"[s]ince the functioning of the EU PNR and the EU-Canada schemes are similar, the answer of the Court may have a significant impact on the validity of all other PNR instruments"*.[248]

Other data sharing agreements such as the Privacy Shield between the EU and the US[249] , the SWIFT Agreement[250] or the above-mentioned EES will most probably also be affected by this Opinion of the Court.[251]

VIII. Looking ahead: Another Brick in the Wall (Part "No-Idea-How-Many-More")?

The implications of the *Tele2* judgment for legislation on EU and national level have been discussed by several working groups within the EU institutions, trying to find solutions on how to make data retention laws compatible with the CJEU's requirements.[252] Without a doubt, national laws stipulating the indiscriminate retention of all metadata will no longer be possible and violate the

---

247. Raphael Bossong, 'Passenger Name Records—from Canada back to the EU', *Verfassungsblog*, http://verfassungsblog.de/passenger-name-records-from-canada-back-to-the-eu/.

248. EDPS, 'Second Opinion 5/2015 on the Proposal for a Directive of the European Parliament and of the Council on the use of Passenger Name Record data for the prevention, detection, investigation and prosecution of terrorist offences and serious crime', 24 September 2015, https://edps.europa.eu/sites/edp/files/publication/15-09-24_pnr_en.pdf, para 18.

249. Pending Cases T-670/16 *Digital Rights Ireland v Commission* (21 October 2016) and T-738/16, *La Quadrature du Net and Others v Commission* (25 October 2016).

250. Agreement Between the European Union and the United States of America on the processing and transfer of Financial Messaging Data from the European Union to the United States for purposes of the Terrorist Finance Tracking Program, [2010] OJ L 8/11.

251. Steve Peers, *'Transferring Personal Data Outside the EU: Clarification from the ECJ?'*, accessed August 8, 2017, http://eulawanalysis.blogspot.com/2017/08/transferring-personal-data-outside-eu.html. Cf. further Mark D. Cole and Teresa Quintel, "Data Retention under the Proposal for an EU Entry/Exit-System (EES). Analysis of the impact on and limitations for the EES by Opinion 1/15 on the EU/Canada PNR Agreement of the Court of Justice of the European Union", https://www.greens-efa.eu/files/doc/docs/c1dc866168f947309cc1f26835a07c14.PDF.

252. See for instance: Discussions during an informal meeting of the justice and home affairs ministers on 26th and 27th January 2017, a Working Party on General Matters on 9 February 2017, the Presidency concerning the retention of electronic communication data on 1 March 2017 and 5 April 2017, the Working Party on Information Exchange and Data Protection (DAPIX) on 10 April 2017 as well as the different agencies, such as Eurojust.

benchmarks established first in *Digital Rights Ireland* and then in reinforced manner in *Tele2*.[253] In April 2017, the Working Party on Information Exchange and Data Protection ("DAPIX") of the European Council reflected on factors to be considered in order to adjust national legislation and make it compatible with the judgments along the limitations regarding the geographical area, the data retention periods and the oversight requirements stipulated by the Court.[254]

Member States, reluctant to give up their national data retention rules, are discussing on alternatives to legally retain metadata and preserve the possibility for LEAs to access and process such data.[255] The German data retention law, albeit not sufficiently clear as to prescribing geographical limitations, the number of subscribers potentially affected, or links to serious crime as prerequisites for retention requests, in its own view is regarded as being constitutional by the German Government, despite the pending examination of the *Tele2* implications.[256] This is all the more noteworthy as Germany originally was the only Member State that was without a transposition of the original data retention obligations resulting from Directive 2006/24/EC when this was declared void by the CJEU, because the German Constitutional Court had earlier struck down the national implementation law as unconstitutional.[257] Very recently, although only in an interim proceeding, a Higher Administrative Court has regarded the German law to be in violation of EU law and therefore declared it inapplicable until a final decision is reached.[258]

In the meanwhile, the competent ministries in several Member States discuss possibilities of surveillance of online messaging services such as WhatsApp,

---

253. Information Note from the Legal Service of the Council of the European Union on the *Tele2* Judgment and the Compatibility with EU law of national legislations on general data retention for the purpose of fighting crime, 5884/17, Brussels 1 February 2017, p. 6.

254. Council of the European Union: 'Reflection Process on data retention issues', 7597/17, Brussels, 5 April 2017.

255. For instance, the so-called "quick freeze" method. According to this method, communications traffic data is not retained preventively but only after a judicial warrant. Usually, providers delete data in a timely manner, but if they receive a warrant they would "freeze" the data currently held and from then onwards to make it available for law enforcement purposes.

256. Bundesregierung, '*Aktuelles, Regierungspressekonferenz vom 6. Februar*', https://www.bundesregierung.de/Content/DE/Mitschrift/Pressekonferenzen/2017/02/2017-02-06-regpk.html.

257. On the developments in Germany concerning the national data retention law cf. Christina Ettelbrück, 'Higher Administrative Court of Northrhine Westphalia Declares German Data Retention Law Violates EU Law', (2017) 3(3) EDPL, p. 394–398.

258. Ibid.

and push companies to weaken end-to-end encryption on their products.[259] In the UK there have been developments towards legislation to dismantle encryption in order to facilitate interception of metadata via secondary legislation to the Investigatory Powers Act (IPA), an amended version of the defeated DRIPA.[260] The different sections of the IPA that came into force from December 2016, expand the powers of the British intelligence agencies and lack notification rights for persons affected by privacy intrusions. On the other hand, the Act seeks to make the system more transparent and arguably established improved oversight and review mechanisms.[261] In Germany, possible amendments permitting the secret installation of software on suspects' smartphones to enable the reading of encrypted messages and access to archived data are being discussed.[262] Prosecutors would then be able to intercept mail communication, online messages or internet calls, and could retrieve information stored on the phone or even from within the cloud.[263]

On the one hand, proponents of data retention claim that in a world of big data and cloud computing, where the processing of personal data by companies is standard, it would only be logical that these data were also available to LEAs for the prevention of threats to public security. On the other hand, doubts regarding the effectiveness of general data retention measures remain. As has been shown by recent terrorist attacks[264] in countries where data was retained on a general basis, these incidents could not be prevented although the perpetrators were known due to prior investigations by relevant law enforcement and security agencies beforehand.[265] One could therefore ask the question whether it would have

---

259. 'UK Government Pushes for Companies to Weaken Encryption', *EDRi*, 31 May 2017, https://edri.org/uk-government-pushes-for-companies-to-weaken-encryption/.

260. 'UK Draft Investigatory Powers Bill: Missed Opportunity', *EDRi*, 18 November 2015, https://edri.org/investigatory-powers-bill-missed-opportunity/.

261. Cf. Lorna Woods, 'The Investigatory Powers Act 2016', (2017) 3(1) EDPL, p. 103–105 and Lorna Woods, 'Draft Investigatory Powers Bill', (2016) 2(1) EDPL, p. 103–107.

262. On the German situation cf. also Broy, Dominic, 'Extended Rights for the German Foreign Secret Service Concerning Data Recovery from the Internet Infrastructure', (2017) 3(2) EDPL, p. 226–228.

263. 'WhatsApp-Überwachung: Der Staat Wird Zum Hacker', *Tagesschau.de*, https://www.tagesschau.de/inland/whatsapp-ueberwachung-101.html.

264. Examples are the terrorist attack in Berlin on 19 December 2016, attack on the Champs-Élyées in Paris on 20 April 2017, attack in Manchester Arena on 22 May 2017, and attack in London on 4 June 2017.

265. Ian Cobain et al., 'Salman Ramadan Abedi Named by Police as Manchester Arena Attacker', *The Guardian*, 23 May 2017, sec. UK news, http://www.theguardian.com/uk-news/2017/may/23/manchester-arena-attacker-named-salman-abedi-suicide-attack-ariana--grande. 'Champs-Élysées Attacker Was Known to French Police', *France 24*, 21 April 2017,

been advisable to allocate available resources for the surveillance of persons which are suspected or established to be dangerous and not invest a lot of resources on using potentially available data of an entire population on a *"just in case"* basis.

In the near future, as mentioned above, the e-Privacy Regulation as *lex specialis* to the GDPR will repeal the e-Privacy Directive and, due to a broadened scope, also be applicable to so-called Over-The-Top[266] ("OTT") service providers.[267] The proposal does not include any specific provisions in the field of data retention and Member States are therefore free to maintain or establish national data retention frameworks that provide for targeted retention measures as stipulated in the *Tele2* judgment.[268] As that judgment blocked the creation of a legal basis to retain data on a general scale, it is highly questionable whether such a legal basis could be construed in national law (or, although this was not foreseen in the proposal anyway, by the e-Privacy Regulation itself). Any restriction of data subject rights deriving from the GDPR or the e-Privacy Regulation will have to be laid down in national or EU law, will have to be appropriate, proportionate and necessary in a democratic society. The e-Privacy Regulation will certainly change the work of LEAs, as the *Tele2* judgment will in the future also affect OTT-services providers, and metadata will be available to a lesser extent for LEAs than is currently the case.

At the same time, developments on EU level concerning cross-border access to electronic evidence for criminal investigations are ongoing. Because channels for cross-border access to electronic evidence indicate a number of deficiencies, the EU Commission is currently considering options to improve investigations

---

http://www.france24.com/en/20170421-france-paris-champs-elysees-attacker-chelles-known-police. 'Mutmaßlicher Attentäter Amri: Der meistgesuchte Mann Europas', *Frankfurter Allgemeine Zeitung*, 22 December 2016, http://www.faz.net/aktuell/politik/anschlag-in-berlin/nach-anschlag-in-berlin-anis-amri-war-der-polizei-bekannt-14587195.html. (Note that there was no general data retention regime in place in Germany at that time).

266. Over-the-top content (OTT) is the delivery of audio, video, and other media over the Internet without the involvement of a multiple-system operator in the control or distribution of the content. Examples of OTT Services include chat applications (WhatsApp, WeChat, Facebook Messenger); Streaming video services (Netflix, AmazonPrime, YouTube); Voice Calling and Video chatting services (e.g. Skype, Facetime). OTT service providers rely on IP based networks to reach customers.

267. Cf. Frederik J. Zuiderveen Borgesius et al., 'An Assessment of the Commission's Proposal on Privacy and Electronic Communications', Study for the European Parliament's LIBE Committee, May 2017, http://www.europarl.europa.eu/RegData/etudes/STUD/2017/583152/IPOL_STU(2017)583152_EN.pdf

268. European Commission, Proposal for a Regulation of the European Parliament and of the Council concerning the respect for private life and the protection of personal data in electronic communications and repealing Directive 2002/58/EC (Regulation on Privacy and Electronic Communications), COM (2017) 10 final, Brussels, 10 January 2017, p. 3.

into cyber-enabled crimes and to tackle problems of obtaining digital evidence in relation to criminal investigations.[269] The objective is the establishment of more effective mechanisms in order to obtain digital evidence, to improve co-operation with service providers, make mutual legal assistance more efficient and to propose solutions to the problems of determining and enforcing juris-diction in cyberspace.[270] The risks relating to data protection entail situations where access requests by EU Member States to third countries that do not have fundamental rights safeguards comparable to EU standards in place, could trig-ger reciprocity responses and might put at risk the data protection rights of EU citizens.[271]

In reality, the principles of data protection and privacy rights are difficult to reconcile with a world of "Big Data" on the internet and mass surveillance, particularly in the context of concerns over security threats due to terrorism. In a globalized world that is driven by technological developments and contin-uously changing social and economic constellations, the role of nation states is likely to change even more due to the influences by private entities.[272] Big Data by its very nature interferes with the core principles of data protection and privacy and, at the same time, Governments are under pressure to limit privacy and data protection rights by using internet data and extending their surveillance methods to avert threats to public security.[273] Therefore, it does not seem unlikely that LEAs and surveillance agencies will cooperate more with companies (also outside the European Union) in order to obtain data for their investigations.[274] At the same time there is a consistent move of courts on

---

269. European Commission, 'Technical Document: Measures to improve cross-border ac-cess to electronic evidence for criminal investigations following the Conclusions of the Council of the European Union on Improving Criminal Justice in Cyberspace', 19 May 2017, https:// ec.europa.eu/home-affairs/sites/homeaffairs/files/docs/pages/20170522_technical _document_electronic_evidence_en.pdf

270. European Commission, 'E-Evidence', Migration and Home Affairs, 7 February 2017), https://ec.europa.eu/home-affairs/what-we-do/policies/organized-crime-and-human-trafficking/e-evidence_en.

271. European Commission, 'Technical Document: Measures to improve cross-border access to electronic evidence for criminal investigations following the Conclusions of the Council of the European Union on Improving Criminal Justice in Cyberspace', 19 May 2017, p. 25 and 31.

272. Hooghe Liesbet and Marks Gary, 'Unraveling the Central State, but How? Types of Multi-Level Governance', American Political Science Review 97, no. 02 (2003), p. 233.

273. This can be seen e.g. in the press release/statement issued following a joint meeting of the ministers of the interior in Paris on 11 January 2015, http://www.ambafrance-mt.org/ Joint-statement-issued-following-a.

274. Hielke Hijmans, The European Union as Guardian of Internet Privacy: The Story of Art 16 TFEU, Dordrecht 2016., p. 112–113.

national level, but especially as demonstrated in this paper, on the European level to reinforce the fundamental rights protection in connection to data processing activities and being very critical of State actions.

There are further pending cases both in Strasbourg and Luxembourg[275] concerning communications data retention and transfer to third countries. Therefore, each of these cases might turn out to be a further ("another") brick—unclear on how many more to come—in the wall, to close with an even more famous track of that very Pink Floyd "The Wall"-album.[276] A wall stopping State measures as described above or elevating the height of difficulties to overcome in finding a privacy and data protection conform solution.[277]

---

275. See for instance: Case C-207/16, Request for a preliminary ruling from the Audiencia provincial de Tarragona, Sección cuarta (Spain), lodged on 14 April 2016—Ministerio Fiscal or Case C-475/16, Request for a preliminary ruling from the Protodikeio Rethymnis (Greece), lodged on 17 August 2016—Criminal proceeding against K (struck from the list after the CJEU requested the referring court to confirm it still upholds the reference in light of the Tele2 judgment and with no answer the CJEU assumed it is no more relevant) and a preliminary reference by the British Investigatory Powers Tribunal of 8 September 2017, *Privacy International v Secretary of State for Foreign and Commonwealth Affairs, Secretary of State for the Home Department, Government Communications Headquarters, Security Service and Secret Intelligence Service* [2016] UKIPTrib IPT_ 15_110-CH, cf. on this Teresa Quintel, 'Investigatory Powers Tribunal: Privacy International v Secretary of State for Foreign and Commonwealth Affairs and Ors Part II', , (2017) 3(3) EDPL (forthcoming).

276. 'Another Brick in the Wall' is featured as part 1, 2 and 3 on the Album, see footnote 2 supra, the most famous being part 2.

277. Since October 2017, when the manuscript for this article was submitted, amendments to and proposals for new legislative acts have been published by the European Commission and further important developments within the matter of this article have taken place. Just to mention a few, in October 2017, the EES was adopted (for an in-depth analysis of the Opinion, cf. Mark D. Cole and Teresa Quintel, "Data Retention under the Proposal for an EU Entry/Exit-System (EES)", above at Fn. 251); in April 2018, the Commission issued a proposal for a Directive to facilitate law enforcement access to financial data and to enhance cooperation between national FIUs (COM(2018) 213 final) and finally published a proposal on production orders of electronic evidence by internet service providers (and with this so-called e-evidence proposal almost concurrently, the U.S. CLOUD Act was ratified); in Case C-207/ 16, the AG issued his Opinion on 3 May 2018; the EU Data Protection Reform entered into applicability, and so did the PNR Directive; and the ECtHR handed down two very important judgments concerning surveillance and the conditions for accessing personal information when gathering of evidence (*Centrum för Rättvisa v. Sweden*, Application no. 35252/08 and *Benedik v. Slovenia*, Application no. 62357/14), as well as very recently the decision on surveillance data exchange in *Big Brother Watch v. UK*, Application nos. 58170/13, 62322/14, 24960/15.

Johanna Chamberlain and Jane Reichel

The Swedish Understanding of Privacy as a Fundamental Right in a Comparative Perspective — Overview and Possibilities

Swedish discussions regarding the right to privacy[1] are, in many ways, still at an early stage. In the midst of the complex process of getting to know the history, scope and legal consequences of privacy in Sweden, it is worth beginning slowly in order to appreciate differences between the privacy discourse in the EU and the discourse in the US. When working in a 'new' field that is highly dependent on international texts, cases and materials, it is tempting to import arguments from other countries or systems. However, are we always talking about the same thing? In this paper, a general comparison is made between the right to privacy as developed within the European Union, and the American concept of the right to privacy. The goal is to begin a discussion on what this European fundamental right means, and to contrast it with the American, civil liberty concept — or perhaps fundamental right? In particular, we wish to see how the right to privacy functions in these different legal settings, and thereby to see how a better understanding of these two systems can help lead us to new insights in a Swedish legal context. The survey will begin with a discussion of the terminology used in the field, and a brief background of the right to privacy as developed thus far in Sweden.

I. Concepts of Rights and Liberties at the Global Level

The concept of privacy is often vaguely defined, and differing trans-border conceptions of the right make it no easier to define the concept. In this

---

1. As 'privacy' is a term that encompasses many different aspects, physical as well as non-physical, the scope is narrowed here by focusing on the non-physical side of the concept: The handling of information relating to the individual.

section, a number of the key terms that are used will be analyzed. As will be described in detail below, the EU characterizes the right to privacy as fundamental. The fundamental nature of the right is indicated by the fact that the EU guarantees the right to respect for private life, as well as the right to protection of personal data, and both of these rights are articulated in the EU Charter of *Fundamental* Rights (EU Charter), articles 7 and 8, under "freedoms" as opposed to rights listed under the first category, "dignity". The concept of "fundamental rights" is closely linked to "human rights"—the latter being commonly perceived as rights that everyone is entitled to, just by being a human being. In the EU Charter, this distinction is made clear by article 52, which refers to the European Convention of Human Rights and Fundamental Freedoms (ECHR). Human rights are sometimes described as at the core of fundamental rights, i.e. the rights that are set out in the Universal Declaration of Human Rights, enacted by the United Nations (UN) in 1948. The right to privacy is (albeit in a somewhat limited and mainly physical sense) included in this non-binding declaration, in article 12. It can also be found in the ECHR's article 8, under "Rights and Freedoms". The convention draws no distinction between human rights and fundamental rights—nor does it, like the EU Charter, divide them into categories which involve protecting "dignity" and protecting "freedom" respectively. When the legally binding International Covenant on Civil and Political Rights (ICCPR) was developed by the UN in the 1960's, the right to privacy was protected in article 17. Frequently, human rights or fundamental rights are the terms used in international regulations—while civil rights are associated to citizenship. Nevertheless, if civil rights are viewed simply as rights granted by legal means, there is no reason why they should be geographically limited when the same regulation is adopted and applied in different countries. This is exemplified by the inclusion of the right to privacy in the ICCPR. Further, a classic description of the European and the American approaches to privacy provides that the former is focused on dignity, whereas the latter is primarily concerned with liberty.[2] Thus, privacy can also be described as a civil liberty. However, the absence of a division between the protected interests in the ECHR, and the placing of privacy under "freedoms" instead of under "dignity" in the EU Charter, seem to suggest that this classification is more useful in theory than in practice. Differences in the

---

2. Levin, Avner and Nicholson, Mary Jo, Privacy Law of the United States, the EU and Canada: The Allure of the Middle Ground, University of Ottawa Law & Technology Journal Vol 2, pp 382–390; Post, Robert, Three Concepts of Privacy, The Georgetown Law Journal Vol 89; Whitman, James, The Two Western Cultures of Privacy: Dignity versus Liberty, The Yale Law Journal Vol 113.

conceptualization of the right to privacy could perhaps lie in the *functioning* of that right. While the EU uses rights to implement EU law, and thus approaches them instrumentally, in the US the classification of a right as fundamental will make it a protected interest, and abridgments of that right would be subjected to a higher standard of judicial review. The effect of these distinctions, and their potential impact on development of the Swedish right to privacy, will be elaborated on in section IV and V.

II. A Slow Start: The Protection of 'Personal Integrity' in Swedish Law

The term 'privacy' (privatliv) has, for reasons that will be discussed below, traditionally not been favored in the Swedish legal landscape. Instead, we have used the reference 'personal integrity' (personlig integritet). The history of legislation protecting personal integrity can—without exaggerating—be described as rather patchy and somewhat reluctant. An early development can be found in the criminal law, and the constitutional law on the freedom of speech, where rules of defamation have been in force for centuries. The parallel in tort law, rules on economic compensation as redress for defamation, was introduced into the Swedish Civil Code of 1734 (that is, formally—informally these rules had already long existed as a "custom").[3] In the current general Damages Act[4] it is stated (chapter 2, §3) that certain criminal offences, including defamation, can lead to liability.

Apart from the law on defamation, nothing much happened on the Swedish personal integrity scene for a considerable amount of time. There are several reasons for this lack of action, at least from a legislative perspective. The laws on freedom of speech and freedom of the press had early origins, and were regarded as national characteristics, and therefore were accorded a high legal status. Consequently, when other legislation was created, it was designed in conformity with the authority of these rules. In constitutional and administrative law, there has long been a corresponding principle of transparency and openness that favours open public records, and challenges the existence of rules protecting personal integrity through, for example, the classification of information. The collectivistic, social democratic welfare state of the 20th century,

---

3. See, for a comprehensive genealogy of non-pecuniary damages in Swedish tort law, Friberg, Sandra, Non-Pecuniary Damages to Victims of Crime [Kränkningsersättning], Iustus, Uppsala, 2010, p 42 and pp 47–56; and of the defamation legislation Nelson, Law and Honor [Rätt och ära], Lundequist, Uppsala, 1950, pp 1–82.
4. Damages Act [Skadeståndslag, 1972:207].

with its focus on collective rights, has in this area traditionally trumped the individual interests in Sweden.[5] The rules still favor open public access to official documents,[6] with specific regulations—mainly the Public Access to Information and Secrecy Act[7]—providing exceptions.[8]

Another historical key to understanding the lack of attention paid to the legal protection of personal integrity is Scandinavian Legal Realism—a school of thought that was dominant with Swedish legal scholars for most of the 20th century. According to its founder, the philosopher Axel Hägerström, nothing can exist outside the natural context of time and space—meaning that immaterial things such as rights most certainly did not exist.[9] Of course, this way of thinking challenged most of what law, as a non-natural science, might encompass. This strong critique of judicial language and science shook the Swedish legal community of the time and has, among other things, resulted in a belated discovery of the—now so globally important—concept of rights.[10] Given this protracted legal trauma, it is not at all surprising that a right to pri-

---

5. However, it should be noted that an interesting and problematizing discussion regarding this statement has been initiated during recent years. Henrik Berggren and Lars Trägårdh argue throughout their book Is the Swede Human? [Är svensken människa?], Norstedts, Stockholm, 2006, that the radically collectivistic welfare state has in fact, paradoxically, ultimately enabled the Swede to become a highly autonomous individual. Their motivation for this conclusion is that a full system of social security makes it possible to live alone and be minimally dependent on other individuals around us, something that could never be the case in other, more individualistic societies. Berggren and Trägårdh have since met opposition, for instance in the historian Mattias Hessérus' dissertation The Right to Privacy [Rätten till privatlivet], Department of Historical Studies, Uppsala, 2016. Hessérus is of the opinion that the social and legal development of the 20th century has been strongly and truly focused on stately interests.

6. See chapter 2, § 1 of the Freedom of the Press Act [Tryckfrihetsförordningen, 1949:105].

7. Public Access to Information and Secrecy Act [Offentlighets- och sekretesslag, 2009:400].

8. Interestingly, the right to access to documents is not considered an individual right in Swedish law. The lack of remedies regarding the Government's or Parliament's refusal to release documents (chapter 2, § 15 of the Freedom of the Press Act) can thereby not be challenged under Article 6 ECHR, according to the Swedish Supreme Administrative Court, Judgment of May 16, 2017, case number 5670-16.

9. Samuelsson, Joel, Interpretation and Construction [Tolkning och utfyllning], Iustus, Uppsala, 2008, pp 301–301; Mindus, Patricia, A Real Mind, Springer, Dordrecht, 2009, pp 55–58.

10. See Schultz, Mårten, New Lines of Argumentation in the Property Law: Rights Arguments [Nya argumentationslinjer i förmögenhetsrätten: Rättighetsargument], Swedish Lawyers' Journal [SvJT] 2011, pp 991–994.

vacy has traditionally barely existed in Sweden.[11] This could also explain the decision to use the expression 'personal integrity' (as an 'object') instead of 'privacy' (which would perhaps be more natural to connect to a 'right', and thus more sensitive and risky).

III. Technological Development, International Impact and the Call for a Swedish Right to Privacy

Despite the continued existence of the Scandinavian Legal Realism, new technologies from the 1960's woke the Swedish legal community with a start and a discussion regarding personal integrity finally began. From this point the development was impressively rapid: changes were made in the Criminal Code introducing the crimes of eavesdropping, hacking and reading of others' mail. Further, a law concerning the handling of personal data was created—the first national act in the world on that subject!—was adopted in 1973.[12] The Data Act regulated the automatic mass handling of personal data and imposed damages for misuse (§23). This system was more or less replaced by the Personal Data Act,[13] which was enacted when the EU started to harmonize the legal area in light of the Data Protection Directive.[14] In the criminal law area, changes have been recently made to improve the protection of personal integrity against threats posed by the digital age, such as identity theft and offensive photographing.

Following decades of avoiding the sensitive and abstract subject of rights, and instead shifting the focus of legal discourse to the more accepted approach

---

11. The focus on the physical and tangible in legal discourse has resulted in various legacies. For instance, in tort law the development of non-pecuniary damages has been slow. Non-pecuniary damage has been seen as difficult to define, and courts have upheld a traditional principle of only awarding compensation for non-pecuniary damage as an exception, when there are clear legal rules to confirm the claim. (While the opposite is considered a general rule regarding pecuniary damage—no specific legislation is needed for compensation to be awarded.) On this legal development see Friberg, Sandra, Non-Pecuniary Damages to Victims of Crime, pp 347–350; Ekstedt, Olle, Non-Pecuniary Damages for Personal Injury [Ideellt skadestånd för personskada], The Legal Association, Lund, 1977, pp 38–43.

12. Data Act [Datalag, 1973:289]. The first regional data act was the Hessisches Datenschutzgesetz (The Hesse Data Protection Act), Gesetz und Verordungsblatt I (1970), 625, from the German state Hesse.

13. Data Protection Act [Personuppgiftslag, 1998:204].

14. Directive 95/46/EC of the European Parliament and of the Council of 24 October 1995 on the Protection of Individuals with Regard to the Processing of Personal Data and on the Free Movement of such Data (Data Protection Directive).

of 'objects' to protect through law (honour; personal data), the legal climate gradually changed in light of Sweden's international commitments. After becoming a party to the European Convention on Human Rights in the 1950s—and especially since its incorporation into Swedish law in 1995, the same year as Sweden's accession to the EU—the European version of reality overtook Scandinavian Legal Realism, and Sweden was obliged to engage with the European rights discourse. Moreover, while the EU legislation was initially premised upon the four economic freedoms of movement (of capital, persons, services and goods), fundamental rights have taken on an increasingly important role in recent decades.[15] In 2009, an obligation was introduced in the Treaty of the European Union (TEU) for the EU to accede to the ECHR.[16] At the same time, the EU Charter, enacted as a political document in the year 2000, became legally binding.[17] Since the rights expressed in EU law and in the ECHR also apply in Sweden, the EU concept of rights has been 'imported' more or less directly, without any real context or preunderstanding of rights rhetoric, into Swedish legal discourse. This is most probably one reason why the encounter has been complicated. The content of rights is perceived as unclear and is being constantly debated—and while this should be natural and unproblematic given that rights are *per se* dynamic and flexible, this idea is simply hard to accept given the Swedish realist tradition. In addition, the fact that rulings on the breach of rights started arriving from the European Court of Human Rights and the Court of Justice of the European Union (CJEU) came as an uncomfortable surprise. For Sweden—a country recognised as an equitable and flourishing welfare state—the legislature had presumed that ratification of the Convention was more or less a formality, and that the Swedish legislation was at least as generous regarding human rights as the ECHR.[18] This was, however, decidedly not the case.[19] The concept of "rights" have come to Sweden to stay—and we need to learn how to handle them. In the following passage the European, fundamental right to privacy will be discussed in further detail.

---

15. See Spaventa, Eleanor, Fundamental Rights in the European Union, in Barnard, Catherine and Peers, Steve (eds.), European Union Law, Oxford University Press, Oxford, 2014, pp 226–236, where the author explains how the fundamental rights were gradually developed by the CJEU.

16. Article 6.2 TEU. See also Protocol no 14 to the ECHR, Article 59.2.

17. See Article 6.1 TEU.

18. See preparatory work proposition 1951:165, p 11.

19. See Andersson, Håkan, Liability Problems in the Tort Law [Ansvarsproblem i skadeståndsrätten], Iustus, Uppsala, 2013, pp 551–552, on the transformation of this attitude over time.

IV. The European Approach to Fundamental Rights, Privacy and Data Protection

A. Individual Rights in EU Law—A Tool for Constitutional Effectiveness?

Individual rights have a different status and function in EU law as compared to Swedish law. From the beginning, the CJEU identified the role of individuals as rights recipients as being instrumental for achieving an effective implementation of EU law within the Member States. When the CJEU famously established the doctrine of direct effect in its 1962 *Van Gend en Loos* judgment, the court underscored the importance of the 'vigilance of individuals concerned' seeking to protect their European rights in the new legal order through judicial control.[20] The idea is that the EU provides individuals with rights, and if their national legislature is not able to convey these rights in an effective manner, individuals are entitled to turn to national courts who are obliged to guarantee the effective and uniform implementation of EU law at the national level.[21]

The doctrines of direct effect and supremacy, together with the preliminary ruling mechanism in Article 267 Treaty of the Functioning of the European Union (TFEU), has created a direct channel of communication between the national courts and the CJEU, entirely disconnected from the political branches of both the EU and the Member States.[22] These factors have enabled the EU to escape the implementation trap of traditional international law, and improved the chances of EU law being implemented at the Member State level.[23] In the words of Alex Stone Sweet, "litigants are understood to be fuelling the machine operated by judges".[24]

---

20. Case C-26/62 Van Gend en Loos v. the Netherlands, EU:C:1963:1.

21. The obligation is now codified in Article 19 TEU.

22. Andersson, Torbjörn, The Principle of Effective Legal Remedy: EC Law and National Sanctions and Procedural Law from a Swedish Civil Procedures Perspective [Rättsskyddsprincipen: EG-rätt och nationell sanktions- och processrätt ur ett svenskt civilprocessuellt perspektiv], Iustus, Uppsala, 1997, p 276. See also Arnull, Anthony, The Rule of Law in the European Union, Accountability and Legitimacy in the European Union, in Arnull, Anthony and Wincott, Daniel, (eds.), Oxford University Press, Oxford, 2002, p 242.

23. Harlow, Carol, Accountability in the European Union, Oxford University Press, Oxford, 2002, p 147 and Douglas-Scott, Sionaidh, Constitutional Law of the European Union, Longman, Harlow, 2002, p 225.

24. Stone Sweet, Alec, The Judicial Construction of Europe, Oxford University Press, Oxford, 2004, p 21.

The original EU Treaties did not contain any provisions regarding the protection of human rights, which initially resulted in some legal disputes between the CJEU and the national courts, not least the German constitutional court. After the CJEU judgment in the *Internationale Handelsgesselschaft* case, 1970,[25] and the response from the German constitutional court in its *So lange* case,[26] in which the supremacy of EU law was called into question due to a lack of clear protection of fundamental rights, the CJEU took upon itself the task of protecting rights within EU law. Based on the EU Treaties, European Convention of Human Rights and other international treaties to which the Member States have acceded, as well as the constitutional traditions of the Member States, the CJEU developed rather comprehensive protections.[27] Criticism has been raised that the case law is more concerned with defending the supremacy of EU law than actually protecting fundamental rights,[28] but that has to a large extent been accepted by the national courts and legislatures. Further, the case law of the CJEU formed the basis for the development of the EU Charter. According to Article 52.3 of the Charter, any right in the Charter that corresponds to rights guaranteed in the ECHR, must be given the same meaning and scope as in the Convention, unless it is given a more extensive protection. From the point of view of the CJEU, it is clear that the court does not intend to give up its right to have the final say on the interpretation of EU law.[29]

B. A European View on Privacy and Data Protection as Fundamental Rights

As stated above, both the ECHR, and the EU Charter include a right to privacy, Article 8 and 7 respectively, which guarantee everyone the right to respect

---

25. Case 11/70 Internationale Handelsgesellschaft v. Einfuhr- und Vorratsstelle für Geitrade und Futtermittel, EU:C:1970:114.

26. BverfGE 37, 321 [1974] 2 C.M.L.R. 540, Solange I (English translation).

27. Spaventa, Eleanor, Fundamental Rights in the European Union, pp 226–236 and Tridimas, Takis, The General Principles of EU law, 2nd edition, Oxford University Press, Oxford, 2007, p 298.

28. See for example the debate in Coppel, Jason and O'Neill, Aidan, The European Court of Justice: Taking Rights Seriously, Common Market Law Review Vol 29, p 669 and Weiler, Jason and Lockhart, Nicolas, 'Taking Rights Seriously' Seriously: The European Court and its Fundamental Rights Jurisprudence, Common Market Law Review Vol 32, pp 579–627. See also Prechal, Sacha, Competence Creep and General Principles of Law, Review of European Administrative Law Vol 3.

29. Opinion 2/13 of the Court on the Accession to the European Convention on Human Rights, EU:C:2014:2454.

for his or her private and family life, home and communications. In the case law of the European Court of Human Rights, it is established that Article 8 of the ECHR's protection of private life includes both the physical and psychological integrity of individuals, including what is commonly referred to as privacy.[30] The court has held that privacy is not subject to an exhaustive definition and embraces the right to the protection of personal data[31] and the protection of personal integrity.[32] As seen above, under Article 52.3 of the EU Charter, the case law of the European Court of Human Rights is relevant to the interpretation of the EU version of the right to privacy.

The EU Charter further includes a right to data protection, Article 8, which does not have a corresponding article in the ECHR.[33] Article 8 of the Charter states that everyone has a right to the protection of his/her personal data. The Article continues: "such data must be processed fairly for specified purposes and on the basis of the consent of the person concerned or some other legitimate basis laid down by law. Everyone has the right of access to data which has been collected concerning him or her, and the right to have it rectified."[34] Further, the EU legislature has enacted secondary legislation on the topic, most importantly the 1995 Data Protection Directive, that is to be replaced by the 2016 General Data Protection Regulation,[35] applicable as of May 2018. These acts include general rules governing the processing of personal data, directed to private and public organs alike, where the basic point of departure is that all processing of personal data must be lawful; that is, it must be processed under a specific legal basis listed in the statutory law.[36] Further, there is sector specific secondary legislation laying down prerequisites for handling personal data in

---

30. X and Y v. the Netherlands 1985 Series A no 91, p 11, para 22 and Slokenberga, Santa, European Legal Perspectives on Direct-to-Consumer Genetic Testing, Jure, Stockholm, 2016, p 157.

31. S and Marper v. the United Kingdom [GC] ECHR 2008-V, para 67.

32. Pretty v. the United Kingdom ECHR 2002-III, para 61.

33. Data protection is however guaranteed through the Council of Europe Convention for the Protection of Individuals with regard to Automatic Processing of Personal Data [1985] ETS 108.

34. In the final paragraph of the Article it is further stated that compliance with the rules of the Article are to be subject to control by an independent authority.

35. Regulation (EU) 2016/679 of the European Parliament and of the Council on the protection of natural persons with regard to the processing of personal data and on the free movement of such data, and repealing Directive 95/46/EC (General Data Protection Regulation).

36. Articles 6 and 7 of the Data Protection Directive and Articles 5 and 6 of the General Data Protection Regulation.

different fields, for example the e-Privacy Directive in regards to electronic communication.[37]

Under the case law of the CJEU, the rights to privacy and data protection are closely connected, and an unlawful processing of personal data can be considered a breach of privacy rights.[38] On the other hand, the CJEU has emphasized that the interpretation of Article 8 is to be seen as distinct from Article 7 of the Charter. In the *Tele2/Watson* case, the question was raised whether this expansive interpretation of EU data protection law would entail a breach of Article 52.3 of the Charter, and of the obligation to interpret the Charter in the light of the ECHR, where relevant.[39] The CJEU held:[40]

> Further, it must be borne in mind that the explanation on Article 52[41] of the Charter indicates that paragraph 3 of that article is intended to ensure the necessary consistency between the Charter and the ECHR, 'without thereby adversely affecting the autonomy of Union law and … that of the Court of Justice of the European Union'. In particular, as expressly stated in the second sentence of Article 52(3) of the Charter, the first sentence of Article 52(3) does not preclude Union law from providing protection that is more extensive then the ECHR. It should be added, finally, that Article 8 of the Charter concerns a fundamental right which is distinct from that enshrined in Article 7 of the Charter and which has no equivalent in the ECHR.

---

37. Directive 2002/58/EC of the European Parliament and of the Council of 12 July 2002 concerning the processing of personal data and the protection of privacy in the electronic communications sector. The directive is currently under review, see Proposal for a Regulation of the European Parliament and of the Council concerning the respect for private life and the protection of personal data in electronic communications and repealing Directive 2002/58/EC (Regulation on Privacy and Electronic Communications) COM (2017) 10 final.

38. In the case C-362/14 Schrems v. Data Protection Commissioner, EU:C:2015:650, para 94, the CJEU states "In particular, legislation permitting the public authorities to have access on a generalised basis to the content of electronic communications must be regarded as compromising the essence of the fundamental right to respect for private life, as guaranteed by Article 7 of the Charter. Reference to Article 8 is made when discussing the independent status of the national data protection authorities, para 99.

39. Joined Cases C-203/15 and C-698/15 Tele2 Sverige AB v. Post- och telestyrelsen and Secretary of State for the Home Department v. Tom Watson, Peter Brice, Geoffrey Lewis, EU:C:2016:970.

40. Ibid, para 129.

41. Explanations relating to the Charter of Fundamental Rights, OJ C 303, 14.12.2007, p 17–35, providing a background to the Articles of the Charter based on the preparatory works.

From the purposes of this article, it may be emphasized that the right to data protection has gained increasing importance and has developed into a both legal and political factor vis-à-vis the legislatures at both the EU and the Member State level, as well as in third countries. In the following section, some of the more salient case law of the CJEU will be presented.

C. Digital Rights Ireland, Google Spain, Schrems, Tele2/ Watson and Breyer

The CJEU has delivered a series of judgments in recent years in which data protection rights have been granted a prominent role in the legal order. The CJEU has interpreted specific data protection rules extensively, resulting in a wide application of data protection law, and it has attributed far-reaching consequences to breaches of the data protection rules, resulting in the invalidation of EU secondary law and the rejection of national law enacted to implement EU directives.

In the first category, concerning the broad application of data protection law, two cases should be mentioned, the *Google Spain* case[42] and the *Breyer* case.[43] The *Google Spain* case contains several interesting aspects of which two will be mentioned here. First, the CJEU made a broad interpretation of the concept of processing, namely the requirement that a person must handle personal data in a legally relevant manner[44] in order to be held responsible for breaching data protection rights. In that case, the CJEU found that the "activity of a search engine consisting in finding information published or placed on the internet by third parties, indexing it automatically, storing it temporarily and, finally, making it available to internet users according to a particular order of preference" was considered processing within the meaning of the Directive.[45] Google Spain was thereby responsible for processing personal data on its site. Second, the CJEU found that even a non-EU entity that has a relevant establishment within the EU, and whose data processing activities are 'inextricably linked' to that establishment, are to be considered within the scope of the Directive.[46] In this case, the display of advertising in the context of processing

---

42. Case C-131/12, Google Spain SL and Google Inc. v. Agencia Española de Protección de Datos (AEPD) and Mario Costeja González, EU:C:2014:317.
43. Case C-582/14, Patrick Breyer v. Bundesrepublik Deutschland, EU:C:2016:779.
44. Article 2 (b) Data Protection Directive.
45. Case C-131/12, Google Spain, para 41.
46. Ibid, para 56.

personal data through a search engine was deemed sufficient.[47] Because of these two interpretations, the scope of application of the Data protection Directive was widened considerably.[48]

In the *Breyer* case, the core question related to the possibility of identifying a person behind a dynamic IP-address. EU data protection law protects personal data, meaning data that can be related to an identified or identifiable person.[49] As explained in the judgment, a dynamic IP address changes each time there is a new connection to the internet, and unlike static IP addresses, dynamic IP addresses do not enable a link to be established, through files accessible to the public, between a given computer and the physical connection to the network used by the internet service provider.[50] A dynamic IP-address does not permit the operator of a website to identify the web-site visitor directly, but only if the information relating to his identity is communicated by the visitor to his internet service provider.[51] The CJEU found that a visitor to a web-site would be considered identifiable, other than if "the identification of the data subject was prohibited by law or practically impossible on account of the fact that it requires a disproportionate effort in terms of time, cost and man-power".[52] In addition, since there were legal channels available to web-site providers, in the event of cyber-attacks, to contact the competent authorities so that the latter could take the steps necessary to obtain information from the internet service provider and to bring criminal proceedings, it was not considered practically impossible to identify the website visitor, in this case Mr Breyer.[53] The threshold for identifying data as identifiable is accordingly set low, again ensuring a wide scope of application for the Data Protection Directive.[54]

---

47. Ibid, para 57. In an opinion regarding the case, the Article 29 Working Party Group holds the following; "the judgment makes it clear that the scope of current EU law extends to processing carried out by non-EU entities with a 'relevant' establishment whose activities in the EU are 'inextricably linked' to the processing of data, even where the applicability of EU law would not have been triggered based on more traditional criteria", Update of Opinion 8/2010 on Applicable Law in Light of the Court of Justice of the European Union Judgment in Google Spain, 176/16/EN WP 179 update, p 7.

48. Svantesson, Dan, The Google Spain case: Part of a Harmful Trend of Jurisdictional Overreach, EUI Working Paper RSCAS 2015/45.

49. Article 2 (a) Data Protection Directive.

50. Case C-582/14, Breyer, para 16.

51. Ibid, para 24.

52. Ibid, para 46.

53. Ibid, para 47.

54. Compare recital 34 in the preamble to the General Data Protection Regulation, on the conditions for genetic data to be considered identifiable; "Genetic should be defined as personal data relating to the inherited or acquired genetic characteristics of a natural person

The other three cases are listed under the heading, *Digital Rights Ireland*,[55] *Schrems*[56] and *Tele2/Watson*,[57] all of which concern different aspects of data surveillance regimes involving personal data. *Digital Rights Ireland* and *Tele2/Watson* deal with problems arising from general and indiscriminate retention of traffic and location data. Both cases related to directives regulating aspects of data retention, the Data Retention Directive and the e-Privacy Directive.[58] In the *Digital Rights Ireland* case, the CJEU found that the Data Retention Directive was invalid, since it did not "lay down clear and precise rules governing the extent of the interference with the fundamental rights enshrined in Articles 7 and 8 of the Charter."[59] The CJEU held that the purpose of the directive, the prevention of offences and the fight against crime, in particular organized crime, was an objective of general interest,[60] but the interference was not proportionate to the objective.[61] In the *Tele2/Watson* case, the Swedish and British legislation respectively, enacted in order to implement the e-privacy directive, was scrutinized in a preliminary ruling. The CJEU held that "general access to all retained data, regardless of whether there is any link, at least indirect, with the intended purpose [to fight serious crime], cannot be regarded as limited to what is strictly necessary".[62] The CJEU found that the general and indiscriminate retention of traffic and location data was contrary to the fundamental right of privacy and data protection under Article 7 and 8 of the Charter, as well as Article 11, on freedom of expression, and that EU law requirements

---

which result from the analysis of a biological sample from the natural person in question, in particular chromosomal, deoxyribonucleic acid (DNA) or ribonucleic acid (RNA) analysis, or from the analysis of another element enabling equivalent information to be obtained."

55. Case C-293/12 Digital Rights Ireland Ltd v. Minister for Communications, Marine and Natural Resources, Minister for Justice, Equality and Law Reform, Commissioner of the Garda Síochána, Ireland, The Attorney General, EU:C:2014:238.

56. Case C-362/14 Schrems v. Data Protection Commissioner, EU:C:2015:650.

57. Joined cases C-203 & C-698/15 Tele2/Watson.

58. The Digital Rights Ireland case handled the directive 2006/24/EC of the European Parliament and of the Council of 15 March 2006 on the retention of data generated or processed in connection with the provision of publicly available electronic communications services or of public communications networks and the Tele2/Watson case the e-Privacy Directive (Directive 2002/58/EC of the European Parliament and of the Council of 12 July 2002 concerning the processing of personal data and the protection of privacy in the electronic communications sector).

59. Case C-293/12 Digital Rights Ireland, para 65.

60. Ibid, para 44.

61. Ibid, para 69.

62. Joined cases C-203 & C?698/15 Tele2/Watson, para 119.

stemming from the interpretation of the directive and the Charter thus precluded such national legislation.[63]

The *Schrems* case addressed the requirements for transferring personal data between the EU and the US under the Safe Harbor agreement.[64] In addition, here, the case concerned the lack of legal delimitations on the processing of personal data by surveillance authorities, in this case the possibilities for generalized access and storage of the content of data transferred from the EU to the US. The Court's main criticism focused on the obligation for entities within the US to disregard the Safe Harbor principles, in the event "national security, public interest, or law enforcement requirements" so required.[65] As the Court rather laconically stated, the fact that US legislation permitted public authorities, such as the NSA, "to have access on a generalised basis to the content of electronic communications", this constituted a breach of the EU right to privacy as guaranteed by Article 7 of the Charter.[66] There is no legal basis in EU data protection law that would render such indiscriminate surveillance of personal data lawful. Further, the fact that the US legal system did not provide for any effective remedy for EU data subjects was contrary to Article 47 of the EU Charter and the right to effective judicial protection.[67] The CJEU thus found that the Commission's decision to enter into the agreement was invalid.[68]

D. Legislating for Humanity?

The question may be asked why data protection has come to be considered such an important fundamental right in the EU legal order. Why has the right been interpreted so broadly and why are breaches of the right considered so grave? For one thing, it may be considered that this is a fitting area for the EU to regulate, since the Member States do not have long-standing

---

63. Ibid, para 125. See further Cameron, Iain, Balancing data protection and law enforcement needs: *Tele2 Sverige and Watson,* Common Market Law Review, 54:1–28, 2017.

64. Commission Decision 2000/520/EC of 26 July 2000 pursuant to Directive 95/46 on the adequacy of the protection provided by the safe harbour privacy principles and related frequently asked questions issued by the US Department of Commerce (C [2016] 4176 final) (Safe Harbor Decision).

65. C-362/14 Schrems, paras 85–86, referring to Safe Harbor Agreement, Part B of Annex IV.

66. C-362/14 Schrems, para 94.

67. Ibid, para 95.

68. Ibid, para. 106.

traditions on data protection that may render a common understanding of rights more difficult. However, as will be discussed further in section VII below, even though ICTs and data protection first became an object of interest to the Swedish legislature in the 1970s, data protection rights have still been difficult to reconcile with the Swedish constitutional principle of openness, protected since 1767.

Whatever the reason may be, it is clear that the EU is determined to afford personal data strong legal protection within EU law. Accordingly, Svantesson has argued that the EU has the most influential and arguably strictest data privacy laws in the world.[69] As seen in the cases discussed above, EU data protection law not only applies to those who process data within the EU, but also to those processing data who have a connection to the EU[70] as well as to recipients of EU data after it is transferred out of the EU. In the preamble to the General Data Protection Regulation, it is clearly shown that the EU's ambition is grand; "the processing of personal data should be designed to serve mankind".[71] In line with this declaration, one of the architects of the GDPR, Jan Philipp Albrecht, a Member of the European Parliament and Vice-Chair of its Civil Liberties, Home Affairs and Justice, recently stated "it is paramount to understand how the GDPR will change not only the European data protection laws but nothing less than the whole world as we know it."[72]

Benvenisti has analysed the practice of states to unilaterally attempt to prevent or remedy collective action failures that produce global "bads" under the notion of "legislating for humanity".[73] Benvenisti refers to examples such as the early 19th century unilateral UK action ban on slave trading and the modern

---

69. Svantesson, Dan, The Extraterritoriality of EU Data Privacy Law—Its Theoretical Justification and its Practical Effect on U.S. Business, Stanford Journal of International Law Vol 50 p 55. See also Slokenberga, Santa, European Legal Perspectives on Direct-to-Consumer Genetic Testing, chapter 9.

70. The territorial scope of the Data Protection Directive (Article 4) and the General Data Protection Regulation (Article 3) is further very broad.

71. Recital 4 of the General Data Protection Regulation.

72. Albrecht, Jan Philipp, How the GDPR Will Change the Worlds, European Data Protection Law 3/2016, p 287.

73. Benvenisti, Eyal, The Future of Sovereignty: The Nation State in the Global Governance Space, in Research Handbook on Global Administrative Law, Cassese, Sabino (ed), Elgar, Cheltenham, 2016, p 492–493, with further references. See also Reichel, Jane, The Swedish Right to Freedom of Speech, EU Data Protection Law and the Question of Territoriality, in Lind, Anna-Sara, Reichel, Jane and Österdahl, Inger (eds.) Transparency in the Future—Swedish Openness 250 years, Ragulka, Tallinn, 2017, p 204.

US sanctions on public, private and even foreign actors who do not comply with US rules on human trafficking.[74] However, as recognized by Benvenisti, "when states 'legislate for humanity' or otherwise form policies that seek global standards, it is rather evident that they should bear in mind the impact of their policies on others, and that they should balance the other's interest against their own".[75] We will return to this question in section VI.

V. The American Right to Privacy—Civil, Constitutional, Fundamental?

A. Going West

To a Swedish researcher interested in privacy, the USA seems a natural place to turn. At least from an outsider's perspective, the legal discussion on privacy comes across as more established, open, refined and rich than its equivalent in Sweden. Whitman has described American law as being "obsessed with privacy".[76] This may not mean that Americans have reached the ultimate definition of what privacy is (although Westin's,[77] in different versions, is still probably the most used), but at least a clear starting point for the legal area and discourse can be found in Warren and Brandeis' ground-breaking article "The Right to Privacy". This seminal piece of work was published in the Harvard Law Review in 1890 and has—among countless other praise—been described as "the outstanding example of the influence of legal periodicals upon the American law".[78] In this section, the status of the fundamental right to privacy at the American constitutional level will be examined in a general manner.[79] The purpose is to identify which approaches for understanding and protecting privacy can be considered most useful in a Swedish context. First, a brief review of different classifications of the right to privacy will demonstrate the importance of these classifications in the USA.

---

74. Benvenisti, Eyal, The Future of Sovereignty, p 493.

75. Ibid, p 498.

76. Whitman, James, The Two Western Cultures of Privacy: Dignity versus Liberty, The Yale Law Journal Vol 113, pp 1157–1158.

77. "Privacy is the claim of individuals, groups, or institutions to determine for themselves when, how, and to what extent information about them is communicated to others." Westin, Alan, Privacy and Freedom, Atheneum, New York, 1967, p 7.

78. Prosser, William, Privacy, California Law Review Vol 48, p 383.

79. This means procedural rules and other conditions that can be seen as more peripheral to the substantive matter may be omitted or simplified.

B. Basic American Provisions

Having found earlier that any attempt to separate civil rights from human rights, and human rights from fundamental rights, on a global level is an all but easy task, let us turn to the American concept of the right to privacy. In the US, the decision to classify a right as "fundamental"—and not merely "human" (here "civil" rights or liberties appear to be the terms more frequently used[80])— is made after the court has examined the historical foundations and decided whether it has such a longstanding tradition that it deserves the higher status of being a fundamental right.[81] Which rights are considered fundamental can vary according to state, but the civil liberties that are listed in the US Constitution, especially its Bill of Rights, are all recognized as fundamental by the Supreme Court. States cannot infringe on fundamental constitutional rights through legal measures unless they can satisfy a "strict scrutiny" standard of review by the courts.[82] "Strict scrutiny" is the highest standard of judicial review used by the US courts. To pass strict scrutiny, the law or policy tested must be justified by a "compelling governmental interest", be "narrowly tailored" to meet the goal, and represent the "least restrictive means" for achieving the interest in question.[83]

When there is instead an issue of restricting a non-fundamental liberty, courts apply the lesser "rational basis test" under which they examine whether or not a law is "rationally related" to a "legitimate" government interest.[84] The classification of the right to privacy (or rather, different aspects of it) as constitutional and fundamental, or as "simply" a civil liberty, is therefore central to determining the level of legal protection that will be granted. This issue has long been debated between originalists and pragmatists[85] in the US Supreme

---

80. Meaning rights held by all people, as opposed to the "political rights" participants in elections are entitled to.

81. See *Washington v. Glucksberg*, 521 US 702 (1997) and *Chavez v. Martinez*, 538 US 760 (2003) on this assessment.

82. This line of ruling is based on the Fourteenth Amendment's (liberty clause) requirement of "due process" when infringing on rights, which has been awarded a far-reaching meaning regarding fundamental rights. See for examples the cases listed in the previous and following footnote.

83. See *Roe v. Wade*, 410 US 113, 155 (1973), with references to earlier cases gradually establishing the strict scrutiny doctrine.

84. This standard is thus considered to amount to the "due process" required by the Fourteenth Amendment when the rights at hand are not fundamental. See for an example of an assessment *Romer v. Evans*, 517 US 620 (1996).

85. For an in-depth discussion of the originalist approach that the Constitution has not changed since it was created versus the pragmatist view that it is necessary to update constitutional norms in order to observe societal changes over the years, see for example Easter-

Court, as well as between legal scholars.[86] The right to privacy is not expressly mentioned in the Bill of Rights but has nevertheless, over the years and in various ways, been interpreted as emanating from the US Constitution. For instance, constitutional protection of the right of privacy has been read into the First Amendment on freedom of speech and assembly (privacy of beliefs; personal autonomy), the Fourth Amendment protection for persons, houses, papers and effects against unreasonable seizes and searches, the Fifth Amendment's privilege against self-incrimination (regarding personal information), the Ninth Amendment's statement that the rights listed in the Bill of Rights (the first eight amendments) "shall not be construed to deny or disparage others retained by the people" and the Fourteenth Amendment's liberty clause establishing that no state shall deprive any person of life, liberty or property without due process of law. In the following, we shall examine how perceptions regarding the right to privacy as constitutional and fundamental has developed in the Supreme Court's case law over the years.

C. Establishing a Constitutional Right to Privacy

Union Pacific Railway Company v. Botsford (decided 1891, the year after Warren and Brandeis' article on the right to privacy as the right to be let alone), is sometimes described as the first case in which the Supreme Court deduced a right to privacy from the words of the Constitution. Justice Gray wrote:

> No right is held more sacred, or is more carefully guarded, by the common law, than the right of every individual to the possession and control of his own person, free from all restraint or interference of others, unless by clear and unquestionable authority of law. As well said by Judge Cooley: "The right to one's person may be said to be a right of complete immunity: to be let alone."

In 1923, in *Meyer v. Nebraska*, the Supreme Court decided a state law forbidding the teaching of foreign languages to children under ninth grade was unconstitutional and invaded the liberty protected by the Fourteenth Amendment. Two years later, the same legal base was used in *Pierce v. Society of Sisters* to strike down a state law compelling all children to attend public schools. In *Olmstead v. United States* (1928) the Supreme Court did not hold the Fourth

---

brook, Frank, Originalism and Pragmatism: Pragmatism's Role in Interpretation, Harvard Journal of Law and Public Policy Vol 31.

86. See Cohen, Julie, Configuring the Networked Self, Yale University Press, Newhaven and London, 2012, p 108.

Amendment applicable to a non-physical intrusion involving the wiretapping of private telephone conversations. However, in the light of later rulings Justice Brandeis's dissent has probably become more famous than the majority's reasoning. Brandeis concluded:

> The protection guaranteed by the Amendments is much broader in scope. The makers of our Constitution undertook to secure conditions favorable to the pursuit of happiness. They recognized the significance of man's spiritual nature, of his feelings, and of his intellect. They knew that only a part of the pain, pleasure and satisfactions of life are to be found in material things. They sought to protect Americans in their beliefs, their thoughts, their emotions and their sensations. They conferred, as against the Government, the right to be let alone — the most comprehensive of rights, and the right most valued by civilized men. To protect that right, every unjustifiable intrusion by the Government upon the privacy of the individual, whatever the means employed, must be deemed a violation of the Fourth Amendment. And the use, as evidence in a criminal proceeding, of facts ascertained by such intrusion must be deemed a violation of the Fifth.

The Court's restrictive approach, reflected in *Olmstead*, would not be altered until the 1960s. First, in the 1965 landmark case *Griswold v. Connecticut*, a state law prohibiting the possession, sale and distribution of contraceptives to married couples was struck down as violating the constitutional right to marital privacy. The majority argued that the shadows, or *penumbras*, of the Bill of Rights created this right, along with other rights not explicitly mentioned in the words of the Constitution but establishing protected zones of privacy: "We deal with a right of privacy older than the Bill of Rights — older than our political parties, older than our school system.". Justice Goldberg, in his concurrence, instead emphasized the Ninth Amendment and marital privacy as an additional personal right "retained by the people", and Justice Harlan preferred to rely on the Fourteenth Amendment's liberty clause. Justice Black, on the other hand, could not find a legal base for nullifying the state law:

> The Court talks about a constitutional 'right of privacy' as though there is some constitutional provision or provisions forbidding any law ever to be passed which might abridge the 'privacy' of individuals. But there is not.

In *Katz v. United States* (1967) the long-awaited adaption of the Constitution's wording to technological developments resulted in that Government activities of electronically listening to and recording communication made through a telephone booth were considered violative of the caller's justifiable expectation of privacy. Thus, they constituted a search or seizure within the (new) meaning of the Fourth Amendment. Justice Stewart wrote for the majority: "The fact that the electronic device employed to achieve that end did not happen to penetrate the wall of the booth can have no constitutional significance." Determining the protected objects to be "people, rather than places", the Supreme Court took the step from physical to non-physical constitutional protection of privacy. Justice Black again dissented and concluded that the makers of the Constitution had not intended its words to be applied in the pragmatist way of the majority. Nor was he of the opinion that "rewriting" the Fourth Amendment to reach a result desired by popular demand was the proper role for the Supreme Court. Thanks to Justice Harlan's concurring opinion, however, the majority's ruling would not lead to as radical a development as Justice Black feared. Harlan had formulated what would be known as the "reasonable expectation of privacy test": to be protected by the Fourth Amendment a person must 1) have expressed a subjective expectation of privacy, that 2) society recognizes as "reasonable". This model, argued Harlan, would be applicable to issues regarding both private and public places. As we shall see, in later years it has been used in such a way as to narrow the area protected by the Fourth Amendment considerably.

Ironically, in the US, the constitutional right to privacy was more easily accepted in cases less connected to privacy itself, and closer to the concept of autonomy, which has traditionally been regarded as more important in America. Perhaps the most famous privacy case was, like *Griswold*, one where the right to privacy—in a physical sense—led to the creation of other rights. In *Roe v. Wade* (1973) the Court was confronted by a Texas statute that criminalized abortion. Justice Blackmun, who delivered the majority opinion, described the earlier case law as creating constitutionally protected zones of privacy even though the word "privacy" is not mentioned in the Bill of Rights: "These decisions make it clear that only personal rights that can be deemed 'fundamental' or 'implicit in the concept of ordered liberty' [...] are included in this guarantee of personal privacy.". The wording is interesting as privacy qualifies other rights by giving them a certain level of protection. From this perspective, it is not the constitutional right to privacy *per se* that is disputed, but what the right encompasses.[87] So which privacy rights should be regarded as fundamental? In *Roe*, the Court men-

---

87. In Sweden, on the other hand, privacy has never been granted this prestigious function. Instead the reasoning has worked the opposite way, using established rights (or objects ...) such as bodily integrity to also, gradually, incorporate notions of privacy.

tions marriage, procreation, contraception, family, relationships, childrearing and education as constituting the types of rights that the constitutional privacy right protects. In line with these protected interests, the Supreme Court concluded that a woman's decision whether or not to terminate her pregnancy also falls within the constitutionally protected zone—whatever the exact legal foundation (here the Fourteenth Amendment's liberty clause was used). The judgment, with its comprehensive review of abortion history, demonstrates the importance of tradition in determining whether a right should be classified as fundamental. The newly found privacy right was not absolute, but had to be weighed against important state interests in regulation, such as deciding the point at which a pregnancy can be terminated. However, the general provisions in the Texas law statute did not pass strict scrutiny. Justice Rehnquist dissented, leaning on the wording of the Constitution: "To reach its result, the Court necessarily has had to find within the scope of the Fourteenth Amendment a right that was apparently completely unknown to the drafters of the Amendment.". If this is considered the case regarding ancient phenomenon such as abortion, it is not surprising that new technology is having a hard time finding its way into the constitutionally protected privacy zone through the Fourth Amendment.

So far, the slow but steady pragmatist readings of the Constitution expressed by the Supreme Court in the privacy area are both interesting and full of potential from a Swedish perspective. The Swedish system, too, lacks explicit fundamental and constitutional protections for privacy—even though freedom of expression and of the press were the first rights to be acknowledged legally and have been enshrined in entire constitutional laws. Despite recent efforts to strengthen the constitutional privacy protection, Swedish protections are still mainly focused on physical trespass and specifically applicable when certain intrusions occur, rather than being awarded the status of a general right to privacy. However, Sweden may at long last be moving towards a higher awareness of the risks that result from privacy invasions both legally and societally. However, unlike the US, which could recognize privacy rights on its own through Supreme Court cases concerning issues that society regards as legitimate and important constitutionally protected interests, Sweden needed the European Court of Justice and the European Court of Human Rights to direct these changes.[88] If Swedish courts dared to use the Swedish Constitution in a more constructive way, we might be able to avoid falling behind again.

---

88. Another aspect is of course that the legitimacy of the Supreme Court decisions is still under debate among those who are of the opinion that courts should leave the making of new law to politicians, and instead stick to applying it.

D. Second Thoughts: Does the Constitutional Right to Privacy Exist in the Digital Age?

In later years, however, the progressive American development appears to have come to a halt, if not to a decline. After initially using the controversial right of privacy to strike down prohibitions on abortion, in several judgments of 1977 the Supreme Court upheld state laws imposing restrictions on public funding for abortions,[89] and in *Planned Parenthood of Southeastern Pa. v. Casey* (1992) it partially overruled *Roe*. The debate on privacy and reproductive rights will not be further discussed here, as it is of physical character. Instead, the starting point for this section is parallel developments regarding the scope of the Fourth Amendment; more specifically the Court's decision in *Katz*. In cases concerning privacy under *Katz*, it is important to determine when a warrant is required to search certain areas rather than others. In the 1971 case *United States v. White*, the focus was on which expectations of privacy could be considered "reasonable". The Supreme Court held that there was no justifiable expectation when information had been revealed to a government informant wearing a concealed radio transmitter. Justice Douglas, in dissent, wrote: "Today no one perhaps notices, because only a small, obscure criminal is the victim. But every person is the victim, for the technology we exalt today is everyone's master.". Justice Harlan, too, dissented and in his reasoning alluded to technology's new threats and the Orwellian Big Brother.

This more restrictive view regarding the constitutional effects of sharing information continued in cases such as *Smith v. Maryland* (1979), where Justice

---

89. *Maher v. Roe*, 432 US 464, *Beal v. Doe*, 432 US 438 and *Poelker v. Doe*, 432 US 519 (all 1977). On the other hand, in *Lawrence v. Texas*, 539 US 558 (2003), the Court overruled earlier caselaw and struck down on a Texas statute criminalizing gay sex. Here, too, the majority used constitutional privacy as the groundbreaker, emphasizing the history of homosexuality and quoting from an earlier judgment: "These matters, involving the most intimate and personal choices a person may make in a lifetime, choices central to personal dignity and autonomy, are central to the liberty protected by the Fourteenth Amendment. At the heart of liberty is the right to define one's own concept of existence, of meaning, of the universe, and of the mystery of human life. Beliefs about these matters could not define the attributes of personhood were they formed under compulsion of the State.". The Court held that the founders of the Constitution "knew times can blind us to certain truths and later generations can see that laws once thought necessary and proper in fact serve only to oppress.". Justices Scalia and Thomas dissented. Thomas found the majority's reasoning unrooted and unconvincing and Scalia quoted Justice Stewart's dissent in *Griswold*, calling the Court's ruling "uncommonly silly". He admitted no right to privacy according to the Constitution. Thus the privacy conflict of originalists and pragmatists continues in the Supreme Court. Despite the outcome in *Lawrence*, the Court was criticized for not having applied the strict scrutiny test that the fundamental privacy rights require.

Harlan's test was adopted by the majority.[90] The Court decided that there could be no "legitimate" expectation of privacy in numbers that a person dials (which in this case had been recorded by a pen register). The Court reasoned that the telephone user had already chosen to share the numbers with his/her telephone company, where they could be recorded for business purposes, and had thus "assumed the risk that the company would reveal the information". Justices Stewart and Brennan dissented, describing the judgment as simply "describing the basic nature of telephone calls". Justice Marshall, who also dissented, criticized the "third-party doctrine" and connected the assumption of risk to an actual *choice* of sharing information, which in his opinion was absent in the situation at hand.

The third-party doctrine has since become highly problematic in relation to text messages, e-mail accounts and other information. Inevitably, individuals convey such information over the Internet, using third parties such as Internet service providers, cell phone companies, etc.[91] Given this development, the constitutional right to informational privacy itself is called into question—in Justice Scalia's words in *NASA v. Nelson* (2011): "Thirty-three years have passed since the Court first suggested this right may, or may not exist. It is time for the Court to abandon this Alfred Hitchcock line of our jurisprudence.". Considering the lacking data protection in US regulation (no single, comprehensive, federal law), the constitutional protection of personal information comes across as key for the individual. Along these lines it can be noted the Supreme Court adopted a more liberal and up-to-date attitude in the 2014 case *Riley v. California*, where it decided that a warrant is required for the police to search digital information on a cell phone seized from someone who has been arrested. According to the Court's opinion, a digital search implicated "substantially greater individual privacy interests than a brief physical search".

VI. Conclusions

A. Looking to the Future

What can the Swedish legal system learn from The US and the EU? Privacy as a fundamental right is established in both the American and EU legal orders, but in very different ways. While privacy is directly protected in the EU

---

90. See also *US v. Miller*, 425 US 435 (1976) regarding bank records, and *Couch v. US*, 409 US 322 (1973) on business records submitted to an accountant. In both cases the expectation of privacy was considered to have been surrendered.

91. See for example *City of Ontario v. Quon*, 560 US 746 (2010).

Charter, which sets the stage for the realization of individual rights, the US is lagging behind in the creation of legal norms for the digital age. On the other hand, there is—despite the lack of a right to privacy in the US Constitution— a well-developed body of case law regarding the different privacy rights that can or should be included, as well as regarding how privacy as an umbrella term may be used to promote various interests in the legal order.

How can Sweden, as an inexperienced country in the (individual) rights discourse, best benefit from these different traditions? Two routes are available; development via adding rights through the Swedish constitution, or via case law. Unlike the US, we do not consider ourselves bound by 18th century words, and should therefore take the opportunity to—like the EU legislature—codify today's societal values. These values include a critical awareness of the State's and other entities' power and possibilities concerning control of citizens' personal data. When creating a "new" constitutional right to privacy in Sweden— and the legal measures required to implement it—one might look both to the reasoning of the US Supreme Court regarding the content of the right to privacy, and the EU legal order for inspiration on how to make it real.

However, the legislative route will not fix the complexities following from the multilevel protection of privacy and data protection that exists in Swedish law today. The main challenge for the Swedish legislature is to deal with the complex relationship between privacy and our national principles of transparency, freedom of the press and of expression. These clashes cannot be solved by constitutional amendments, but perhaps changing attitudes regarding the right to privacy will, in time, allow for a combination of old and new rights in the digital age. Swedish courts will play a pivotal role in this endeavour.

B. Closing Thoughts on the American Approach

The cases mentioned in section V.D. above are not the only ones where the constitutionally protected zone of privacy, and thus privacy as a fundamental right at the federal level in the US, have resulted in a reduction of that right.[92] Developments in the US Supreme Court raise the question whether the right to privacy, having become so narrow that it only seems to prevail as an exception, can be said to exist at all. However, the fact that there is an ongoing debate at all differs from the Swedish understanding of the constitutional and fundamental right to

---

92. See also, e g, *Laird v. Tatum*, 409 US 824 (1972), *Cox Broadcasting Corporation v. Cohn*, 420 US 469 (1975), *Whalen v. Roe*, 429 US 589 (1977), *Florida Star v. BJF*, 491 US 524 (1989). Regarding the same tendency in tort law cases on privacy issues, see *Doe v. Chao*, 540 US 614 (2004) and *Federal Aviation Administration v. Cooper*, 566 US (2012).

privacy. For various societal and legal reasons described above, Sweden has avoided the topic of what privacy is—not least in a constitutional setting. But it is never too late to commence a serious discussion on why privacy is valuable and when it should be protected as a fundamental right. The US Supreme Court's long history of judgments offer an impressive array of reflections, definitions and elaborations on this matter in different contexts, which could serve as valuable inspiration and motivation for the Swedish legal community. Also, having the latest privacy cases and tendencies in mind, we could hopefully—at a distance—use the conflict between pragmatists and originalists in a way that is beneficial to protecting privacy, and that grants privacy its own status away from autonomy.

The regulation now discussed may be highest in rank in the US, but let us not forget that legal protection of privacy is also provided for in state constitutions (such as the California Constitution, where privacy is mentioned and considered a fundamental right),[93] in federal, state and local statutes (such as the Privacy Act of 1974, with specific provisions for federal agencies, and civil rights laws, such as the New York Civil Right Law's article 5) and through the by now well-established common law torts developed over the years and incorporated into the American Restatement of Torts.[94] In addition, American legal doctrine continues to be "obsessed" with privacy and there are countless publications added to the field every year. It would seem that the right to privacy enjoys a fair deal of attention and protection in the American legal scene—perhaps in every way but as a constitutional fundamental right.[95]

C. Closing Thoughts on the European Approach

In the US, while classification of a right as fundamental will lead to a higher standard of judicial review, the EU approaches fundamental rights instrumentally. Especially in relation to data protection law, the EU legal order provides a fruitful platform for individuals and interest groups to use "rights" as a vehi-

---

93. Section 1, article 1: "All people are by nature free and independent and have inalienable rights. Among these are enjoying and defending life and liberty, acquiring, possessing, and protecting property, and pursuing and obtaining safety, happiness, and privacy."

94. The four main privacy torts were first described by William Prosser, see Privacy, p 389.

95. See, however, for an expression of the opinion that the statutory provisions have been weakened by repeated amendments, Moore, Adam, Privacy Rights: Moral and Legal Foundations, Penn State Press, Pennsylvania, 2010, p 111. Regarding the privacy torts, Moore argues (p 101) that they have all been "either eliminated or severely restricted". Also, as mentioned above, the sparse US regulation on data protection has not been aided by the slow development for constitutional informational privacy.

cle to further their goals; behind the cases discussed in section IV.C above, there are NGOs and individuals committed to their respective causes; the NGO Digital Rights Ireland, the law student Maximilian Schrems (with some help from Digital Rights Ireland), and most recently, the politician and pirate partist Patrick Breyer.[96]

Another important difference between the US and the EU from the perspective of Swedish law, is that the former merely can influence Sweden by way of persuasive ideas and convincing thoughts, while EU law is part of the internal Swedish legal order since Sweden is a Member State of the EU. Swedish law is therefore obliged to apply EU law loyally. The Swedish legislature therefore needs to be more careful in how its responds to EU requirements.

As discussed above, the EU seems to have grand ambitions in promoting high standards of data protection around the world. The question is how this can be reconciled with other traditions within the Member States. Even if Sweden has started to develop a more coherent view on protection of personal integrity, there are other interests that so far have gained more attention, such as transparency, openness and access to public documents. The possible negative effects from the EU on Sweden's longstanding tradition of openness has been an area of discussion ever since the Swedish accession of 1995.[97] The development of EU data protection law has deepened the concerns. As discussed below, Swedish courts have so far upheld Swedish openness laws in cases where conforming to EU interpretations regarding data protection might have produced different results. If the question of balancing between the Swedish right to openness and the EU right to data protection were put before the CJEU, a different outcome might be expected. If the Swedish legislature would like to conduct the balancing test in privacy matters differently than the EU, the legislator ought to carefully build a line of arguments.

D. Possible Lines of Development for the Swedish Legal Order

Coming back to the idea of legislation via constitutional amendments, there is a Swedish tradition of changing the constitution on a regular basis—espe-

---

96. Compare Reichel, Jane and Hellner, Agnes, EU Participatory Democracy from Promise to Practice: The Role of IOs and NGOs, in Wahlgren, Peter, Wrange, Pål and Zamboni, Mauro, Law without State, Scandinavian Studies in Law Vol 62, Stockholm, Hart, 2017.

97. Österdahl, Inger, Transparency Versus Secrecy in an International Context: A Swedish Dilemma, in Lind, Anna-Sara, Reichel, Jane and Österdahl, Inger (eds.), Freedom of Speech, Internet, Privacy and Democracy, Liber, Stockholm, 2015.

cially the section on the protection of fundamental rights. This means that there is potential space to explicitly convey the values underpinning today's Swedish legal order, such as the wish to combine a modern protection for privacy with certain historical principles. Defining a more comprehensive Swedish version of the right to privacy in the Swedish Constitution, perhaps with guidance from the elaborate American legal discourse on its content, could better the legal situation both internally in the Swedish legal order and vis-à-vis the EU. In Article 4.2 TEU it is stated that the EU "shall respect the equality of the Member States before the Treaties as well as their national identities, inherent in their fundamental structures, political and constitutional, inclusive of regional and local self-government". The dialogue with the EU in this respect would benefit from a clear and transparent articulation of the Swedish view in the Constitution itself, not least since the principle of openness, against which privacy is often balanced, is extensively regulated in constitutional texts.

Regarding case law development, this is one area where the Swedish courts, especially the Supreme Administrative Court, is in need of inspiration from CJEU and American courts. This is important without regard to the changes in the constitutional texts discussed above, since the letter of a constitutional text must always be interpreted and applied in the context of a specific case, and, more importantly, interpreted and applied taking due account of rights stemming from European sources, the ECHR and EU law. As noted, section II, Swedish legal tradition has shied away from the concept of rights and Swedish courts may still be hesitant to engage in rights based analysis in the development of Swedish law.[98] In recent years, the Swedish Supreme Administrative Court has decided several cases where the balance between data protection and the Freedom of the Press Act and the Swedish principle of openness has been at the fore, namely HFD 2014 ref. 66, HFD 2015 ref. 61 and HFD 2015 ref. 71. The Supreme Administrative Court has continuously given priority to the Freedom of the Press Act and the principle of openness without offering any analysis on how and on what grounds the two competing rights, data protection and transparency, should be balanced. Neither the European Convention of Human Rights, nor the EU Charter, are referred to in any of

---

98. The Swedish Supreme Court has been more progressive in this respect, see for example NJA 2014 p 323, NJA 2014 p 332 and Andersson, Håkan, Compensation and the Instrument of Government [RF och ersättningsrätten], De lege 2014, Iustus, Uppsala, pp 109–138, on the awarding of damages based on the constitutional rights catalogue. See also, regarding damages granted for breaches of the rights expressed in the ECHR, for example NJA 2005 p 462, NJA 2007 p 583 and NJA 2012 p 211 I–II.

the cases. In a case decided in the Spring 2017, Greenpeace invoked the right to court access under Article 6 of the European Convention of Human Rights, the Aarhus Convention,[99] and Article 47 of the EU Charter, against the Swedish Government's decision to refuse to release documents regarding a controversial affair on coal mines in Germany.[100] Without revealing any reasoning or grounds, the Supreme Administrative Court found that no right to appeal existed since the right to access to documents was not considered a "civil right," the criteria in Swedish law, referring back to Article 6 of the European Convention. The Court simply referred to a 2007 judgment,[101] which was also very short and unreasoned, and stated that it did not find that the subsequent European Court of Human Rights case law provided a reason to render a different interpretation. The same tendency can be found in the Supreme Court's judgments, where for example the interpretation of journalistic exceptions from the Data Protection Act has been generous to say the least.[102]

If the Swedish view on transparency and its principle of openness are to be prioritized over the right to privacy and data protection, the Swedish courts will have to explain the justification. In a globalized and connected world, Swedish courts would benefit from a judicial dialogue with other courts at an international level, or by being inspired by other national courts, such as the US Supreme Court. Privacy need not necessarily be seen as contrary to openness and transparency. After all, protecting individuals—journalists, for instance—from privacy threats will ultimately also allow them to continue speaking their mind.[103]

---

99. The UNECE Convention on Access to Information, Public Participation in Decision-making and Access to Justice in Environmental Matters, Aarhus, 25 June 1998, entered into force the 10 October 2001, in relevant parts implemented in Swedish law via the EU Directive 2003/4/EC of the European Parliament and the CouncilL of 28 January 2003 on public access to environmental information.

100. Judgment of the Supreme Administrative Court on March 23, 2017, case number 7074-15, not yet reported. According to the Freedom of the Press Act, Chapter 2, § 15, decisions of the Government on access to documents cannot be appealed.

101. RÅ 2007 not 202.

102. NJA 2001 p 409.

103. See further on this topic, Koltay, András, Internet Gatekeepers as Editors—The Case of Online Comments, in this book.

András Koltay, Professor of Law,
Pázmány Péter Catholic University

Internet Gatekeepers as Editors— The Case of Online Comments

I. Introduction

Back in the nineties, the Internet, then a recent channel of public communication, was likened by many to the *frontier*, i.e. the 19th century American borderland, where the presence of central government was barely noticeable, and where associations, institutions and communities could freely grow and flourish without state oversight or guardianship.[1] Under this view, the Internet as a *frontier* is mostly free from state intervention and regulation and its stakeholders (content and infrastructure providers, as well as the users) set the rules for their activities. As such, the borders of free speech involve setting the legal rules aside. This view necessarily leads, in the absence of state intervention, to a stronger role for freedom of speech.[2]

Although this paradigm is often cited in the literature[3], it is in reality a fleeting fantasy. In the past two decades, it has become clear that states will not forgo Internet regulation, and that Internet businesses are themselves keen to restrict the free flow of opinions because they perceive that their (primarily economic) interests so require.[4] Restrictions on speech from the offline world can also be ap-

---

1. William C. Davis, *American Frontier: Pioneers, Settlers, and Cowboys 1800–1899* (New York: Smithmark 1995).
2. Thomas G. Krattenmaker, LA Powe Jr., 'Converging First Amendment Principles for Converging Communications Media' 104 *Yale Law Journal* (1994–95) 1719.; Eugene Volokh, 'Cheap Speech and what It will Do' 104 *Yale Law Journal* (1994–95) 1805.
3. Andrew Tutt, 'The New Speech', 41 *Hastings Constitutional Law Quarterly* (2013–2014) 235, 237.
4. See e.g. James Curran, Neil Fenton, Des Freedman, D (eds.), *Misunderstanding the Internet* (London—New York: Routledge 2016. 2nd ed.); Jacob Rowbottom, *Democracy Distorted. Wealth, Influence and Democratic Politics* (Cambridge—New York: Cambridge University Press 2010); Evgeniy Morozov, *The Net Delusion. The Dark Side of Internet Freedom* (New York: Public Affairs Publishing 2011).

plied in the online environment, and rules applicable to the traditional media apply to content displayed via the Internet, even without a separate act by the legislator, and these rules include criminal law and private law standards.[5]

In Internet communication, while Internet services are of major importance, including those that produce content (and which are traditionally squeezed under the umbrella concept of "media", so are those that transmit content to the public (Internet intermediaries or gatekeepers). Thus, the Internet is like prior communications technologies in that there has always been an intermediary between the medium and the public, whether it be a newsstand, postman or broadcaster. However, in the Internet environment the role of intermediaries has become much more significant. Gatekeepers are not only unavoidable in the communications process, but they are capable of materially influencing the public sphere by making certain content inaccessible or accessible only with great difficulty while transmitting other content to large audiences. Compared to a newsstand or a printing press, Internet intermediaries often have an interest in intervening in the communications process.[6] Laidlaw distinguished between high influence "macro-gatekeepers" (who are unavoidable, such as Internet service providers (ISPs) or search engine providers), "authority gatekeepers" (service providers of websites with large traffic that can make decisions on the content appearing there, such as social media sites), and "micro-gatekeepers" (blog providers, or moderators of websites with less traffic, which still provide an interface for opinions participating in democratic public sphere, where the displayed content can be controlled by the content provider).[7]

The role of gatekeepers is therefore not only passive, but active in the communication process; they make decisions on a daily basis on what to display to their users and what cannot be accessed by them, or that can be accessed but only with great difficulty. The EU Directive partly regulates the activities of

---

5. Perry Keller, *European and International Media Law. Liberal Democracy, Trade, and the New Media* (OUP, 2011) Chapters 8 to 13. See furthermore from the case law of the European Court of Human Rights the restriction of obscene views: *Perrin v. the United Kingdom*, application no. 5446/03, decision of 18 October 2005; violation of reputation: *Times Newspapers Ltd. v. the United Kingdom* (nos. 1 and 2), application nos. 3002/03 and 23676/03, judgment of 10 March 2009; *Mosley v. the United Kingdom*, application no. 48009/08, judgment of 10 May 2011; Editorial Board of Pravoye Delo and Shtekel v. Ukraine, application no. 33014/05. judgment of 5 May 2011; violation of privacy: K.U. v. Finland, application no. 2872/02. judgment of 2 December 2008; or protection of copyrights: *Ashby Donald and Others v. France*, application no. 36769/08, judgment of 10 January 2013.

6. Emily Laidlaw, *Regulating Speech in Cyberspace. Gatekeepers, Human Rights and Corporate Responsibility* (CUP 2015) 40–44.

7. Ibid., 53–54.

gatekeepers,[8] enabling them to be called to account for infringements, and releasing them from liability if they do not actively take part in the transmission of unlawful content to the public, and if they are unaware of its unlawful nature.[9] Under to the current legal approach, gatekeepers do not qualify as "media," and therefore their activities are not restricted by legal guarantees that secure individual a right of access to media,[10] and they are not viewed as subject to the same obligations that the media, as private institutions granted constitutional rank,[11] are expected to fulfil.[12] As a result, it is not only the subjects of the freedom of press that should beware of the state. Nunziato cites numerous examples to illustrate the ways in which Internet intermediaries intervene in the free flow of opinions. He claims that the largest U.S. Internet businesses, contrary to public belief, make such interventions not only to protect their economic interests, but also to restrict the political opinions of others, applying a kind of censorship that is usually not banned by law. This is true for ISPs, which can restrict outgoing emails or transmission of certain content to the public, as well as news aggregators which can ignore specific news items that might otherwise deserve reporting, and search engines which can restrict access to certain content.[13]

This paper discusses certain liability issues related to a specific type of micro-gatekeeper, namely "comments", i.e., the reader's input on a piece of content appearing on a website, typically published in such a manner that the contributor cannot be identified (i.e., anonymously). The right to freedom of the press initially served the purpose of defending the "media" in the sense of content produced by using professional methods. However, content created by users is also protected under the right to freedom of speech, even where compliance with professional-ethical standards cannot be expected or imposed. At the same time, the media, or other content providers who record such their

---

8. Directive 2000/31/EC of the European Parliament and of the Council of 8 June 2000 on certain legal aspects of information society services, in particular electronic commerce, in the Internal Market ('Directive on electronic commerce').

9. Ibid., Articles 12–15.

10. András Sajó, Monroe Price (eds.), *Rights Of Access To The Media* (Kluwer Law International 1995).

11. William J. Brennan, 'Address' 32 *Rutgers Law Review* (1979) 173.

12. Commission on Freedom of the Press, *A Free and Responsible Press. A General Report on Mass Communication: Newspapers, Radio, Motion Pictures, Magazines, and Books* (University of Chicago Press 1947); John C Nerone, *Last Rites: Revisiting four Theories of the Press* (University of Illinois Press 1995) 77–100.

13. Dawn C. Nunziato, *Virtual Freedom. Net Neutrality and Free Speech in the Internet Age* (Stanford, Ca., Stanford University Press 2009) 5–17, 110–114.

content, or provide an interface that permits comments, can theoretically be liable for content created by their users, and therefore they must decide whether to allow potentially unlawful user content to be posted (or whether to consent to its publication on their interfaces).[14]

In addition to a general overview of gatekeepers' "editorial" activity, this paper discusses three comment-related cases that have emerged from the case law of the European Court of Human Rights (hereinafter "ECtHR"), focusing on when a website's content provider can be considered an "editor" with regard to comments, and when it can be held responsible for unlawful user-written views. These cases reveal the conflict between the rights afforded in two Articles of the European Convention on Human Rights (hereinafter "ECHR"): Article 10 protects freedom of expression and Article 8 protects the right to privacy. In the ECtHR's case law, Article 8 also protects the right to respect for one's reputation, and the right to honour,[15] the violation of which is most often raised in comment-related cases. However, comments can also display personal information that violates the right to privacy.[16]

II. Internet gatekeepers as "editors"

For a long time, the concept of "media" could be defined with relative precision, despite the emergence of newer media. The media consist of printed media, and television and radio broadcasters, in the current legal sense. Conversely, from the point of view of regulation, we do not regard feature films projected in the cinema, books and fliers distributed on the street, or the products of organisations dealing with the collection and publication of information, such as credit agencies, financial service providers, travel agencies and weather forecasters, as "media" products.[17]

---

14. Lorna Woods, 'User Generated Content: Freedom of Expression and the Role of the Media in a Digital Age' in Merris Amos, Jackie Harrison, Lorna Woods (eds.), *Freedom of Expression and the Media* (Leiden & Boston, Nijhoff 2012) 168.

15. David Harris, Michael O'Boyle, Ed Bates, Carla Buckley, *Law of the European Convention on Human Rights* (OUP 2014, 3rd ed.); Eric Barendt, 'Balancing Freedom of Expression and Privacy: The Jurisprudence of the Strasbourg Court' 1 *Journal of Media Law* (2009) 49.

16. See a judgment in Hungary by the Pécs High Court of Appeal on a comment (BDT2013. 2941): "A public expression relating to another person's sexual orientation not outstandingly vulgar but with offensive purpose and degrading effect can qualify as violation of rights relating to personality."

17. David A. Anderson, 'Freedom of the Press' 80 *Texas Law Review* (2002) 429, 442–444.

A characteristic element of the current concept of "media" is editorial activity. According to the European Union's AVMS Directive, an "audiovisual media service" is defined as a service:

- defined in Articles 56 and 57 of the Treaty on the functioning of the European Union (i.e. usually provided for a consideration, as an economic service),
- for which a media service provider bears editorial responsibility,
- the principal purpose of which is to transmit programmes to the public for information, entertainment or education,
- via an electronic communications network within the meaning of Article 2 (a) of Directive 2002/21/EC.[18]

In theory, this definition could be extended to other types of media, and thus include not only radio and the printed press as well as the Internet press, although the Directive fails to do so. In the *New Online Media* case[19], the Court of Justice of the European Union held that if online press products and news portals publish audiovisual content as well, they can qualify as media services in certain cases, and therefore the definition can be interpreted broadly, and applied not only to television (broadcasting), websites of television services or services broadcasting exclusively content that is expressly similar to television programmes. Further, given revisions to the AVMS Directive, ongoing since May 2016,[20] it is likely to result in the partial extension of the scope of the regulation to video-sharing platforms and social media services if publication of audiovisual content is an important element in their activity.[21] These new provisions of the Directive would clearly cover user-created content without the knowledge and intention of the service provider, which becomes available on its website without its direct involvement.

It is important to note that, since the EU's Directive mainly regulates the single media market, it thus regulates only services of an economic nature

---

18. Directive 2010/13/EU of the European Parliament and of the Council of 10 March 2010 on the coordination of certain provisions laid down by law, regulation or administrative action in Member States concerning the provision of audiovisual media services (AVMS Directive), article 1. (1) (a).

19. C-347/14. New Media Online GmbH v. Bundeskommunikationssenat, Judgment of the Court, (Second Chamber) 21 October 2015.

20. Revision of the Audiovisual Media Services Directive (AVMSD), see https://ec.europa.eu/digital-single-market/en/revision-audiovisual-media-services-directive-avmsd.

21. Adapting to technological changes, preserving European competitiveness and fundamental values in audiovisual services (Press release of the Council of the European Union), see http://www.consilium.europa.eu/en/press/press-releases/2017/05/23-audiovisual-services/.

(provided on a commercial basis, for financial gain and subject to financial risk). Irrespective, it is beyond dispute that the general concept of "media" includes editorial activity, editorial decision-making and the associated legal responsibility. Editing means actual control over the content published in the relevant medium which involves decisions regarding the content that should appear on the interface of the relevant medium and in what manner. Traditionally, media content is created by persons (journalists) connected to the medium in some way, but these days user content must be taken into account, and the question arises as to when the publication of user content (for example, a comment) can be regarded as the outcome of an editorial decision.

The most important gatekeepers make numerous editorial decisions on a daily basis. Google's search engine service, unavoidable for most Internet users, does not create any content but it does list Internet sites at the user's request, in an order specified by the service.[22] At the same time, a search engine unavoidably "edits" as the essence of its activity, by ranking content and prioritising it, making certain content nearly invisible and other content easily accessible. Under the "right to be forgotten", created by the case law of the Court of Justice of the European Union, certain links to websites containing personal data, which may be harmful to the applicant, must be removed from the search hits.[23] This is undoubtedly a kind of editorial activity, where Google must take a decision on the accessibility of certain content, even though that content affect the distribution of political opinions, and thus shape the scope of democratic debate.[24]

In May 2016, news spread that Facebook editors had side-lined conservative opinions in the United States,[25] and then in November the election of Donald

---

22. James Grimmelmann, 'The Structure of Search Engine Law' 93 *Iowa Law Review* (2007) 1.; James Grimmelmann, 'Some Skepticism About Search Neutrality' in Berin Szoka—Adam Marcus (eds.), *The Next Digital Decade: Essays on the Future of the Internet. Is Search Now an "Essential Facility"?* (TechFreedom, 2010) 438.

23. C-131/12. Google Spain SL, Google Inc. v. Agencia Espanola de Proteccion Datos Mario Costeja Gonzalez, Judgment of the Court (Grand Chamber), 13 May 2014. For the legal analysis of the case see David Lindsay, 'The "Right to be Forgotten" by Search Engines under Data Privacy Law: A Legal Analysis of the Costeja Ruling' 6 *Journal of Media Law* (2014) no. 2. 159.

24. Robert C. Post, 'Data Privacy and Dignitary Privacy: Google Spain, the Right To Be Forgotten, and the Construction of the Public Sphere', 67 *Duke Law Journal* (2018) 981, Lawrence Siry, 'Forget Me, Forget Me Not: Reconciling Two Different Paradigms of the Right to be Forgotten' 103 *Kentucky Law Journal* (2014–2015) 311., Amy Gajda, 'Privacy, Press, and a Right to Be Forgotten in the United States' (draft manuscript, on file with author).

25. Sam Thielmann, 'Facebook's News Selection is in Hands of Editors, not Algorithms, Documents Show' *The Guardian*, 12 May 2016.

Trump as President was attributed to lax Facebook editorial decision-making, in that the Social media site had failed to filter out fake news from its news feed, thus contributing to the discrediting of Trump's rival.[26] The fake news panic is ongoing. In May 2017, the British daily *The Guardian* published Facebook's leaked editorial guidelines, confirming the widely held belief that Facebook moderators are "editors" in the sense that they make decisions regarding which content shall be available on the service and that should be removed, including provisions for sanctioning users for violating "community guidelines". Obviously, this "editing" is not like the editing that is done by a traditional daily paper in that it takes place prior to publication. In theory, Facebook's guidelines are designed to "clean" offensive content from the service (the user news feed), and is mainly done by algorithms rather than by actual people; however, it becomes increasingly difficult to deny that, all in all, this activity qualifies as "editing" in that the service is controlling the range of content accessible to the user.[27]

Other services facilitating user comments (online press products, blogs, other websites) face similar questions although to a lesser degree than Google or Facebook. Comment posting can be allowed by large media businesses, as well as by not-for-profit civil organisations, associations or private individuals. Moreover, the possibility of posting comments to content posted or shared by a user is a basic feature of Facebook and other SNSs, although, according to the terms and conditions, it must be done by displaying the user's real name. Editorial activity occurs also in the context of comments, either in the form of prior filtering or subsequent decision-making following a complaint. In this regard, the fundamental question is when a content provider can be held accountable for an unlawful comment, and when it is exempted from legal responsibility. This issue is only rarely raised in the United States, because § 230 of the Communications Decency Act largely precludes the liability of content providers for user content.[28] However, European regulations are not as clear-cut.

---

26. Olivia Solon, 'Facebook's Failure: Did Fake News and Polarized Politics Get Trump Elected?' *The Guardian*, 10 November 2016.

27. Stuart Minor Benjamin, 'Algorithms and Speech' 103 *University of Pennsylvania Law Review* (2013) 1445.

28. Anthony L. Fargo, 'ISP liability in the United States and Europe: Finding middle ground in an ocean of possibilities' in András Koltay (ed.), *Comparative Perspectives on the Fundamental Freedom of Expression* (Budapest: Wolters Kluwer 2015) 191.; Andrew M. Sevanian, 'Section 230 of the Communications Decency Act: A "Good Samaritan" Law Without the Requirement of Acting as a "Good Samaritan"' 21 *UCLA Entertainment Law Review* (2014) 121.

III. General issues of responsibility for comments

A. Comments as "speech"

A comment involves reader input on a piece of content published on a website (news portal, blog, forum, social media profile etc.) by the content provider of that website (the editorial office, the blogger, the holder of the profile). A comment cannot exist independently, "on its own"; but rather it necessarily relates to a piece of content published on the site. This characteristic helps explain the potential liability of the content provider since the comment would not "exist" in the absence of the provider's activity.

User opinions on online content typically appear anonymously (by displaying a nickname only), in a manner usually not suitable for identifying the user. At the same time, under Facebook posts, comments can be posted only with the real name of the user, who hands over his/her personal data when registering for the service. Although the intention of the service provider is to preclude anonymity, this policy can be fairly easily circumvented, but this does not alter the fact that most Facebook users specify their true details on the website.

A single comment or comment feed can either be moderated or unmoderated. In the latter case, the service provider provides only the opportunity to comment, and does not interfere with the process either before or after posting. As a result, the provider is not aware that a comment has been posted, or its possible unlawful nature, unless somebody draws their attention to it. Moderation can be either prior or *ex post*; in the former case, the posting of the comment, in the latter the further accessibility or the removal of a comment which has already been posted, depends on the service provider's decision.

B. Anonymity

A possible feature of comment is thus the anonymity of the author. Recent literature considers the right to anonymity as an inseparable component right of freedom of speech;[29] i.e., the protection of freedom of speech must extend to anonymous speech. In recent decades, as the scope of freedom of speech has grown, the range of component rights that can be derived from freedom of speech has also increased with the emergence of new means of communica-

---

29. Dirk Voorhoof, 'Internet and the right of anonymity', in Jelena Surculija (ed.), *Proceedings of the conference Regulating the Internet* (Belgrade, Center for Internet Development, 2010) 163.; Connor Francis Linehan, 'Anonymous Speech on the Internet' (unpublished paper), see https://works.bepress.com/conor_linehan/2/.

tion. For example, in Europe, it is undisputed that the media is entitled to keep the identity of their information sources confidential,[30] and in most states this is ensured by a separate statutory provision.[31] However, so far, the "right" to anonymity has only been recognised by the US Supreme Court in *McIntyre v. Ohio Elections Commission*,[32] where the Court declared that anonymous communication is generally protected by the First Amendment.[33]

The reasons offered in defence of the constitutional protection of anonymity are similar to the arguments on which the unprecedentedly wide protection of freedom of speech is based, including the fear of the despotism of the majority, i.e. the additional protection afforded to minority opinions, as well as a reluctance to apply any kind of content based regulation. If we consider the name of the author as part of the text, i.e. "content," then insisting that this be displayed qualifies as interference with the content.[34]

The European approach puts greater emphasis on the interests of the audience of the speech, and thus it is less supportive of those who wish to engage in anonymous expression. That approach focuses on the "true", or at least well-founded, nature of published speech, the possible assessment of an opinion's credibility, the possible avoidance of misleading publications, and the identifiability of the person violating the law, all of which are factors that are viewed as serving the public interest.[35]

In general, Internet communication magnifies or casts old issues of freedom of speech in a new light that raises question regarding the further sustainability of earlier approaches of the legal system to those issues. In the context of the Internet content, the power of legal doctrines that are well-established in the offline world are weaker. The same applies to the issue of anonymity: it is much easier to maintain anonymity on the Internet in the sense that it is more difficult to identify the author. The Internet is unique in that many more people are able to speak, with or without giving their names. This is due to the Internet's democratic nature, compared to earlier types of media, its virtually

---

30. Jan Oster, *Media Freedom as a Fundamental Right* (CUP 2015) 87–91.

31. Final Report—ELSA's International Legal Research Group, *Freedom of Expression and Protection of Journalistic Sources*. See https://files.elsa.org/AA/LRG_FoE_Final_Report.pdf.

32. 514 US 334 [1995].

33. It is true that in the case at hand the subject of the case was an election flyer, on which the publisher of the flyer should have been displayed under a local law. Nevertheless, the general right of anonymity *mutatis mutandis* covers online communication.

34. Eric Barendt, *Anonymous Speech. Literature, Law and Politics* (Oxford—Portland, Hart 2016), Chapter 3.

35. Ibid., pp. 4–8.

free and unrestricted access, and the ease with which infringements of freedom of speech can be committed, and the difficulties of identification. All of these factors lead to the conclusion that, due to the difficulties of enforcement being disproportionately larger in scale relative to the targeted goal, no legal recourse is needed for minor infringements of personality rights committed anonymously. However, the additional difficulties caused by technology provides a solid basis *per se* for extending the limits of freedom of speech without there being a foundation in principle.

Accordingly, in Europe, anonymous speech is only a possibility that can be guaranteed by the service provider, but it is not regarded as a generally enforceable right. Hence, by using the available measures of criminal prosecution, even an anonymous person can be identified on the basis of his/her MAC address. In addition, those entitled to complain about comments usually initiate civil procedures, in which the investigating authority has no role, but the applicant and the court often have no effective means of identifying the person who posted the comment. Each of the three ECtHR cases to be discussed fell into this category, and in all three cases the civil law responsibility of the comment's author was examined by the acting courts.

C. Moderation

The existence or non-existence of moderation, and its prior or *ex post* nature, can have important implications for the establishment of liability. If the service provider performs prior moderation then it makes an intentional decision to publish or not publish certain comments, which is undoubtedly an editorial decision. When the service provider decides in advance to publish (approve the comment), then it makes the comment in essence part of its edited content. Hence, it assumes the possible legal consequences of an infringement, that is, civil law liability, and when the service provider itself is subject to press or media regulation then the liability arises from that status.[36]

The case is not as straightforward for *ex post* moderation, when the service provider decides on the removal or non-removal of a comment afterwards rather than before the posting. If moderation is subsequent (after the publication), it is arguable whether the service provider's responsibility for the unlawful comment

---

36. This was the Estonian Government's argument in the Delfi case, see *Delfi AS v. Estonia*, application no. 64569/09, judgment of 15 June 2015 [GC] (hereinafter: *Delfi* [GC]) Paragraphs 85., 125.

(1) relates only to the removal after an external signal received or

(2) is subject to a continuous monitoring obligation after the publication, on the basis of which unlawful comments must be identified and removed, even in the absence of an eventual external signal,

(3) the publication of an unlawful comment is an objective infringement, which can only be mitigated by its subsequent removal.

Options (1) and (3) are relevant also in the case of websites without automatic moderation; therefore, the question is whether the publication of the comment itself is an infringement or only the failure to remove it immediately after notification qualifies as infringement.

In a broader sense, this issue can be raised relating to what "duties and responsibilities" a content provider is subject to under Article 10 (2) of the ECHR, with regard to controlling comments posted or intended to be posted there.[37]

D. Basis of responsibility for unlawful comments

In the context of comments, the EU Directive on e-commerce, and the national law,[38] implementing it might be applied, and treats the website's content provider as "hosting." Affected content providers used this argument before the ECtHR, both in the Estonian and Hungarian cases to be discussed later. Under this approach, a content provider that allows commenting is an "intermediary service provider" for those comments that store the information provided by the user (hosting).[39] However, as a rule, the hosting provider is not responsible for the information provided by others, and is simply transmitted, stored or made available through the information society services provided by the intermediary service provider.[40] The hosting provider is also not responsible for unlawful content when "the provider does not have actual knowledge of illegal activity or information and, as regards claims for damages, is not aware of facts or circumstances from which the illegal activity or information is apparent; or the provider, upon obtaining such knowledge or awareness, acts expeditiously to remove or to disable access to the information."[41]

---

37. *Delfi* [GC], Paragraph 115.

38. Act CVIII of 2001 on certain issues of electronic commerce services and information society services (hereinafter as: E-Commerce Act).

39. Directive on electronic commerce, Article 14 (1).

40. Directive on electronic commerce, Article 14 (1).

41. Directive on electronic commerce, Article 14 (1) (a)–(b).

The concept of the hosting service, however, can only be applied to commenting with great difficulty. The hosting service provider is clearly different from the content provider which publishes the content in the storage place; the latter provides the infrastructure for the publication (an element of it), and although it might technically be able to amend the content, it does not generate the content itself, and those using its services do not "connect" to the content of the hosting provider. By contrast, the content provider of a website which permits the posting of comments does not create the comments itself, but they are nonetheless inseparable from its own content, and would be meaningless without its own content since they respond to it. The content provider who allows commenting has its own hosting provider (a third actor) who enables and permits the operation of the website on its servers, and therefore the relationship between the commenter and the content provider is completely different from the relationship between the content provider and the hosting provider. If the provision of commenting a hosting service, then there would be two separate hosting providers for that content, one being the website's content provider and one being the website operation. The legal differentiation between service providers, who have a role in the publication of a given website, and identification of the liability rules applying to them, is not always simple. For instance MTE itself was the blog host, the Blog.hu platform was the (blog) provider, while a third party was the hosting service provider. In theory the liability for the infringing comment may be established against all of them, but according to different rules and under different circumstances.

In theory, one can assume a close relationship between the comment and the article being commented on, since the former reacts to the latter. However, this is not necessarily the case. The actual article can be just an excuse for speaking out, and there might be no content correlation between the article and the comments on it. Indeed, some of the comments may be "off-topic" or written by "trolls"[42]. The importance of this distinction did not, however, emerge in the cases before the ECtHR.

Identifying the provision of commenting as a hosting service is indirectly supported by the case law of the Court of Justice of the European Union. In the *Delfi* case, three decisions of the Luxembourg tribunal were mentioned.[43]

---

42. See the entry "Internet troll" on Wikipedia, https://en.wikipedia.org/wiki/ Internet_troll.

43. Case C-324/09 *L'Oréal and Others*, judgment of 12 July 2011; Case C-70/10 *Scarlet Extended*, judgment of 24 November 2011; Case C-360/10 *SABAM*, judgment of 16 February 2012.

In these decisions, the EU Court held that the providers of services who provide access to unlawful content (search engine, webshop, Internet service provider) are only liable under Article 14 of the E-commerce Directive[44] if they gained knowledge of the unlawful content and failed to take steps to remove it. Hence, by analogy, the content provider who allows commenting could be a hosting provider, although it is true that, in the above-mentioned cases, the relationship between the service provider and the content published by the person committing the infringement may be much more remote, and search engines, webshops and Internet service providers (ISPs) are more akin to a "classic" hosting provider providing the infrastructure than the hosts of the websites containing the comments (for ISPs, this is not in question but in the other two cases, no related content exists). However, the ECtHR rejected this broad interpretation of the "hosting provider" concept in the three judgments on comments, and focused on the civil law responsibility of content providers.

Hungarian case law considers comments to be "*dissemination*" involving the. transmission of information originating from others.[45] If this information is unlawful, the distributor is also liable in the sense that. the website's content provider can be liable for a comment, and in the absence of the author's identification it can have exclusive liability.

In the Hungarian Civil Code, "dissemination" is covered in the section on violation of reputation. "Dissemination" can take place by transmitting a piece of information, typically one containing an untrue statement of facts, but it assumes active conduct and a conscious decision by the content provider. For comments which are not moderated in advance, the content provider does not engage in such active conduct. Where prior moderation does exist, however, this constitutes active conduct and thus a conscious decision has been made; hence there is no obstacle to the establishment of an infringement via dissemination.

Liability for breaching civil law rules on personality rights was also the starting point in the other two relevant cases. The background to the *Delfi case reveals* that the Estonian authorities established that an infringement had been committed by the service provider, applying civil law liability rules.[46] Hence, similarly to Hungary, not only the author but also the content provider in-

---

44. Directive on electronic commerce, Article 14.

45. *Hungarian Association of Content Providers and Index.hu Zrt v. Hungary*, application no. 22947/13, judgment of 6 February 2016. [hereinafter: *MTE*] Paragraphs 26 and 42, New (2013) Civil Code, Section 2:45. §(2), Old (1959) Civil Code, Section 78.

46. *Delfi* [GC], Paragraphs 21–43.

volved in the transmission to the public is liable under civil law for defamatory statements that violate personality rights. In the most recent judgment by the ECtHR related to comments, delivered in the *Pihl* case, the applicant originally claimed a violation of his personality rights in the Swedish court, in a similar way to the plaintiffs in the Estonian and Hungarian cases.[47]

Although the issue of dissemination did not come up in the majority statement of reasons in the Hungarian Constitutional Court's resolution made in the comment case [resolution no. 19/2014. (V. 30.) AB] it was raised in the dissenting opinion of Judge Stumpf, where he refers to a decision made by the Pécs High Court of Appeal in another case.[48] The latter sought to clarify the exact definition of dissemination and held that:

> [D]issemination means the forwarding of news, i.e. to communicate a thought and share information [...]. This assumes active and conscious conduct, i.e. the consciousness of the person violating the right must cover the unlawful claim and expression of opinion, and must share it with the public as the content of their own consciousness, in a communicative manner. [...] In this case, the defendant is capable of removing the unlawful content and it can moderate the comments. Provided that they become aware of the comments' unlawful nature. The website operator cannot be expected to monitor all inputs and entries continuously, in particular in relation to larger content providers. However, it can be expected that, when they become aware of unlawful content on the website operated by it, they shall remove it as soon as possible. Failure to remove it expresses its agreement with the unlawful content. In this case, however, it performs the violation of reputation as set out in Section 78 of the Civil Code."

On this basis, the High Court of Appeal declared, establishing a principle, that:

> [t]he operator of the website accessible via the Internet (intermediary service provider) is subject to civil law liability for the content of comments violating reputation uploaded by another to the website, if it fails to act for the removal immediately upon gaining knowledge of it.

---

47. *Pihl v. Sweden*, application no. 4742/14, decision of 9 March 2017. (hereinafter: *Pihl*).

48. Pécs High Court of Appeal Pf.VI.20.776/2012/5., BDT2013. 2904 See: Constitutional Court resolution no. 19/2014. (V. 30.) AB, Paragraphs 84–88.

This means, according to the High Court of Appeal, that where the content provider removes the challenged content upon request, it will not be liable. However, if it consciously refuses to fulfill the request, it can be considered to disseminate, and consequently, for comments of an unlawful nature, will be liable for the infringement. However, the Constitutional Court chose a different path, and took a step towards the recognition of objective liability—in which case, the free posting of the comment by another person can be considered in itself as an infringement by the content provider.

This raises the question: If we consider the posting of a specific comment to be unlawful (violating personality rights), what then is the legal basis for the content provider's exemption from civil law liability if the comment is removed? The approach taken by the Constitutional Court may be justified to the extent that traditionally the civil law fails to differentiate between unlawful situations of differing duration-this can only be taken into account when imposing the sanction rather than when establishing the infringement.

Alongside the notions of a hosting service and of dissemination, possible third interpretation is that the comment is nothing more than a "reader's letter," making it very similar to the genre well known from the traditional press and so it can be assessed in a similar way.[49] This would mean unconditional liability of the content provider for the content. However, the analogy to the reader's letter could emerge consistently only with regard to comments moderated in advance and passed through the filter, since in the printed press each reader's letter is published as a result of a conscious editorial decision, and so the analogy would require such a decision to have been taken for comments before are displayed. A comment moderated subsequently, or not moderated at all, can hardly be regarded as equivalent to a reader's letter.

IV. The ECtHR's case law relating to comments

A. Overview of the cases

The *Delfi* case[50] was the first ECtHR case on comments. Delfi is a popular news website in Estonia, on which seriously defamatory comments were

---

49. Nádori Péter, 'Kommentek a magyar interneten: polgári jogi gyakorlat' ['Comments on the Hungarian Internet: civil law practice'] *In Medias Res* 2012/2. 319.

50. *Delfi* [GC] and its background: *Delfi v. Estonia*, application no. 64569/09, judgment of 10 October 2013 (hereinafter: *Delfi*).

posted by readers regarding a company referred to in an article.[51] Although the Estonian court of first instance applied the law on e-commerce, classifying the news portal's service provider as a hosting provider, the court of appeal and the Supreme Court decided the case on the basis of the law on civil law obligations, establishing a violation of the rights of the plaintiff (the owner and at the same time the member of the supervisory board of the affected company).[52] The application of the service provider was turned down in 2013 by the First Section of the ECtHR, and in 2015 by the Grand Chamber, declaring that its call to account does not violate Article 10 of the ECHR.

In the *MTE* case, the Fourth Section of the ECtHR decided in favour of the applicant. One of the two applicants in the case was a professional association, and the other a large news portal. As in the *Delfi* case, personal rights procedures were initiated related to defamatory readers' comments attached to an article criticising a company's operation.[53] None of the Hungarian courts considered the rules on hosting providers to be applicable, so they decided that the Civil Code's rules on the protection of reputation had been violated.[54] However, the ECtHR established that the judgment of the Hungarian courts was contrary to Article 10, primarily due to the less defamatory nature of comments compared to the comments in the *Delfi* case.[55]

---

51. A few examples of the 20 comments cited by the EctHR in its judgment:
    - open water is closer to the places you referred to, and the ice is thinner. Proposal—let's do as in 1905, let's go to [K]uressaare with sticks and put [L.] and [Le.] in a bag
    - good that [La.'s] initiative has not broken down the lines of the web flamers. go ahead, guys, [L.] into the oven!
    - [little L.] go and drown yourself
    - What are you whining, kill this bastard once[.] In the future the other ones … will know what they will risk, even they will only have one little life.
    - and can't anyone defy the shits?
52. *Delfi* [GC], Paragraphs 22., 38.
53. The three comments found to be unlawful were as follows:
    - They have talked about these two rubbish real estate websites a thousand times already.
    - Is this not that Benkō-Sándor-sort-of sly, rubbish, mug company again? I ran into it two years ago, since then they have kept sending me emails about my overdue debts and this and that. I am above 100,000 [Hungarian forints] now. I have not paid and I am not going to. That's it."
    - People like this should go and shit a hedgehog and spend all their money on their mothers' tombs until they drop dead.
54. *MTE*, Paragraphs 15–25.
55. *MTE*, Paragraphs 76, 91.

The applicant in *Pihl*, this time not a legal entity, unsuccessfully resorted to the Swedish courts regarding the violation of his personal rights by comments posted about an article written about him.[56] In its decision, the ECtHR did not establish the violation of Article 8. In the Swedish legal system, there are separate regulations regarding comments, based on which seriously unlawful comments (certain statutory definitions of criminal law offences, and violating copyrights) must be removed. However, the Swedish courts concluded that this law did not apply to comments that are "merely" defamatory.[57] According to the Third Section of the ECtHR, the comments were not so seriously unlawful that not sanctioning them would result in the violation of Article 8.[58]

B. Set of criteria shown in the cases before the ECtHR

In these three judgments of the ECtHR, the outlines of a multi-element set of criteria are taking shape, albeit without any guidance regarding the degree to which each criterion is relevant. We discuss the criteria below. The common starting point for the decisions is that the establishment of the gatekeeper content provider's liability in itself does not infringe its right to freedom of speech.

1) The content of the comment

MTE establishes the idea that the subject of the original article (to which comments were posted) concerned a public matter,[59] and that this is of material importance. When a post concerns public matters, there should be increased protection for freedom of speech.[60]

Several authors have argued that certain parts of Internet communications, such as comments, should be assessed according to different criteria than others, since they are often less well thought-out due to their nature, often written in anger, fail to reflect actual considerations, and do not suggest actual intentions to act, hence their nature is different from that of the opinions published in the traditional media.[61] This (properly substantiated) approach is partly

---

56. The only affected comment:
   • that guy pihl is also a real hash-junkie according to several people I have spoken to.
57. *Pihl*, Paragraph 12.
58. *Pihl*, Paragraph 36.
59. *MTE*, Paragraph 72.
60. Eric Barendt, *Freedom of Speech* (OUP, 2005, 2nd ed.) pp. 155–62.
61. Jacob H. Rowbottom, 'To Rant, Vent and Converse: Protecting Low Level Digital Speech' 71 *Cambridge Law Journal* (2012) No. 2. 355.; Ian Cram, *Citizen Journalists Newer Media, Republican Moments and the Constitution* (Cheltenham: Edward Elgar 2015) pp. 73–111. Péter Nádori, 'Anonymous Mass Speech on the Internet and the Balancing of Fundamental Rights' in Koltay (ed.), *Comparative*, pp. 217, 245–246.

contradicted by the ECtHR which considers not only the relevant articles but also the comments posted on them as deserving protection, due to their involvement in the public debate, thereby attributing key importance to them.[62] According to the former approach, comments (or other similar online phenomena) need not be taken completely seriously, and it is unnecessary to restrict them due to their relative immateriality, while the ECtHR consider comments as public/political opinion and deserving of the strictest protection, although it declares their lower stylistic value, which is typical of numerous websites and mitigates the effect related to such infringements.[63] With that said, the ECtHR considers that such content can still be restricted according to the usual tests applied to public debates. It is to be noted too that this reference to their "low value" can be turned on its head: if comments are less capable of shaping the public debate, their restriction obviously affects the public in a less negative way.

Some of the comments in *Delfi* were assessed by the Grand Chamber as "hate speech",[64] and this interpretation was taken over later by *MTE* and *Pihl*, although in *Delfi*, the First Section itself did not make such an assessment.[65] While the Grand Chamber made unusually frequent repetitions in *Delfi*, by talking about "clearly unlawful" comments,[66] the *MTE* and the *Pihl* judgments reject the restriction on freedom of speech on exactly this basis, saying that, contrary to the comments encouraging hate and violence to be assessed in *Delfi*, comments in the other two cases, although offensive[67] and defamatory,[68] are altogether less serious, and thus they can be subjected to the protection afforded to freedom of speech by Article 10.

The common lesson to be learned from these three cases is that an assessment of the comment's content is of essential importance in assessing the content provider's responsibility.

2) Identifiability of the commenter

It has already been noted that identification of the communicator depends on the type of procedure initiated in regard to the comment being complained

---

62. *Delfi* [GC], Paragraphs 11, 28, 29; *MTE*, Paragraph 72.

63. *MTE*, Paragraph 77.

64. *Delfi* [GC], Paragraph 117.

65. It only highlights that the original article caused a "higher than average risk" for comments containing hate speech, see *Delfi*, Paragraph 86.

66. *Delfi* [GC], Paragraphs 128, 140, 141, 153, 156, 159.

67. *MTE*, Paragraphs 76, 91.

68. *Pihl*, Paragraph 25.

about. In a criminal procedure (after a report for criminal defamation), identification of the perpetrator is more likely. The ECtHR has taken the position that uncertainties in identification, existing in each case, provide a sufficient reason for the procedure on the grounds that an unlawful comment can be initiated directly against the content provider.[69] That is, an attempt at identification (or the absence of it), and the choice between the available procedures, will not affect the decision on the content provider's responsibility. At the same time, in *Pihl* the ECtHR imputes to the applicant that, although it acquired the IP address of the computer used by the comment's author, it failed to take further steps to identify the author.[70] Nevertheless, the weight of this circumstance in the adjudication of the case is not completely clear from the decision.

The argument brought up in the comment cases is not only relevant in connection with anonymous comments. The arguments for the content provider's responsibility in the ECtHR's decisions raise the possibility of establishing the content provider's responsibility, even for comments published when the author's name is given. Hence, for a comment posted to a Facebook post, the user of the social media profile (be it a private individual, a public figure or a content provider itself) can be responsible for the post, the author of which can be identified (provided that the particulars specified are true) with a single click. The Hungarian case law holds that the responsibility of the profile holder, who published the post that was commented on by another user, can be established for violation of reputation.[71]

3) The content provider's person

In *Delfi*, the ECtHR put great emphasis on the economic interests of the content provider.[72] According to the ECtHR, provision of the opportunity to post comments served the economic interests of the news portal's publisher; comments themselves attracted the public to the site. In *MTE*, there were two applicants; one of them was a news portal with economic interests and the

---

69. *Delfi* [GC], Paragraphs 147–151.

70. *Pihl*, Paragraph 34.

71. However, the two decisions published so far are not completely compatible with each other. See: BH2016. 330 ("The holder of a Facebook profile is liable for communications with unlawful content"), and BDT2017. 65 ("The content provider fulfils the requirement of conduct that can be expected under the circumstances where, in the event of a complaint against a comment posted to a content published on its Internet portal (Facebook site), it removes that comment without delay"—but in the event of failure to do so, it might be liable for the infringement.).

72. *Delfi*, Paragraph 94; *Delfi* [GC] Paragraphs 115, 116, 128, 144.

other a professional (not-for-profit) organisation; the difference between these two was noted by the ECtHR,[73] but it failed to draw the relevant consequences from the distinction.[74] This ultimately did not have any negative effect for the not-for-profit applicant since the ECtHR upheld the applications as to both of them. In *Pihl*, however, the statement of reasons on the judgment highlighted that low traffic on the website and the not-for-profit nature of the content provider were important considerations.[75]

4) *The person of the affected party*

Another relevant consideration involves who the comments are targeted against. In *the MTE case*, the target of the comments was a legal entity, the operation and criticism of which clearly qualified as a public matter. In any case, the protection of a legal entity's rights should be assessed differently than those of natural persons; the "moral" rights of legal entities deserve less strict protection.[76] In *MTE*, the ECtHR articulated the need for this differentiation.[77] It would be interesting to see whether the ECtHR's assessment of the comments would have changed if the actual targets of the comments, the managers of the company, had initiated the case in their own name and not in the name of the affected company as a legal person, since their honour could be seriously violated by the comments. In *Pihl* it is not evident from the ECtHR judgment whether the applicant was a private individual or a public figure. From the content of the article it can be assumed that he qualified to some extent as the latter, but this remains an assumption only and a circumstance that would have justified more thorough examination by the ECtHR.

5) *The effect of the comment on the attacked party*

The *Delfi* and the *Pihl* judgments failed to examine the effect of the state authorities' decision on the attacked party, but *MTE* suggested that this factor might be relevant.[78] Here it is necessary to distinguish between the violation of

---

73. *MTE*, Paragraph 73.
74. Dirk Voorhoof, 'Pihl v. Sweden: non-profit blog operator is not liable for defamatory users' comments in case of prompt removal upon notice', *Strasbourg Observers Blog*, 20 March 2017. See https://strasbourgobservers.com/2017/03/20/pihl-v-sweden-non-profit-blog-operator-is-not-liable-for-defamatory-users-comments-in-case-of-prompt-removal-upon-notice/.
75. *Pihl*, Paragraphs 31, 37.
76. *Uj v. Hungary*, application no. 23954/10., judgment of 19 July 2011. Par. 22.
77. *MTE*, Paragraph 65.
78. *MTE*, Paragraph 85.

a company's business reputation, and a comment which negatively affects the social status of a private individual, because this latter interest is protected more thoroughly.[79]

6) The conduct of the content provider

The content provider's conduct is of key importance. In *Delfi*, the Grand Chamber established that, although the content provider immediately removed the comment after its attention was drawn to it (i.e. it performed *ex post* moderation), that act was not sufficient to escape liability, since the provider should have prevented the publication of the "clearly unlawful" comments (i.e., it should have performed prior moderation).[80] This requirement *mutatis mutandis* assumes the preliminary assessment of all comments, by which the content provider would clearly become an "editor".

In *Delfi*, the news portal had a separate comment policy, which set content boundaries for users. In addition, it included a disclaimer on the website, i.e. that authors are responsible for the content of comments. Furthermore, the portal operated an efficient notice-and-takedown system which it used to remove unlawful comments after notification. As a result, the content provider could not be considered a "passive, clearly technical" service provider.[81] In *Delfi* the unlawful comments were accessible for six weeks even though the service provider removed it upon notification. However, the harmful content was accessible on the website for a lengthy period (in particular considering the "lifespan" of an online article and the related comments).

In *MTE*, the affected websites operated in a similar manner, displaying a disclaimer, and for index.hu there was a published moderation policy, and both content providers operated notice-and-takedown systems. The offended company failed to request the removal of comments but went to court immediately.[82]

In *Pihl*, the content provider removed not only the comment but also the related article, since it contained a false factual claim regarding the applicant's membership in the Nazi Party, thereby violating his reputation.[83] The comment was removed by the service provider the day after notification, on the ninth day after publication.[84]

---

79. *MTE*, Paragraph 84.
80. *Delfi* [GC], Paragraph 141.
81. *Delfi* [GC], Paragraphs 144–146, 155, 159.
82. *MTE*, Paragraphs 80, 81, 83.
83. *Pihl*, Paragraph 30.
84. *Pihl*, Paragraphs 32, 37.

7) *Sanction applied*

The gravity of the sanction against the content provider is another criterion that might be analysed in examining the violation of Article 10. In *Delfi*, the EUR 320 damages imposed as compensation by the Estonian courts was not found to be disproportionate by the ECtHR, nor the possible indirect consequences of the decision. As the Grand Chamber put it, following the decisions made by the Estonian courts, the news portal was not forced to change its business model and no additional costs were incurred. Indeed, Delfi remained one of the most popular news portal in Estonia, in terms of receiving the largest number of anonymous comments, and had in any event already employed moderators earlier.[85]

Contrary to this, in *MTE*, the Second Section considered the legal consequences imposed on the content providers to be grave, even in the absence of ordering compensation.[86] By establishing the infringement in court, and ordering the content providers to pay the not excessively high court fees, the Hungarian court, according to the ECtHR, incurred wider consequences from its decision, encouraging them to close down their sections for commenting in the future and not to provide this option to their readers.[87]

8) *Summary*

The gravity of the above criteria and their relationship is still unclear. Two extreme situations can be identified. Comments with gravely offensive (hateful, threatening, encouraging violence) content, which appear through the offices of a service provider with economic interests related to the publication of the comment, and which attack a natural person, without prior moderation, with lenient court sanctions, can surely be restricted on the basis of these three ECtHR judgments. On the other hand, comments that are "only" defamatory or violate other personal rights (such as privacy), that are published on a not-for-profit website, are made against a legal entity and removed immediately upon notification and subject to grave official sanctions, can surely be covered by the protection afforded by Article 10 of the ECHR. The numerous situations that arise between these two extremes are to be assessed on a case by case basis, by weighing the relevant circumstances and determining their weight in the relevant case.

---

85. *Delfi* [GC], Paragraphs 160–161.
86. *MTE*, Paragraph 86.
87. Ibid.

V. Main criticism of the ECtHR's judgments

A. Liability of a content provider

The main criticism considers the element of the ECtHR practice present in all three cases, that in certain cases the content provider can be held liable for comments. In other words, it cannot clearly be considered an intermediary service provider, the obligation of which to remove unlawful content emerges only upon notification. It is certain that legal systems that expect more than this—that impose a kind of special editorial obligation on content providers—do not breach Article 10 by this alone. It is still too early to establish whether the ECtHR *expects* such an attitude from legal systems towards this issue, i.e. the violation of Article 8 can be established in the absence of a mandatory requirement in the state's legal system to moderate gravely unlawful content automatically (without a separate notification). On the basis of *Pihl*, one might think that this probably does not hold, but in that case the violation was "not serious" according to the ECtHR (defamation), and it follows from the Swedish regulations that, in the event of the hate speech, the actual threat and incitement to violence referred to in *Delfi*, the Swedish authorities would have acted. Regulations providing almost complete (U.S.-type) exemption for the content provider would probably not be compatible with Article 8 of the ECHR.

The European approach has been criticised by many, amongst others Judge Sajó, who wrote a lengthy dissenting opinion to the Grand Chamber's judgment in *Delfi*, which drew attention to the risk of "collateral censorship" caused by the decision which encourages interference from the content provider.[88] Nádori[89] and Cheung[90] also fear restriction of freedom of speech in the future. According to Voorhoof, *Delfi* may have far-reaching consequences for the expression of opinion online. It seems that only prior moderation can offer full security for content providers; subsequent removal in itself does not secure full exemption from liability. This would create a new paradigm of online media, enabling personal involvement in debates, and might lead to the termination of comment-posting opportunities, in order to cut costs and

---

88. *Delfi* [GC], Judge Sajó's dissenting opinion, Paragraphs 1–3.
89. Nádori, 'Anonymous Mass Speech', 217.
90. Anne SY Cheung, 'Liability of Internet Host Providers in Defamation Actions: From Gatekeepers to Identifiers' in András Koltay (ed.), *Media Freedom and Regulation in the New Media World* (Budapest: Wolters Kluwer 2014) pp. 289, 293.

avoid the possible danger of liability.[91] *MTE* and *Pihl* somewhat mitigate this worry but, being aware of these, one can still assume that full security can be afforded only by prior moderation which inevitably filters out borderline content in addition to "clearly" unlawful comments.

It is true that while many bells were rung for the freedom of online speech after the ECtHR decisions, especially after *Delfi*, only a few were concerned with the effective protection of personality rights in the context of anonymous comments. This issue is usually negated by reference to the "inferior" or low style of Internet communication and the insignificant effect of comments on the assessment of the attacked person. Angelopoulos and Smet, at the same time, argued that European legal thinking generally is incompatible with the full exemption of content providers from legal liability, and with tipping the balance between freedom of speech and personality rights towards the former.[92]

B. Importance of the "economic service"

The economic interest of the content provider should not be a decisive argument in establishing legal liability for comments. Had we imputed the financial interests of the media as a kind of "aggravating circumstance", professional media cannot exist in the absence of proper economic foundations. Even subject to this, the ECtHR approach of identifying an economic interest in allowing the posting of comments, and considering it a circumstance linking the article published by the content provider and the comments posted thereto, thus refuting the content provider's hosting provider status in the context of comments (since the latter must be completely independent from the user content posted on its storage space), is not totally unfounded. The different assessment of not-for-profit websites and large news portals can be justifiable in certain cases.

---

91. Dirk Voorhoof, 'Qualification of news portal as publisher of users' comment may have far-reaching consequences for online freedom of expression: Delfi AS v. Estonia' *Strasbourg Observers Blog*, 25 October 2013. See https://strasbourgobservers.com/2013/10/25/qualification-of-news-portal-as-publisher-of-users-comment-may-have-far-reaching-consequences-for-online-freedom-of-expression-delfi-as-v-estonia/; Dirk Voorhoof, 'Delfi AS v. Estonia: Grand Chamber confirms liability of online news portal for offensive comments posted by its readers' *Strasbourg Observers Blog*, 18 June 2015. See https://strasbourgobservers.com/2015/06/18/delfi-as-v-estonia-grand-chamber-confirms-liability-of-online-news-portal-for-offensive-comments-posted-by-its-readers/.

92. Christina Angelopoulos—Stijn Smet, Notice-and-fair-balance: How to Reach a Compromise Between Fundamental Rights in European Intermediary Liability' 8 *Journal of Media Law* (2016), no. 2. 266, 287.

Even though *MTE* did little to settle this issue, in *Pihl* the ECtHR already emphasised the small scale and freedom from financial interests of the affected side.[93]

C. Expecting moderation

As we noted above, it follows from the current practice of the ECtHR that, where a content provider wants to avoid liability completely, it must moderate all comments in advance or at the latest directly after their posting, in no way relying on notification from the injured party.[94] This indeed puts a heavy burden on content providers, even if most comments are not unlawful and it is not excessively complicated to establish this for them. For providers, the theoretical possibility of being held liable is the real threat rather than the actual legal proceedings which are initiated against them quite rarely.

D. Assessment of the comment's content

From these three cases, it turns out that comments embodying "hate speech", "threat" or "incitement to violence" are to be assessed as most serious because they are "clearly unlawful"[95], while it is a lot more difficult to establish the content provider's liability for "merely" defamatory comments. Some of the comments in *Delfi* were classified by the ECtHR as hate speech. In this context the issue arises that, while the owner of the affected company initiated the procedure in Estonian courts to protect the personality rights of that company, and the Estonian courts held the news portal's service provider liable for protecting these rights, hate speech is traditionally a criminal law concept, which needs to be restricted to protect some kind of common interest or the public order.[96] As such, the ECtHR created the category of hate speech to be prosecuted at the individual's request and to protect his rights in *Delfi*, which merges the various limitations on freedom of speech, each of which are legitimate and justifiable in themselves, but which are otherwise clearly separable.

Highlighting "threat" and "incitement to violence" is also problematic. On the one hand, the ECtHR claims that the stylistic value of expression of opinions on the Internet is generally low, and this is why it is not warranted to assess it according to the content scales established for the traditional media. But

---

93. Voorhoof, 'Pihl v. Sweden'.
94. *Delfi* [GC], Paragraph 159, Voorhoof, 'Pihl v. Sweden'.
95. *Delfi* [GC], Paragraph 128, 140, 141, 153, 156, 159.
96. See Ivan Hare—James Weinstein (eds.), *Extreme Speech and Democracy* (OUP 2009).

if this is true then why take threats and incitement to violence seriously and why assess them as causing more serious harm than defamation?

The main issue of decision-making left to the content provider is as to the procedure and criteria used in considering challenged content necessarily differ from the content and procedural rules set out by the law. The content provider can decide arbitrarily; it is not tied by constitutional guarantees; it can have its own policies and set of rules and take decisions that are not transparent; their details and justifications cannot be studied, and there are no clear-cut remedies against them.[97] Currently, content or platform service providers (social media, video-sharing platforms) can decide freely regarding the removal of content. Considering the influence these services have on the public sphere (of course this is primarily true for social media and not for the comment feeds available on certain less popular websites), this is rather dangerous from the point of view of freedom of speech.

The service provider and the moderator acting on its behalf are not law enforcement agencies; they decide on content on the basis of different standards and reasons, for example by primarily defending the economic interests and smooth operation of the service provider. They cannot be expected to take over the court's role, in the absence of the necessary background and guarantees, but their decisionmaking should be somehow in line with at least some basic principles, which take into account both freedom of speech and the interests of the democratic public sphere. It is not completely satisfactory to leave the handling of these issues to the notice-and-takedown procedure; the E-commerce Directive links the emergence of the obligations of the intermediary service provider to the awareness of the infringement,[98] while under the civil law rules applied in the comment cases, a near-immediate or at least very quick takedown also exempts the service provider from liability, while the unlawful nature of comments can only be established to a satisfactory manner by the courts in a rather lengthy procedure.[99] It follows that a service provider necessarily overperforms i.e. takes down lawful content that it deems to be risky.

According to my assessment, in its case law so far, the ECtHR has not been completely principled. While it has made it clear that it expects some active in-

---

97. Dirk Voorhoof—Eva Lievens, 'Offensive Online Comments—New ECtHR Judgment' *ECHR Blog*, 15 February 2016. See http://echrblog.blogspot.hu/2016/02/offensive-online-comments-new-ecthr.html.

98. Directive on electronic commerce, Articles 12–14.

99. See this issue in Angelopoulos—Smit, 'Notice-and-fair-balance' 285.

volvement from content providers in their assessment of comments, the court has failed to specify the criteria for such involvement. Also, by selecting among the various types of free speech restrictions, classifying some of them as more serious than others, based on unclear justifications, the ECtHR has itself contributed to the reinforcement of problems related to the "private censorship" of freedom of speech, which in any case inevitably proliferate in the era of online gatekeepers.

VI. Conclusion

In the era of Facebook, comments can seem to be a relic from the past. However, numerous Internet content providers provide space for comments in their social media systems, and general user communication has largely moved to social media. Even with this in mind, the issues present are worthy of in-depth investigation, since the issue raised by comments raise important societal questions. Content providers who allow comment posting are Internet gatekeepers, many other types of which are known (infrastructure providers, platform providers: social media, video sharing portals, or search engines, webshops, etc.), and in connection with which similar liability issues may emerge. So far the ECtHR has not yet raised these questions. In *Delfi*, the ECtHR expressly declared that the decision did not apply to other forums of Internet communication that permit the publication of third party comments.[100] However, this does not exclude this does not exclude the possibility that the reasoning of the decisions could be used in the future in cases involving other services.[101] The obligations of gatekeepers, the conditions for establishing their legal liability, and user rights against them are issues that will determine the future framework of freedom of speech in Internet communication.

European legal systems opt for balancing the opposing rights,[102] aiming for a "fair balance".[103] This approach is contrary to the clear-cut rules in the U.S.

---

100. Delfi [GC], Paragraph 116.

101. For instance, certain European courts established the liability of Facebook for publication of user content committing the tort of misuse of private information, in those cases when the content concerned was not removed, despite the provider having knowledge of the respective infringement. See: the decision of the court of appeal of Northern Ireland in the CG v. Facebook case ([2016] NICA 54). For an analysis of this decision, see: Lorna Woods, 'When is Facebook Liable for Illegal Content under the E-commerce Directive? CG v. Facebook in the Northern Ireland Courts' EU Law Analysis, 19 January 2017. Available here: http://eulawanalysis.blogspot.hu/2017/01/when-is-facebook-liable-for-illegal.html.

102. Barendt, *Freedom of Speech*, pp. 205–27.

103. Angelopoulos—Smit, 'Notice-and-fair-balance' 275.

that generally exempt gatekeepers from liability. In Europe, proper balancing would be greatly enhanced by statutory legislation (adopted for example in the United Kingdom in 2013[104]), because it is clear that neither the e-commerce rules nor the general private law liability rules are fully capable of dealing with the issue of comments, and in general with the liability of online gatekeepers.

The debate on the obligation of content providers and the preservation of freedom of speech will doubtless continue. However, in Europe it can no longer be questioned whether content providers necessarily perform "editing" regarding users' comments. The traditional concept of media in the era of on-line gatekeepers cannot be fully maintained; there is already an unavoidable intervention in the communication process and content by those who do not take part in content production itself. This is a different type of editing from the traditional model, but it is similar in many aspects. Aligning the regulation of media and freedom of speech to this phenomenon is unavoidable.

---

104. James Price—Felicity McMahon (eds.): *Blackstone's Guide to the Defamation Act 2013* (OUP 2013); Alastair Mullis—Andrew Scott, 'Tilting at Windmills: the Defamation Act 2013' 77 *Modern Law Review* (January 2014) 87.

Mariette Jones*

Privilege, Power, and the Perversion of Privacy Protection

At the start of summer 2017, England found itself trying to come to terms with three major terrorist attacks in as many months. The attacks targeting tourists at the Houses of Parliament, youngsters at a pop concert in Manchester, and late night revellers enjoying rare warm weather at pubs and restaurants near London Bridge,[1] are themselves only the latest in a string of Islamist terrorist atrocities facing Western Europe over the past few years. Death tolls are substantial: The November 2015 attack on the Bataclan nightclub in Paris claimed 130 lives,[2] the Nice 2016 Bastille Day vehicle ramming attack cost 85 lives,[3] the Berlin Christmas market attack 12,[4] the explosions in Brussels 32.[5] In fact, these terrorist attacks have become such a regular oc-

---

* Senior Lecturer in Law and Fellow of the Higher Education Academy, Middlesex University London, School of Law.

1. *See* Dominic Casciani, *London Attack: What we have learned,* BBC (Jun. 4, 2017), http://www.bbc.co.uk/news/uk-40154268. *See also* Vikram Dodd, Helen Pidd, et al, *At least 22 killed, 59 injured in suicide attack at Manchester Arena,* THE GUARDIAN, (May 23, 2017) https://www.theguardian.com/uk-news/2017/may/22/manchester-arena-police-explosion-ariana-grande-concert-england. For an interesting analysis of the Westminster and other Islamist terror attacks, *see* Jason Burke, *The myth of the 'lone wolf' terrorist,* THE GUARDIAN (March 30, 2017). https://www.theguardian.com/news/2017/mar/30/myth-lone-wolf-terrorist.

2. *See Paris attacks death toll rises to 130,* RTE NEWS (Nov. 20 2015) https://www.rte.ie/news/2015/1120/747897-paris/. *See also Houses of Parliament attack: four dead including police officer,* THE GUARDIAN (Mar. 22, 2017) https://www.theguardian.com/uk-news/2017/mar/22/westminster-attack-man-shot-by-police-and-several-hurt-in-nearby-incident.

3. Death toll from France truck attack rises to 85, BNO NEWS. (Aug.4, 2016) http://bnonews.com/news/index.php/news/id4998.

4. Cath Levett, Glenn Swann, et. al., *Berlin Christmas market attack: a graphical guide to what we know so far,* THE GUARDIAN (Dec.23, 2017) https://www.theguardian.com/world/2016/dec/21/berlin-christmas-market-attack-a-graphical-guide-to-what-we-know-so-far.

5. *Another bomb found in Brussels after attacks kill at least 34; Islamic State claims responsibility,* THE LOS ANGELES TIMES (Mar. 22, 2016).

currence that even the mainstream media is beginning to refer to the situation as the 'new normal'.[6]

If the death toll and attacks continue, it may reach a point where it could well be argued that a *de facto* state of civil war exists. Thus it is not surprising that in the wake of such events, calls invariably follow for more powers to be given to the security services to monitor suspects. Are average citizens prepared to sacrifice some (or depending on how one looks at it, more) of their democratic liberties in order to secure safety? And even if they are, would it make any difference? In the digital age, surveillance capabilities are truly astounding: Individuals going about their daily lives are routinely monitored to such an extent that the picture that emerges using such metadata is a profiler's dream.[7] And still successful attacks continue against this background of already unprecedented public and state access to private information: Modern day terrorists, by all accounts fully engaged in online and public activity and as such subject to routine surveillance the same as everybody else, continue to slip through the net. Nevertheless let's suppose, for the sake of argument, that increased surveillance capabilities (and the concomitant intrusion on privacy) would, or could, make a difference. It could even be argued that a single life saved might tilt the balance in this argument. In that case, it may be time for jurists to take a step back and reflect again on privacy, and its democratic price.

Against this background, this essay will focus on the current state of privacy protection in the United Kingdom, and will seek to elicit debate on two contrasting propositions. The first is that privacy protection runs the risk of becoming a tool of the powerful, analogous to the (alleged) abuse of pre-reform libel laws. The second proposition is that the nature of modern life demands a *de facto* surrender of privacy rights, and that any discussion of privacy needs to acknowledge this. Warren and Brandeis,[8] following Judge Cooley,[9] famously stated that

---

6. *Cf.* Prof Cas Mudde, *The Brussels Attacks and the New Normal of Terrorism in Western Europe*, THE HUFFINGTON POST (Mar. 26 2016) http://www.huffingtonpost.com/cas-mudde/the-brussels-attacks-and_b_9521360.html.

7. *See* Mariette Jones, *Double-Lock or Double-Bind? The Investigatory Powers Bill and Freedom of Expression in the United Kingdom* IN VI THE GLOBAL PAPERS SERIES, CYBERSURVEILLANCE IN A POST-SNOWDEN WORLD: BALANCING THE FIGHT AGAINST TERRORISM AGAINST FUNDAMENTAL RIGHTS 3, 5–7 (Russell L. Weaver, Steven I. Friedland, et al. eds., 2017).

8. Samuel Warren & Louis Brandeis, *The Right to Privacy* 4 HARVARD LR 193 (1890).

9. THOMAS MCINTYRE COOLEY, A TREATISE ON THE LAW OF TORTS OR THE WRONGS WHICH ARISE INDEPENDENTLY OF CONTRACT 29 (2 ed. 1888).

privacy entails the 'right to be left alone'. A true understanding of life lived fully in a modern state reveals that the average person is almost *never* 'left alone'. This reality cannot be ignored in any privacy discussion or policy formulation.

Having examined these two disparate propositions, the context of increased uncertainty about basic security will be used in the final section to colour the questions that are raised about the law's handling of privacy concerns in the UK. In the end, the purpose of this essay is to elicit debate in this critical area.

I. Privacy protection in the United Kingdom

First, however, we have to contextualise the discussion by briefly summarising the current UK legal approach to privacy. 'Privacy' itself is not a monolithic concept. American jurists recognise privacy to consist of '... not one tort, but a complex of four'.[10] In the UK and EU it has also been recognised that the concept is an umbrella term for a myriad of interests. Article 8 of the European Convention of Human Rights (ECHR) which confers the right to privacy and family life, in particular, spans such a large range of possible contexts that Lord Walker described it as the 'Indefinite Article 8'.[11]

With the adoption of the Human Rights Act 1998 (the HRA) the judiciary had to give effect to the ECHR in English law. [12] When Article 8 came in for

---

10. DEAN PROSSER, THE LAW OF TORTS 804 (4 ed. 1971).

11. Robert Walker, Justice of the Supreme Court, The Indefinite Article 8, Thomas Moore Lecture, Lincoln's Inn, (Nov.9, 2011) (transcript available at https://www.supremecourt.uk/docs/speech_111109.pdf).

12. In terms of the HRA, English courts are under a duty to develop the law in accordance with the various rights and freedoms contained in the European Convention of Human Rights (ECHR). This means that their decisions should, as far as not in conflict with primary legislation, be compatible with these rights. Section 2 of the HRA reads: "— Interpretation of Convention rights.

(1) A court or tribunal determining a question which has arisen in connection with a Convention right must take into account any—

(a) judgment, decision, declaration or advisory opinion of the European Court of Human Rights,

(b) opinion of the Commission given in a report adopted under Article 31 of the Convention,

(c) decision of the Commission in connection with Article 26 or 27(2) of the Convention, or

(d) decision of the Committee of Ministers taken under Article 46 of the Convention,

whenever made or given, so far as, in the opinion of the court or tribunal, it is relevant to the proceedings in which that question has arisen." See also s 6(1), (2) and s 3(1).

scrutiny, the courts declined to recognise or develop a general tort of privacy invasion. Instead the judiciary developed the tort of misuse of private information from the test for breach of confidence,[13] and stated that the other aspects of privacy invasion are likewise sufficiently covered by existing torts. Where gaps remain this was to be filled by the legislature.

While recognising the various manifestations of privacy, this essay will focus on a theme that runs through most privacy jurisprudence in the UK, namely the expectation of privacy, and the public interest as a countervailing argument, as concepts linking the two propositions under examination.

A. Invasion of privacy not a tort in itself

A good starting point for discussing common law privacy protection in the UK is *Wainwright v Home Office*.[14] The House of Lords[15] confirmed that a general right to privacy has never been (and continued not to be) formally accepted as a stand-alone cause of action in English jurisprudence. It is worthwhile spending some time reflecting on this case. The claimants, (Mrs Wainwright) and her son (21 year old Alan, who happened to be mentally impaired and suffered from cerebral palsy), were fruitlessly strip-searched for drugs on a prison visit in 1997. The search was very invasive and not conducted according to the relevant prison rules. For instance, the search consent form was given after, not before the fact; Mrs Wainwright was searched in a room with an un-curtained window to the outside instead of a private room, and instead of no physical contact, Alan had to endure one prison officer touching his penis to lift the foreskin. Understandably, both claimants were left humiliated and distressed, and Alan was affected to such an extent that he developed post-traumatic stress syndrome.

In their claim for trespass to the person, the court was asked to declare that the UK recognised a tort of invasion of privacy under which the searches of both Wainwrights were actionable, and damages for emotional distress recoverable. Lord Hoffmann summed up the prevailing judicial attitude in his classic dictum on whether or not such a tort exists, or should exist in the English common law:

---

13. *Campbell v Mirror Group Newspapers Ltd* [2004] UKHL 22; [2004] 2 A.C. 457, see discussion below.

14. *Wainwright v Home Office* [2003] UKHL 53 [2004] 2 AC 406.

15. Until replaced by the Supreme Court of the United Kingdom on 1 October 2009, the House of Lords functioned as the highest appeal court in the UK.

There seems to me a great difference between identifying privacy as a value which underlies the existence of a rule of law (and may point the direction in which the law should develop) and privacy as a principle of law in itself. The English common law is familiar with the notion of underlying values — principles only in the broadest sense — which direct its development. A famous example is *Derbyshire County Council v Times Newspapers Ltd [1993] AC 534*, in which freedom of speech was the underlying value which supported the decision to lay down the specific rule that a local authority could not sue for libel. But no one has suggested that freedom of speech is in itself a legal principle which is capable of sufficient definition to enable one to deduce specific rules to be applied in concrete cases. That is not the way the common law works.[16]

Turning to the duty to give effect to Article 8 of the ECHR, Lord Hoffmann noted that the European Court of Human Rights (ECtHR) only asks whether English law provides an adequate remedy in any given case where it had come to the conclusion that an invasion of privacy contrary to article 8(1) had occurred which was not justifiable under article 8(2), '… and its jurisprudence did not suggest that anything more is required, such as adopting 'some high level principle of privacy'.[17]

In the final analysis the Court concluded that this was an area which required legislation to provide the necessary detail, rather than the broad brush of common law principle.[18] Lord Hoffmann further noted that even if the court had found that there was a breach of Article 8 (which on the facts it found not to have happened), such a breach would only have demonstrated that there was a gap in the English remedies for invasion of privacy, which he then argued had since been filled by sections 6 and 7 of the Human Rights Act 1998.[19] Going further than that would have required the courts to distort the principles of the common law (for example, awarding damages sounding in

---

16. Para. 31.

17. At para. 32.

18. At para. 33.

19. Section 6(1) states: "It is unlawful for a public authority to act in a way which is incompatible with a Convention right" and Section 7 gives a corresponding right of action. Section 7(1) states: "A person who claims that a public authority has acted (or proposes to act) in a way which is made unlawful by section 6(1) may — (a) bring proceedings against the authority under this Act in the appropriate court or tribunal, or (b) rely on the Convention right or rights concerned in any legal proceedings, but only if he is (or would be) a victim of the unlawful act.

Mariette Jones

mere distress for privacy invasion, whereas in the tort of negligence damages are awarded only for a recognized physical or psychiatric injury).

Since then, and despite academics joining the courts in calling for legislative intervention, parliament has so far declined to furnish individuals with the right to sue for privacy infringements by other private individuals (there is of course vertical application via the Human Rights Act as illustrated above). Instead the courts developed the tort of misuse of private information from the common law tort of breach of confidentiality in line with the legal requirement to give effect to Article 8.[20] The tort of misuse of private information enables an individual who feels that another had misused their private information, to seek damages or injunctive relief. As such, it could be argued that for all intents and purposes the right to enforce privacy does indeed exist—albeit in a form of claim that 'dare not speak its name.'[21]

B. Reasonable expectation of privacy

Article 8 rights are engaged when the claimant had a reasonable expectation of privacy.[22] This, in turn, means that privacy may be reasonably expected

---

20. *See* especially the reasoning in *Campbell* and also *Douglas v Hello! Ltd* [2001] 2 WLR 992.

21. With apologies to Lord Douglas and Oscar Wilde.

22. Frustratingly, English case law to date have failed to formulate a satisfactory objective test as to what, exactly, a 'reasonable expectation of privacy' means. A circularity of argument is evident from *Campbell*, where it was merely held (at par. 95) that it was 'obvious' that the information being disclosed was private, through cases such as *McKennitt v Ash* [2006] EWCA Civ 1714; [2008] QB 73, and *HRH Prince of Wales v Associated Newspapers Ltd* [2008] Ch 57, where likewise the question of a reasonable expectation of privacy was treated as being obviously evident by the court. Where it is not 'obvious' that information is private, the court in *Campbell* held that it should be asked whether disclosure would cause offence to a 'person of ordinary sensibilities' (at para. 166), although it is doubtful that the ordinary person would find herself at the receiving end of the kind of attention most privacy litigants receive. This test is faintly analogous to the formulation in the US *Second Restatement of Torts* and the Australian case of *Australian Broadcasting Commission v Lenah Game Meats* [2001] 208 CLR 199 (HC (AUS)) but falls short of the 'highly offensive' criterion of either. The lack of legal certainty surrounding the application of this bizarre subjective-objective test is further evident from cases such as *Jagger v Darling* [2005] EWHC 683; *ERY v Associated Newspapers Ltd* [2016] EWHC 2760; and *Middleton and Another v Person or Persons Unknown* [2016] EWHC 2354. *See* also Nicole Moreham, *Privacy in Public Places* CLJ 606 (2006). Similar concerns about the objectivity of the 'reasonable expectation of privacy' test, and the casuistic way in which the test is applied, are also raised in the U.S.—*cf.* Russell L. Weaver, *The Fourth Amendment, Privacy and Advancing Technology*, 80 MISS. L.J. 1131, 1154–55 (2011).

when engaged in an activity in a private place. What about public places? In English law, it is now established law that an expectation of privacy could extend to public places. In addition a claimant's Article 8 Rights have been extended to also apply to *horizontal* relationships.

The development of the tort of misuse of private information out of the tort of breach of confidence is illustrative of this. A twofold test is followed, first formulated in the leading case of *Campbell v Mirror Group Newspapers Ltd*.[23] As a threshold test, the claimant first has to satisfy the court that the information generated a reasonable expectation of privacy. Then follows a balancing exercise, weighing the privacy expectation against the defendant's reason for intrusion, in most instances the right to free speech. The supermodel Naomi Campbell was pictured leaving a Narcotics Anonymous meeting, after having denied any drug problems previously. Regardless of the public place where the photos were taken, the court held that Ms Campbell's expectation of privacy outweighed publication. Similar reasoning was followed by Patten J in *Murray v Express Newspapers plc*,[24] which concerned the publication of a photograph of the famous Harry Potter author, J.K. Rowling's 19 month old baby, taken while he was out for a stroll in public with his parents. Here, too, an expectation of privacy in a public place was recognised by the court, and then the balance was tilted in favour of privacy.[25]

C. Public interest

In American jurisprudence, the concept of 'public interest' seems to be well developed, favouring transparency and free speech. Things that are said in public, that are part of public proceedings, that are matters of public records, or for that matter relates to public figures, are all subject to first amendment protection favouring dissemination.

Things are not as clear in England or in Europe. Although the Court of Appeal had described the process of identifying the public interest in publication as the "decisive factor" in determining the outcome of the claim,[26] there is arguably no real clarity on what precisely 'public interest' means or how the concept should be contextualised. From a lawyer's perspective the public interest

---

23. *See* paras 133–137, 141, 146–160, 165–171.

24. *Murray v Express Newspapers plc and Big Pictures (UK) Ltd* [2007] EWHC 1908 (Ch) [2007] ECDR 20 [2007] EMLR 22.

25. *See* paragraphs 56–61.

26. *K v News Group Newspapers Ltd* [2011] EWCA Civ 439; [2011] 1 W.L.R. 1827.

could even be said to be a mess at present. There are different interpretations of the concept depending on whether you are defending a libel case or a privacy case, and yet again for copyright and yet again for the Data Protection Act.[27] The point is, absent jury trials in civil cases[28] the way in which the issue of what is and what is not in the public interest is decided, is questionable. This brings us to our first proposition.

II. Notion One: Is Privacy protection a tool for the powerful only?

> I see the battle over privacy as being part of a wider war that is raging about who controls access to information: Is it the state in its many manifestations? Is it an elected body of representatives? Is it the courts? Is it the individual?

Gill Phillips, director of editorial legal services, *The Guardian*[29]

To these questions one must add: Is it corporations? This question is examined in the discussion of the second issue raised in this essay, namely to what extent individuals retain *de facto* control over private information. For now, this question: Is privacy protection in reality a workable right only for the powerful, in whose hands it may chill freedom of speech? A quick trawl of misuse of privacy protection cases does seem to involve a slew of famous, rich and powerful claimants. Of course the obvious answer to this is that there is little interest in the private shenanigans of ordinary people, who hence do not need to enforce their rights in courts. Perhaps the better question is whether, powerful, rich, public figures nonetheless, the courts are too biased in favour of privacy over public interest/free speech? Two further issues need to be noted here: the secrecy surrounding these issues accorded by the use of so-called 'super injunctions', and the seeming increased use of Data Protection laws to enforce privacy.

---

27. Gill Phillips, Press freedom v privacy: time for parliament to draw the line?' , Address at the annual UCL and Bindmans debate (Feb. 8, 2012) (transcript available at https://www.theguardian.com/gnm-press-office/phillips-speech-press-freedom-versus-privacy).

28. Libel remains the only civil action that could theoretically be decided by jury trial, although the practical effect of the Defamation Act 2013 means that for all intents and purposes here too jury trials have been abolished.

29. *See* Phillips *supra.*

A. Privacy injunctions and super injunctions

The primary remedy in privacy cases is an injunction prior to disclosure.[30] Further, the identity of the parties may also be kept secret through an anonymised privacy injunction.[31] In addition, since 2010, 'super-injunctions' are available under certain circumstances. These are injunctions which prevent the reporting of the existence of proceedings.[32] Thus, not only is it possible to keep information obtained in public and/or about public personas secret through injunctive relief, the very existence of the privacy suit could also be kept secret.[33] Understandably, there was an outcry over this and a committee was established to scrutinise the situation. It acknowledged that historically it was impossible to say how many super injunctions had been granted, and that it was advisable in future to keep record.[34] In response a practice direction was given for the recording/statistical noting of these injunctions, which provides for " ... the recording, and transmission to the Ministry of Justice for analysis, of certain data in relation to injunctions prohibiting publication of private or confidential information. The purpose of the scheme is to enable the Ministry of Justice to collate and publish, in anonymised form, information about applications for injunctions where section 12 of the Human Rights Act 1998 is engaged." [35]

For the last six years therefore data has been collected as a result of the Master of the Rolls' Report. At first glance, it seems as if the incidences of super-injunctions being granted are very scarce, and may even be dwindling. For example according to the latest official statistics on privacy injunctions from

---

30. Of course once private information has been disclosed, damages become the primary remedy.

31. Lord Neuberger, Master of the Rolls, 'Report of the Committee on Super-Injunctions: Super-Injunctions, Anonymised Injunctions and Open Justice' (May 20, 2011), at iv defines this as 'an interim injunction which restrains a person from publishing information which concerns the applicant and is said to be confidential or private where the names of either or both of the parties to the proceedings are not stated'. (Report available at https://www.judiciary.gov.uk/publications/committee-reports-super-injunctions/).

32. Lord Neuberger, *Id.*, defines a super-injunction as: " ... an interim injunction which restrains a person from: (i) publishing information which concerns the applicant and is said to be confidential or private; and (ii) publicising or informing others of the existence of the order and the proceedings". Practice Direction 40F—Non-Disclosure Injunctions Information Collection Scheme (available at https://www.justice.gov.uk/courts/procedure-rules/civil/rules/part40/practice-direction-40f-non-disclosure-injunctions-information-collection-scheme).

33. *See JIH v News Group Newspapers Ltd* [2011] EWCA Civ 42 for the courts' approach to anonymization.

34. Lord Neuberger, *id.*

35. Practice Direction 40F *Id.*

January to December 2016 there were only three such proceedings in the High Court. [36] However, there are grave doubts about the accuracy of statistics generated in compliance with this direction. It is important to note that judges are not compelled to record the occurrence of these cases, and it seems that they do not bother unless prompted by either of the parties, who in turn have little reason to do so. Commentators rightly query whether this results in accurate statistics.[37] The plain answer to how many super-injunctions are granted therefore remains 'we do not know'.

Nevertheless, let us accept for the sake of argument that the statistics are accurate and that super-injunctions are therefore very rare. There are still other legal tools available to those who wish to avoid public scrutiny. One of these is the use of data protection laws.

B. Is 'Data Protection the New Defamation'?

To American eyes, English and European laws protecting personality rights must seem to come at a significant cost to (especially) free speech. Indeed, where competing rights are not given pre-determined relative weights, but are to be weighed up in ad hoc balancing exercises according to context and circumstance—as they are in European Jurisprudence—the risk exists that a skewed picture may emerge. The UK's recent scrap with its own defamation laws illustrates this point. As a background discussion, it serves as a cautionary example to policymakers who should be wary of replacing one set of rules favouring the powerful just as they'd finished trying to level the playing field in another. To explain what this means, the reader's indulgence is begged here for a brief detour to the law of defamation.

A few years ago, it was deemed necessary to wholly reform the UK's defamation law by enacting the Defamation Act 2013. This was largely prompted by concerns about the common law of libel's chilling effect on free speech. Why this was

---

36. Ministry of Justice, Civil Justice Statistics Quarterly, England and Wales, January to March 2017 (provisional) and Royal Courts of Justice 2016, (Jun. 1 2017), (available at: https://www.gov.uk/government/statistics/civil-justice-statistics-quarterly-january-to-march-2017). Of the three cases, one went on appeal to the Court of Appeal and thereafter the Supreme Court. It can safely be assumed that this was the well-publicised case of *PJS v. News Group Newspapers* [2016] UKSC 26; [2016] A.C. 1081; [2016] 2 W.L.R. 1253.

37. *See* Judith Townend, 'Where did all the privacy injunctions go? A response to the Queen's Bench 'Media List' consultations' (at https://inforrm.wordpress.com/2017/05/31/where-did-all-the-privacy-injunctions-go-a-response-to-the-queens-bench-media-list-consultation-judith-townend/) last accessed 31 May 2017.

so can best be explained by contrasting the (then) UK libel law to the US position. It is well known that perhaps nowhere else on earth is free speech protected as robustly as in the United States. First Amendment, i.e. constitutional, rights accord defendants in libel claims with very powerful protection. Since the landmark decision in *Sullivan*,[38] it is established that public figures suing in libel bear a substantial burden of proof: to make out with convincing clarity not only that the allegedly defamatory statement is false, but also that it was made with actual malice and resulted in actual loss/injury. In this way the evidentiary burden strongly tilts in favour of free speech and is placed squarely on the claimant.

In England the situation was almost the opposite, not only because the burden of proof largely rested on the defendant,[39] but also because of three distinct characteristics of the common law of defamation: the presumption of falsity, strict liability and the presumption of damages.[40] In effect the claimant merely had to produce a *prima facie* defamatory statement, whereupon the court presumed harm and falsity—and the presumption of harm itself was irrebuttable.[41] Further, the burden then shifted to the *defendant* to prove that the statement was true, subject to privilege, or fell under a list of possible defences, each with a substantial evidentiary burden. The suit was both actionable *per se* and of strict liability, and neither party was allowed legal aid. All of this meant that defendants knew, *a priori*, that they would be facing an uphill battle in court. As a result in many instances, the mere threat of being sued in libel was enough to ensure the silence of potential critics—thus chilling free speech.[42] What is more, the claimant-friendly nature of the English common law of libel made this a prime destination for libel tourists,[43] to such an extent that the European Parliament named the UK the 'libel capital of the world', and the

---

38. *New York Times Company v. L. B. Sullivan*, 376 U.S. 254 (1964).

39. Even in the newly operational Defamation Act 2013 this remains the case. Although the initial hurdles for bringing a claim are set higher (in terms of actual damage to reputation required in s.1, and in terms of jurisdiction), the burden still largely shifts to the defendant to raise one of a number of defences set out at length in the act.

40. DARIO MILO, DEFAMATION AND FREEDOM OF SPEECH 11 (OUP 2008). In this seminal work Milo terms these the 'potent trilogy of fundamental principles' of the common law of defamation in the UK.

41. *Jameel v Dow Jones & Co Inc* [2005] 2 W.L.R. 1614.

42. For an interesting personal account of a scientist's experience of the censoring effect of UK common law libel actions, *see* Hardeep Singh, *The libel survivor* 13(32) LEGAL WEEK, 20–21 (2011).

43. *See* for example the case of *Bin Mahfouz v Ehrenfeld*[2005] EWHC 1156, where neither the claimant nor the defendant were domiciled or based in the UK, the defamatory statement was found in a book, of which only 23 copies had been sold in the UK, and nevertheless the judgement went in favour of the claimant.

United States felt it had to protect its citizens against libel suits in the UK by promulgating legislation that made English libel judgements unenforceable in the USA.[44] Recognising this as a 'national humiliation',[45] the British legislature attempted to level the playing field between libel claimants and defendants with the adoption of the Defamation Act 2013.

Whether or not the Act succeeds in this is of course another question, and beyond the scope of this article.[46] The point is that one personality right (the right to vindicate one's reputation) became a tool of the powerful to stifle dissent, a state of affairs regarded by the legislature as sufficiently serious to warrant wholesale legislative reform. The question is: Are we heading in the same direction with another personality right, this time the right to privacy? Put another way: could invasion of privacy suits in the UK potentially replace libel actions by the powerful as preferred weapon of silencing critics? Privacy suits in the form mostly of misuse of private information suits have already been looked at, but what about data protection suits?

The most recent statistics indicate that for 2016, issued defamation claims are at the lowest recorded number ever.[47] However, it is pointed out that there is no separate record of the number of privacy and data protection claims, and that they are presumably included in the 956 "miscellaneous" claims issued. At least anecdotally there is evidence that suggests that data protection claims against the media are on the increase. However, this is not verifiable from the official statistics.[48] In what follows the use of Data Protection laws read in conjunction with European jurisprudence will be examined.

---

44. Securing the Protection of our Enduring and Established Constitutional Heritage (SPEECH) Act, 124 Stat. 2480–2484 (2010).

45. House of Commons Culture Select Committee report on press standards, privacy & libel 2.

46. At least, the Act discourages frivolous claims being entertained due to its threshold requirement of 'serious harm' to reputation (financial/likely financial damage in case of bodies corporate). *See* the interesting case of *Monroe v Hopkins* [2017] EWHC 433 (QB) in which the 'serious harm' test under the Defamation Act 2013 has been applied to tweets for the first time. Jurisdiction criteria have been tightened as well to try and prevent libel tourism. However, the burden of proof is still mostly on the defendant.

47. Ministry of Justice, Civil Justice Statistics Quarterly, England and Wales, January to March 2017 (provisional) and Royal Courts of Justice 2016, (Jun. 1, 2017), https://www.gov.uk/government/statistics/civil-justice-statistics-quarterly-january-to-march-2017.

48. INFORRM, Judicial Statistics, 2016: Issued defamation claims down by 17%, lowest recorded number in modern times, Law and Media Round-up (Jun. 6, 2017) at https://inforrm.wordpress.com/2017/06/06/judicial-statistics-2016-issued-defamation-claims-down-by-17-lowest-recorded-number-for-any-year-for-which-records-are-available/.

C. Data protection in the UK

A closer look here at current data protection regulation in the UK shows that, although it allows us to 'hide from each other' as it were (similar to the operation of the 'right to be forgotten' post *Google Spain*,[49] below), real privacy protection arguably remains somewhat illusory. The overall picture that emerges is that we can hide from each other but not from corporations or the state. The modern economy can only function with de facto data intrusion, and security concerns necessitate ever-more intrusive surveillance. Yet an unintended consequence of corporate data profiling and content tailoring means that the growing prevalence of confirmation bias, amplified in online echo chambers, can lead to ever increasing societal polarisation. In a society where people don't talk to each other anymore, the last thing that is needed is a mechanism to enforce more silence.

1. Data Protection Act 1998

The Data Protection Act (DPA) provides for the regulation of the processing by data controllers of information relating to individuals, including the obtaining, holding, use or disclosure of such information. [50] In other words, the DPA applies whenever anyone collects, retains, uses, or discloses any information about a living person. As such it implements the European Data Protection Regulation, which is scrutinised below. Article 9 of the EU Data Protection Directive permits Member States to provide for exemptions or derogations from its provisions for the processing of personal data carried out solely for journalistic purposes or the purpose of artistic or literary expression, but only if they are necessary to reconcile the right to privacy with the rules governing freedom of expression. It is here that the analogy with defamation comes to light.

The DPA is an attempt at providing a framework of rights and duties designed to balance the individual's right to information privacy against the legitimate needs of others to collect and use people's details (including purposes such as freedom of expression and journalism). Albeit there are recent indications from the High Court in *Stunt v Associated Newspapers*[51] that the UK's margin of appreciation in terms of Article 9 above should be exercised more robustly in favour of free speech to avoid prior constraint, journalists have for

---

49. *Google Spain SL and Google Inc. v. Agencia Espanola de Proteccion de Datos (AEPD) and Mario Costeja Gonzalez,* Case C-131/12 (Google Spain).

50. Preamble to the Data Protection Act 1998 c. 29.

51. [2017] EWHC 695 (QB).

some time now been complaining that claimants have been abusing data protection laws to stifle or interfere with legitimate journalistic activity.[52]

What is more, suits based on the DPA 1998 are profitable: In contrast to negligence claims, where non-pecuniary damages are not recoverable, DPA claimants can recover damages for distress. In *Vidal-Hall v Google Inc*[53] it was held that because the EU Data Protection Directive allowed those suffering damage falling short of pecuniary damage to make a claim under the concept of "moral damages", the DPA had to be interpreted in such a way as to allow any damage suffered through a data controller's breaches to be recovered.[54]

2. EU General Data Protection Regulation

Any celebration of the media-friendly decision in *Stunt* may be premature, given that the law around data protection is changing substantively. The EU General Data Protection Regulation (GDPR),[55] which came into force in May 2018, represents the biggest change to the UK data protection regime in 20 years.[56] It may prove to be even more protective of privacy than its predecessor.

The changes brought by the GDPR are substantial. First, the GDPR will include direct obligations on data processors, not just data controllers. This widens the net of potential defendants. Further, substantial new rights are included for data subjects, such as the right to data portability and to object to profiling. In certain circumstances mandatory notifications must be given of

---

52. Keith Mathieson, '*Case Law: Stunt v Associated Newspapers, Mail heads off attempt by businessman to prevent use of personal data in important decision on the Data Protection Act*' (Apr. 6, 2017) at https://inforrm.wordpress.com/2017/04/06/case-law-stunt-v-associated-newspapers-mail-heads-off-attempt-by-businessman-to-prevent-use-of-personal-data-in-important-decision-on-the-data-protection-act-keith-mathieson/.

53. *See Vidal-Hall v Google Inc* [2015] EWCA Civ 311; [2016] Q.B. 1003.

54. Under §.13(1).

55. Regulation (EU) 2016/679 ('GDPR') was adopted on 27 April 2016. The government has confirmed that the UK's decision to leave the EU will not affect the commencement of the GDPR, and thus it will in effect replace the DPA on the day of its coming into force.

56. Article 5 of the GDPR states that personal data must be: a. Processed fairly, lawfully and in a transparent manner in relation to the data subject. b. Collected for specified, explicit and legitimate purposes and not further processed in a manner that is incompatible with those purposes. c. Adequate, relevant and limited to what is necessary in relation to the purposes for which they are processed. d. Accurate and, where necessary, kept up to date. e. Kept in a form that permits identification of data subjects for no longer than is necessary for the purposes for which the personal data are processed. f. Processed in a manner that ensures appropriate security of the personal data including protection against unauthorised or unlawful processing and against accidental loss, destruction or damage, using appropriate technical or organisational measures.

data breaches. Some organisations will be required by mandate to appoint a data officer, and the Regulations will be given extra-territorial scope to regulate those companies located outside of the European Union but who target goods or services at European citizens or monitor online behaviour of European citizens. Finally, the GDPR also contains new concepts of accountability, and of privacy by design and privacy by default. It must also be noted that these new changes are set against a backdrop of potential fines of up to 120 million Euros or 4% of annual worldwide turnover, whichever is higher.[57]

This brings us to the question: how practicable is all of this? The GDPR embodies an ambitious and far-reaching change in a legal regime that some would argue already provides adequate privacy protection. In the next section a reality check is attempted.

III. Notion Two: Modern life entails a de facto surrender of privacy rights

Lord Justice Greer famously called the average person in Britain 'the man on the Clapham Omnibus' and described him as rather nondescript.[58] His modern incarnation lives in a world where his every move is monitored—in or outside his home.

A. State sanctioned privacy intrusion

The Snowden revelations still form the touchstone for reflection on the massive extent to which the modern state monitors its subjects, be that covert, overt, on a legal basis, by means of exploiting legal loopholes or even illegally.[59] In addition to terrorism legislation, current UK laws provide for the legal surveillance of subjects on arguably the largest scale in the world.[60] Two recent statutes deserve mention. The Investigatory Powers Act consolidates the powers available to law enforcement and security and intelligence agencies to obtain communications and data about communications. It also overhauled the way these powers are authorised and overseen, mostly by the introduction of

---

57. Article 83(4) of the GDPR.

58. *Hall v. Brooklands Auto-Racing Club* [1933] 1 K.B. 205.

59. *See* VII The Global Papers Series, Cybersurveillance in a Post-Snowden World: Balancing the Fight Against Terrorism Against Fundamental Rights, (Russell L. Weaver et al, eds., 2017).

60. *See* Mariette Jones, *supra* at 24.

a 'double-lock' for interception warrants, entailing both state and judicial oversight. But it also hands law enforcement agencies more access to individuals' Internet connection records than ever before: It requires web and phone companies to store records of websites visited by every citizen for 12 months for access by police, security services and other public bodies. For the first time ever it makes it legally explicit that security services have the power to collect in bulk large volumes of personal communications data, and security services and police have the power to hack into and bug computers and phones and what is more, a new legal obligation is placed on companies to assist in these operations to bypass encryption.[61]

The Digital Economy Act, which was enacted on 27 April 2017, attempts to address various issues relating to online services and electronic communications. [62] Most importantly for this discussion, it attempts to liberalise data sharing across government agencies and public bodies. The Conservative Government in the explanatory notes to the 2017 Act had stated a commitment to finding a way of 'overcoming the legal barriers to the better delivery of public services, better research and better statistics'. They argued that the best way to do this was to enable data sharing, or more precisely, to 'provide the necessary legal framework to enable data sharing for a public benefit'.[63] The notes went on to state that a single gateway was envisaged to enable specified public authorities to share personal information for tightly constrained reasons that had to be agreed by Parliament, and only when the purpose of such sharing was 'to improve the welfare of the individual in question'. Mirroring the now familiar language used in legally sanctified privacy intrusions, the proposed sharing of

---

61. Alan Travis, *Investigatory powers bill: the key points*, THE GUARDIAN, (Nov. 4, 2015) https://www.theguardian.com/world/2015/nov/04/investigatory-powers-bill-the-key-points.

62. The preamble to the Digital Economy Act 2017, C.30 reads as follows: An Act to make provision about electronic communications infrastructure and services; to provide for restricting access to online pornography; to make provision about protection of intellectual property in connection with electronic communications; to make provision about data-sharing; to make provision in connection with section 68 of the Telecommunications Act 1984; to make provision about functions of OFCOM in relation to the BBC; to provide for determination by the BBC of age-related TV licence fee concessions; to make provision about the regulation of direct marketing; to make other provision about OFCOM and its functions; to make provision about internet filters; to make provision about preventing or restricting the use of communication devices in connection with drug dealing offences; to confer power to create an offence of breaching limits on ticket sales; to make provision about the payment of charges to the Information Commissioner; to make provision about payment systems and securities settlement systems; to make provision about qualifications in information technology; and for connected purposes.

63. Explanatory notes, para. 29.

information 'must be for the purpose of one of the specified objectives, which will be set out in regulations'.[64] Whilst aiming towards joined-up thinking and the provision of seamless services to the public are laudable, it needs to be borne in mind that this comes at the sharing of data and metadata at a previously unthinkable scale. The Act is in fact couched widely, even more so when the regulations are added and come into effect, which will result in data sharing allowed across multiple agencies, and for multiple purposes.[65]

As stated, to this must be added monitoring sanctions by terrorism laws. The cumulative effect is that the man on the Clapham omnibus can expect routine monitoring by the state on an unprecedented scale. Next, the way in which he is tracked by companies will be examined, but first one needs to briefly note the framework that attempts to regulate such activity.

B. The European data protection framework

At the time of writing the Data Protection Directive remains the European Union's primary legislative instrument in respect of data protection.[66] The Directive defines personal data as "any information relating to an identified or identifiable natural person".[67] The processing of personal data is then in turn subject to a range of substantive provisions.[68] With the coming into effect of the GDPR in May 2018, data protection is set to be tightened up under far more stringent rules, as described above. Nevertheless it can be argued that the notion of real privacy protection in this regard is at the least problematic and at most, an illusion. The same critique can thus be levelled against both the current and future regulatory regimes.

For instance, Pearce points out how modern big data capabilities mean that the core Data Protection Directive principles do not reflect reality any more. [69] First, the most fundamental concept of data protection law is that of personal data itself, which is defined in the Directive as 'any information relating to an

---

64. Para. 31.

65. Annex B of the notes lists the type of information sharing objectives that are envisaged, as well as the public authorities who are likely to be permitted to use the power.

66. Directive 95/46 on the protection of individuals with regard to the processing of personal data and on the free movement of such data.

67. Data Protection Directive art.2(a).

68. For a critique of the Data Protection Directive, and in particular how big data makes the distinction between personal and other information obsolete, *see* Henry Pearce, *A systems approach to data protection law and policy in a world of big data?*, 22(4) CTLR. 90, 90–93 (2016).

69. *Id.*

identified or identifiable natural person'[70] which are then subject to a wide range of substantive regulation. By implication non-personal information are not subject to data protection laws. And yet big data capabilities mean that the difference between personal and non-personal data is blurred. The second fundamental principle of the European data protection framework is that of the individual's informed consent as a basis for legitimate data processing. But data processing operations in the big data age are hugely complex, which arguably makes it almost impossible for individuals to make informed and meaningful decisions about how their personal data are used.[71] It will also be argued below that consent as a *sine qua non* of access to certain services mean that we cannot speak of real consent, informed or otherwise. The third fundamental EU data protection principle is that of data minimisation, contained in article 6 of the Data Protection Directive. This tenet entails that the only personal data that ought to be collected, stored and processed by any parties are those which are necessary to realise specified and legitimate goals, and that all such data should be destroyed once they are no longer relevant to the achievement of the said goals. Yet big data, by its very nature, depends on the acquisition, analysis and use of huge quantities of data. As such it is completely at odds with the principle in article 6.

C. Deconstructing data protection

In section II above, the ways in which data protection laws may be used to evade public scrutiny through the press was examined. To this must be added EU citizens' "right to be forgotten".

1. The right to be forgotten — but by whom?

Since the decision in *Google Spain*[72] was handed down the right to be forgotten has received much attention,[73] but the impact of the ruling should not be exaggerated.[74] To a large extent the case merely reiterated principles now fa-

---

70. Article 2(a).

71. Henry Pearce, *Online data transactions, consent, and big data: technological solutions to technological problems?* 21 CTLR 149 (2015).

72. *Google Spain SL and Google Inc. v. Agencia Espanola de Proteccion de Datos (AEPD) and Mario Costeja Gonzalez,* Case C-131/12 (Google Spain).

73. *See* e.g. Irène Bouhadana & William Gilles, *From the Right to Be Let Alone to the Right to Be Forgotten: How Privacy Is Moving in the Collecting Data Age in* IV The Global Papers Series, Privacy in a Digital Age: Perspectives from Two Continents 3 (Russell L. Weaver et al, eds., 2017).

74. *See* Susanna Lindroos-Hovinheimo, *Legal Subjectivity and the 'Right to be Forgotten': A Rancièrean Analysis of Google* 27(3) Law and Critique 289, 289 (2016).

miliar in the data protection context: Personal data must be processed fairly for specified purposes and primarily on the basis of the consent of the person concerned. Everyone also has the right of access to data which have been collected concerning him or her and the right to have that data rectified. So far, so much reaffirmation of the existing rights in the EU Charter and Data Protection Directive.[75] The rub lies in noting that the key question that should arise about the right to be forgotten confirmed by this case is: 'Forgotten by whom?' In many instances (such as public information of the kind that formed the subject of the *Google Spain* case) the right would merely entail that search engine links to the information are disabled. So the information usually remains 'out there'—it is just more difficult to find. [76] The answer to the question is thus that in practical terms the right to be forgotten more correctly stated means the right to be forgotten *by the public*.

So one's privacy is protected from intrusion by others—but to what extent does this include the state and corporations? Is there a right to be forgotten by companies?

2. Informed consent and the (im)practicability of data minimisation

As an experiment, readers with a smartphone are invited to download almost any application (such as Facebook) and have a look at the permissions that are required for installation. Access to location, satellite tracking, access to contacts and their details, names, etc. are requested as standard. How many people really thoroughly read the 'permissions' they agree to when they use applications on their smartphones and other devices to access search engines, social media, online banking and so on? And even if they do, what choice do they have apart from accepting the intrusion or disengaging from the activity—which in reality is not an option for many people. Functions that were fulfilled by High Street businesses (such as travel agencies) are increasingly being replaced by online services. For example, in Britain High Street bank branches are disappearing at an alarming rate, forcing more and more people to do their banking exclusively online.

---

75. *Google, supra* sections 97, 99.

76. Lindroos-Hovenheimo *supra* at 299 noted the irony of this case: Mr Gonzalez affirmed his voice and presence in law by demanding his non-presence in the internet. He asked for a right to be forgotten but by staging his act on the legal stage, in court, he simultaneously ensured that he will never be forgotten. He signs his history as 'I, Mr Gonzalez, whose real-estate was auctioned'. The case solidifies his legacy instead of consigning him to oblivion.

When one looks up Google's privacy policy,[77] the first sentence on their website reads: "When you use Google services, you trust us with your information."[78] Reading the policy it becomes almost shockingly clear how far users are expected to trust Google with their information. Google solicits information directly from users, including the user's name, email address, telephone number and even credit card details. To take full advantage of the service that Google offers, they also ask users to create a publicly visible Google Profile, which may then include their name and photo.

In addition to this information directly garnered from users, Google also harvests information from the user's online activity. These are described as follows: [79]

> We collect information about the services that you use and how you use them, like when you watch a video on YouTube, visit a website that uses our advertising services or view and interact with our ads and content. This information includes: Device information ... Log information ... Location information ... Local storage [which means that] [w]e may collect and store information (including personal information) locally on your device ...

Google is also upfront about its data analytics and profiling:

> We use information collected from cookies and other technologies ... to improve your user experience.... One of the products we use ... is Google Analytics ... Our automated systems analyse your content (including emails) to provide you personally relevant product features, such as customised search results, tailored advertising ... We may combine personal information from one service with information, including personal information, from other Google services—for example, to make it easier to share things with people you know. Depending on your account settings, your activity on other sites and apps may be associated with your personal information ... [80]

Suffice it to say that reading the entire privacy policy of this multinational giant used by millions of people on a daily basis, fully elucidates the massive intelligence-gathering and profiling capabilities of metadata. No wonder states

---

77. Recently, Google has been requiring its UK users to agree to its new conditions (probably to comply with the *Shrems* decision).

78. https://www.google.com/policies/privacy/ (May 6, 2017).

79. *Id.*

80. *Id.*

including the USA and the UK find it hard to keep their hands off the intelligence 'voluntarily' given by individual users.

The differing levels of state access to commercially gathered data came to the fore recently in the *Schrems*[81] case, where a challenge was made to the Irish Data Protection Commissioner, and in turn, the ECJ, about protection for personal data transfers from the European Economic Area to the U.S., due to the access that U.S. authorities had to European data once it reaches US shores. The Court found the then extant 'Safe Harbor' framework lacking. As a result, European authorities sought to agree an alternative. On 12 July 2016, the European Commission adopted the "Privacy Shield" as an adequate means of transferring personal data to the US. The central tenets of European data protection (such as consent and data minimisation) feature in the principles of the Privacy Shield, which include providing consent and opt-out protocols to data subjects and assuring that data is processed only for the purposes for which it has been collected.

Under the GDPR consent will have to be positively solicited. That is, instead of an opt-out, it will be an opt-in feature. But even so, the question remains: Does this qualify as 'real' consent if the alternative is non-engagement with the service concerned?

From the business perspective it is clear that restricting data access is problematic. In the information age, data has become more than a currency. It is the lifeblood of many industries, from large multinational corporations such as Google and Facebook, to smaller businesses. So the conundrum seems to be: if the pretence of consent to commercial data gathering is replaced by real consent, many businesses might be unable to function properly or even go out of business.[82]

On the other hand, unfettered data processing capabilities may have grave if unintended consequences which also deserve careful scrutiny.

3. Echo chambers and confirmation bias: the unintended consequences of content tailoring

Data gathered from millions of users allow ever more sophisticated data analytics algorithms to profile customers with eerie accuracy. While tailored content can be a massive boon to users, it may also lead to negative effects, espe-

---

81. Case C-362/14, *Maximillian Schrems v Data Protection Commissioner, joined party: Digital Rights Ireland Ltd*, 6 October 2015.

82. Liliia Oprysk, *The Forthcoming General Data Protection Regulation in the EU: Higher Compliance Costs Might Slow Down Small and Medium-sized Enterprises' Adoption of Infrastructure as a Service* 24 JURIDICA INTERNATIONAL 23(2016).

cially when other content is also filtered in this way, such as political content. It has been documented how online forums such as Facebook in using filtered content, become huge echo-chambers characterised by confirmation bias. In this way users who are not challenged in their thinking, and who do not become used to being challenged, show an increasing unwillingness, even an inability, to engage with challenging or subversive thought. This is especially true for younger generations who rely on social media for much of their information gathering. Studies indicate that democratic debate is experienced by many of this generation not as an intellectual exercise, but as emotional distress.[83] One only needs to look at the dismay and incomprehension with which the polarised populations of Brexit UK and Trump America regard each other to understand the very real threat posed to civil discourse in recent years.

IV. Concluding remarks

It is clear that the notion of 'privacy' is more nuanced than a single tort could encompass. Even so, it is submitted that the judicial attitude to privacy in the UK is fragmented, based on a complex of common law and legislative regulation that arguably sometimes recognise privacy more in the authorisation of invasion than in an actionable right. In this sense, it becomes 'visible' less often as a substantive right, but more so in state sanctioned infringements. For more powerful individuals, data protection laws have the potential to replace libel claims as a silencing mechanism.

A. Some are more equal than others

We need to face the reality that, at least in the world of law, privacy has become a double edged sword. For the ordinary person who of necessity engages in the digital world, privacy—in the sense of being left alone, not being watched, not being tracked and profiled—has become a mirage. We routinely 'consent' to extreme intrusion that invade not only our individual rights but may even sound in societal harm. Commercial intelligence driven by increasingly 'intelligent' algorithms track, profile, pigeonhole and target us to such an extent that it may well end up driving democratic distortion. At the same time states accord themselves increasingly invasive powers.

---

83. *See*, for an interesting study in this regard, CLAIRE FOX, I FIND THAT OFFENSIVE (2016).

But for the powerful, privacy may well have become a blunt instrument to protect carefully crafted images, to stifle critique and adverse publicity, and to disappear from public scrutiny. In the UK, when considering public interest, it falls not to the public to decide what they are interested in, but rather paternalistically for the courts to decide what the public should be interested in. Those interested in playing identity politics could make much of the composition of the judiciary making up these courts, even today. The result could very well be that the law, intended to protect all equally, end up yet again protecting the powerful from public scrutiny and stifling free speech. It is argued that regardless elite distaste for the seemingly prurient taste of the British hoi polloi, " ... the public should be entitled to scrutinise and censure the conduct of people—it needs to be remembered that privacy injunctions allow deceit and fraud and lying and cheating to be covered up."[84]

B. Unintended consequences

Ours is called the 'information age'—but taking into account privacy practice in the EU and the UK, it may be more correct to talk about the 'disinformation (or even misinformation) age'. The reason is because current privacy laws allow for, or at least inadvertently lead to, the distortion of information. Public profiles are easily manipulated vis-à-vis ordinary citizens (via the right to be forgotten and privacy injunctions) whilst at the same time there is increasingly constant and seemingly ever-widening monitoring from the state. And so in the final analysis it could be said that our privacy is protected, yes, but only against each other.

C. Security

Finally, the security crisis facing ordinary citizens in the UK should not be forgotten. Epstein,[85] in his discussion of the ECJ's *Schrems* decision, rightly points out that in privacy jurisprudence, the theoretical/philosophical dimension (the' jurisprudence of concepts, or '*Begriffsjurisprudenz*") seems to be given precedence over consideration of the practical consequences of regulation. In considering privacy protection in the light of security concerns, he argues from the perspective of a tort lawyer, pointing out that much of the law

---

84. Gill Phillips *supra*.

85. Richard A. Epstein, *The ECJ's Fatal Imbalance Its cavalier treatment of national security issues poses serious risk to public safety and sound commercial practices* 12(2) European Constitutional Law Review 330 (2016).

of tort, and huge portions of the regulatory system, are not concerned with giving the proper legal interpretation to legal concepts. Instead the question is framed in terms of how best to balance two types of error:

> Type I error and Type II error. The first addresses a false positive, acting as if some dangerous condition exists when none is apparent. The second is a false negative, which assumes that the condition is safe when in fact some dangerous condition exists. In our context, Type I error involves an invasion of privacy when there is no need to do so. Type II error involves missing a terrorist threat that causes serious harm in order to protect privacy. [M]any attach a higher severity to the first type of error than to the second. But the greater the importance of Type II error, the more willing governments should be to reduce its occurrence. If what is sought is to minimise the sum of the two types of error, then at the margin we should be willing to accept a far higher level of false positives than false negatives.[86]

Or put simply, in weighing up privacy and security, the scales should be tilted in favour of security. But this brings us back to the question: Can it be proven that giving up more privacy rights would necessarily improve the security situation? The difficulty lies with judging the efficacy of privacy intrusion be that data gathering, profiling based on metadata, or old-fashioned surveillance of communication and movement. Security surveillance is of necessity veiled in secrecy and intelligence agencies rightly play their cards close to their chests when it comes to suspected terrorists. When these agencies insist that they'd prevented incidents from happening, the public has to take their word for it. And it is difficult to gauge whether increased powers to intrude on privacy would have a positive effect on preventing future atrocities when it seems that many of those that do happen seemingly could have been prevented without much intrusion on privacy. For example, questions are raised about the authorities' failure to take repeated alerts about the Manchester bomber seriously.

In the light of all this, it may be time to revisit, regarding the right to privacy, the question: Qui bono?

---

86. At 336.

Ellen S. Podgor[1] and Louis J. Virelli III[2]

Accountability in Criminal Discovery

Administrative agency decisions impact nearly every aspect of American life. In exchange for the benefits of administrative government, we require agencies to exercise their considerable authority within carefully drawn limits—with great power comes great responsibility.[3] This tension between agency power and responsibility was on clear display in a recent dispute about an internal criminal discovery policy of the Department of Justice (DOJ).

In *National Association of Criminal Defense Lawyers v. Executive Office for United States Attorneys* (the "Blue Book Litigation"),[4] the court was asked to help draw the line between the DOJ's discovery authority in handling criminal prosecutions and the public's need to know what its institutions—especially those entrusted with prosecutorial power—are up to. More specifically, the case involved the question of whether criminal defense attorneys and the public generally should be allowed to view the DOJ's Federal Criminal Discovery Blue Book (Blue Book), a DOJ policy document that "contains information and advice for prosecutors about conducting discovery in their cases, including guidance about the government's various obligations to provide discovery to defendants."[5] This issue arose from a Freedom of Information Act (FOIA) request by the National Association of Criminal Defense Lawyers (NACDL) for DOJ disclosure of the Blue Book. NACDL is a criminal defense organization

---

1. Gary R. Trombley Family White Collar Research Professor of Law, Stetson University College of Law. Although the opinions expressed in this Essay are those of the Author, the Author discloses that she was a signatory of the Brief of Sixty-Three Law Professors as Amici in Support of the Appellant and Reversal. *See* William D. Douglas, *Law Reviews and Full Disclosure*, 40 WASH. L. REV. 227, 232 (1965).

2. Professor of Law, Stetson University College of Law.

3. This sentiment has been attributed to several famous sources over the centuries, from the Bible to FDR and Spiderman. *See, e.g., Luke* 12:48; Franklin Delano Roosevelt, *Text of Speech Written by Franklin Delano Roosevelt on the Night Before His Death*, DAILY ILLINOIS STATE JOURNAL, Apr. 14, 1945, at 2; Stan Lee, *Spider-Man!*, Aug. 1962 (cover page).

4. 844 F.3d 246 (D.C. Cir. 2016).

5. *Id.* at 249.

with "10,000 direct members and 40,000 state, local, and international affiliate members," including public, private and active-duty military defense counsel, judges, and law professors.[6] FOIA requires government agencies to provide public documents to citizens, except when excluded by statute.[7] In this case, DOJ refused the NACDL's FOIA request. NACDL then filed a lawsuit to compel access to the Blue Book. DOJ's opposition was premised on the Blue Book being protected work product within FOIA's Exemption 5, "which exempts from disclosure certain agency records that would be privileged from discovery in a lawsuit with the agency."[8]

The United States District Court for the District of Columbia agreed with the government's position that the Blue Book was exempt work product and denied NACDL's request. A panel of the D.C. Circuit affirmed, but remanded the case to the district court to assess "whether the Blue Book also contains non-exempt policy statements amenable to reasonable segregation from the privileged work product."[9] The case was remanded to the district court for *in camera* review to determine if there are non-privileged materials in the Blue Book that can be disclosed to the NACDL.[10]

The Blue Book Litigation raises more issues than it resolves. On its face, it addresses the scope of FOIA when government policy is the subject of review and whether criminal discovery obligations should be limited by the work product doctrine. These questions could have serious practical consequences for criminal defense lawyers and the criminal justice system, and as such should be carefully vetted by the courts. What is potentially lost in the current litigation, however, are the bigger issues at stake. More than a dispute over the publication of government records, the Blue Book Litigation highlights broader concerns about government secrecy. A government decision to shield its policies from public view raises a series of constitutional and administrative

---

6. *See* Complaint for Declaratory and Injunctive Relief, *Nat'l Ass'n Crim. Defense Lawyers v. Exec. Office for U.S. Attorneys*, Civil Action No. 14-CV-269, at ¶ 10 (D.D.C. Feb. 21, 2014) (hereinafter "NACDL v. EOUSA"), *available at* https://www.nacdl.org/BlueBook FOIALitigation/.

7. *See* 5 U.S.C. §552. The statute includes nine exclusions. *Id.* at §§552(b)(1)–(9).

8. *Id.* at §552(b)(5). The government also argued that the Blue Book was exempt under subsection (b)(7)(E) "as a document compiled for law enforcement purposes." Brief of Appellees, *NACDL v. EOUSA*, 2015 WL 5081706, at *25 (D.C. Cir. Aug. 28, 2015).

9. 844 F.3d at 249.

10. *See* Memorandum Regarding Segregability and Reply re: Segregability, *available at* https://www.nacdl.org/BlueBookFOIALitigation/. Upon remand the DOJ did release Chapter One of the Blue Book. At the time of this writing, the case was still on remand to the district court.

law questions that cannot be fully addressed by an analysis of whether a DOJ policy is exempt from FOIA disclosure requirements.

This Essay seeks to draw attention to the larger issues implemented by the Blue Book Litigation, both to reorient the court's perspective in that case, as well as to initiate a broader conversation about the challenges associated with government decisions to conceal information more generally.[11] Part II looks at the ramifications of the Blue Book Litigation for individual liberty and criminal justice. It scrutinizes the overarching due process issues presented by discovery doctrine under the Supreme Court's decision in *Brady v. Maryland*[12] and its progeny, the Federal Rules of Criminal Procedure, professional responsibility mandates, and existing statutory authority. Part III considers the case from an administrative law perspective. It looks at the importance of transparency and accountability to our administrative state and preliminarily discusses how the Blue Book fits within the structure and expectations of administrative law.

I. Discovery as a Due Process Obligation

A. Blue Book Litigation

The genesis of the DOJ Blue Book was in part an attempt by DOJ to thwart congressional legislation that would mandate discovery obligations.[13] Senator Theodore "Ted" Stevens, a sitting Senator in the height of a re-election campaign, was tried on charges of public corruption without exculpatory evidence

---

11. A fuller treatment of the constitutional and administrative ramifications of secret government policies is part of the authors' ongoing work in the area.

12. 373 U.S. 83 (1963).

13. In a Statement on the Record to the Senate Judiciary Committee following a report that disclosed the failures in the Senator Ted Stevens case, the DOJ stated, "[i]n light of these internal reforms, the Department does not believe that legislation is needed to address the problems that came to light in the *Stevens* prosecution." *See* U.S. Dep't of Justice, Statement for the Record, Senate Comm. on the Judiciary, *Hearing on the Special Counsel's Report on the Prosecution of Senator Ted Stevens* 1 (March 28, 2012) (hereinafter "Special Counsel's Report Hearing"), *available at* https://www.judiciary.senate.gov/imo/media/doc/12-3-28SchuelkeTestimony.pdf. The DOJ later noted that one of the steps taken was "[a] Federal Criminal Discovery Blue Book—which comprehensively covers the law, policy, and practice of prosecutors' disclosure obligations—was created and distributed to prosecutors nationwide in 2011. It is now electronically available on the desktop of every federal prosecutor and paralegal." *Id.* at 4.

being provided to the defense.[14] Following Senator Steven's conviction, the Hon. Emmet G. Sullivan, the judge who had presided over the trial, ordered an investigation of suspected discovery violations. He appointed Attorney Henry F. Schuelke III to oversee the investigation. Schuelke, who was designated as Special Counsel for the investigation, provided the court with a 525 page report ("Schuelke Report") that confirmed the failure by DOJ to provide this "significant exculpatory evidence" to the defense.[15] The government eventually moved to dismiss the *Stevens* case, and the district court set aside the verdict.[16] This case set the groundwork for proposed Senate legislation that would statutorily mandate the DOJ to provide discovery to those accused of crimes.[17]

The DOJ opposed this new legislation and responded that internal DOJ policy rectified the existing problems that occurred in the *Stevens* case. In a statement to the Senate Judiciary Committee, the DOJ provided the steps that they had taken to correct past deficiencies. These steps included a host of reforms such as a New Prosecutor Boot Camp to educate new attorneys on their obligations under the Supreme Court's decisions in *Brady v. Maryland* and *Giglio v. United States*.[18] The DOJ also stated that a discovery Blue Book was electronically available on the desktop of prosecutors nationwide.[19]

Although the bill died in the Senate,[20] the hearing on the Schuelke Report alerted the NACDL to the existence of a Blue Book that provided a treatise "which comprehensively covers the law, policy, and practice of prosecutors'

---

14. "The investigation and prosecution of U.S. Senator Ted Stevens were permeated by the systemic concealment of significant exculpatory evidence which would have independently corroborated Senator Steven's defense and his testimony, and seriously damaged the testimony and credibility of the government's key witness." Report to Hon. Emmet G. Sullivan of Investigation Conduct Pursuant to the Court's Order dated April 7, 2009, In re Special Proceedings, No. 09 Misc. 0198 (D.D.C. March 15, 2012), *available at* http://legaltimes.typepad.com/files/stevens_report.pdf (commonly known as the "Schuelke Report").

15. *Id.* at 12.

16. United States v. Stevens, No. 09 Crim. 231 (D.D.C. Apr. 7, 2009). *See also* Rob Cary, Not Guilty: The Unlawful Prosecution of U.S. Senator Ted Stevens (2014) (providing a detailed account by Senator Stevens' attorney of the pre-trial, trial, and post-trial occurrences in the case).

17. *See* Brief of Appellant, *NACDL v. EOUSA*, 2015 WL 4320471, at *3–4 (D.C. Cir. July 15, 2015) (discussing the introduction of the Fairness in Disclosure of Evidence Act).

18. For further discussion of these cases and the resultant obligations on the government, see *infra* Part II.B.

19. *See* Special Counsel's Report Hearing, *supra* note 13, at 4.

20. Fairness in Disclosure of Evidence Act. *See* Brief of Appellant, *NACDL v. EOUSA*, 2015 WL 4320471, at *5 (D.C. Cir. July 15, 2015).

disclosure obligations."[21] NACDL's subsequent FOIA request for the Blue Book sought to obtain this new discovery policy, which the DOJ claimed as one of the antidotes for correcting its discovery problems.

Despite DOJ's claim to the Senate Judiciary Committee that it instituted new discovery policies, the NACDL's FOIA request for the Blue Book was rejected by the Executive Office for United States Attorneys as falling under Exemptions 5 and 7(E) of FOIA.[22] The NACDL exhausted its administrative remedies and then proceeded to federal district court to litigate the release of the Blue Book. NACDL presented its complaint, but as with many *in camera* reviews, the NACDL was left to argue for the release of information without access to the very information that could assist them in their arguments to the court.

The district court reviewed the Blue Book *in camera* and granted DOJ's summary judgment motion[23] on the basis of FOIA's Exemption 5 and the work product doctrine. The D.C. Circuit, in an opinion authored by Judge Srinivasan, affirmed this decision. In an amended opinion, however, the court remanded the case to consider whether the Blue Book also contained nonexempt policy statements that could be separated from the protected attorney work product and therefore produced to the NACDL.[24]

Judge Srinivasan's initial opinion focused on FOIA, rejecting the NACDL's arguments that "(i) the Blue Book was not prepared in anticipation of litigating a specific claim or case; (ii) the Blue Book principally serves a non-adversarial function; and (iii) the Blue Book's content resembles that of a neutral treatise."[25] The court's opinion provided an exhaustive discussion of the work product doctrine and its accompanying case law. It also distinguished this case from existing cases such as *Coastal States Gas Corporation v. Department of Energy*,[26] which involved a memorandum that the court believed was not in anticipation of litigation,[27] by holding that a specific claim was not a prerequisite for being "in anticipation" of litigation under the work product doctrine. The court stated that, "in the case of a document like the Blue Book, prepared en-

---

21. *See* Special Counsel's Report Hearing, *supra* note 13, at 4.

22. *See* Complaint for Declaratory and Injunctive Relief, *NACDL v. EOUSA*, Civil Action No. 14-CV-269 (D.D.C. Feb. 21, 2014), *available at* https://www.nacdl.org/BlueBook FOIALitigation/.

23. 75 F. Supp. 3d 552 (D.D.C. 2014).

24. 844 F.3d 246 (D.C. Cir. 2016).

25. *Id.* at 252.

26. 617 F.2d 854 (D.C. Cir. 1980).

27. 844 F.3d at 253. The D.C. Circuit also distinguished this from *Sealed Case*, 146 F.3d 881 (D.C. Cir. 1998), finding that a specific claim was not required for implicating the privilege. 844 F.3d at 254.

tirely for use in wholly foreseeable (even inevitable) litigation, there is no need to apply any specific-claim test to conclude that litigation is sufficiently likely to warrant application of the work-product privilege."[28] The court also distinguished the Blue Book from the United States Attorneys' Manual, which is available to the public, finding that "the Blue Book imparts litigation strategy to government lawyers."[29] The court's opinion recognized that DOJ already publicized "general policy statements about federal prosecutors' discovery obligations."[30] In the end the court's focus did not deviate from an analysis of FOIA and the work product issues applicable to that statute.

A concurring opinion was less content with the results in the case. Judge Sentelle, joined by Judge Edwards, expressed dismay with having to follow the precedent that mandated this decision. They believed that a limited interpretation of FOIA, specifically Exemption 5, was necessitated by *Schiller v. NLRB*,[31] a case they believed "was wrongly decided in the first instance."[32] Their concurring opinion noted that "[a]lthough ... the normative and perhaps ethical implications of extending this protection to a prosecutorial manual are sufficient to give pause, I cannot see any legal difference between this case and *Schiller* which would permit us to reach a different result."[33] Thus, although dissatisfied with the current state of the court's FOIA-related precedent, even the concurring opinion focused on resolving the issue in this limited context.

This FOIA-focused decision omits the overriding discovery concerns that led the NACDL to bring this action in the first place. There is no mention of the discovery violation in the *Stevens* case that inspired the creation of the Blue Book. The findings housed in the Schuelke Report do not even get a passing mention in the D.C. Circuit opinion. Finally, there is no balancing of the important due process rights of providing knowledge of the discovery process to the accused.

B. Beyond FOIA

A key event in the genesis of the Blue Book, the botched public corruption prosecution of Senator Ted Stevens, turned on the DOJ's failure to provide the defense with exculpatory evidence as required by *Brady v. Maryland*,[34] a

---

28. *Id.* at 255.
29. *Id.* at 256.
30. *Id.* at 257.
31. 964 F.2d 1205 (D.C. Cir. 1992).
32. 844 F.3d at 258–59.
33. *Id.* at 258.
34. 373 U.S. 83 (1963).

Supreme Court opinion recognizing the importance of discovery in assuring due process to those accused of crimes. The *Brady* Court held that "suppression by the prosecutor of evidence favorable to an accused upon request violates due process where the evidence is material either to guilt or to punishment, irrespective of the good faith or bad faith of the prosecution."[35] This landmark opinion was extended to include impeachment evidence in *Giglio v. United States*.[36] A three-prong test is used by courts in reviewing whether there has been a *Brady* violation, a test that examines whether the evidence was "favorable to the accused," whether the government had suppressed that evidence, and whether there was resulting prejudice.[37] Although courts have dissected accompanying issues of materiality, inadmissible evidence, discovery obligations when the accused is entering a plea, and evidence destruction by the government, *Brady* obligations have continually been a key component in assuring that defendants receive due process.[38]

Brady obligations have not been limited to Supreme Court doctrine. Its principles are replicated in ethical, procedural, and statutory obligations. ABA Model Rules of Professional Conduct Rule 3.8 requires prosecutors to "make timely disclosure to the defense of all evidence or information known to the prosecutor that tends to negate the guilt of the accused or mitigates the offense." It also includes obligations related to disclosure for sentencing. The only exemption provided in the ethical rule rests on when "the prosecutor is relieved of this responsibility by a protective order of the tribunal."[39]

Equally persuasive sources of the obligations to disclose favorable evidence to the accused are found in the Federal Rules of Criminal Procedure. For example, Federal Rule of Criminal Procedure 16 provides the mechanics of providing discovery, and Rule 26.2 requires disclosure of witness statements.[40] Federal statutes also mandate discovery obligations. The government is statu-

---

35. *Id.* at 87.

36. 405 U.S. 105 (1972) (holding that "evidence of any understanding or agreement as to a future prosecution would be relevant to his credibility and the jury was entitled to know of it").

37. Strickler v. Green, 527 U.S. 263 (1999).

38. Peter J. Henning, Andrew Taslitz, Margaret Parris, Cynthia Jones, & Ellen S. Podgor, Mastering Criminal Procedure, Vol. 2 — The Adjudicatory Stage 2d 136-44 (2015) (discussing *Brady* and its progeny).

39. ABA Model Rules of Professional Conduct, Rule 3.8.

40. *See generally* Ellen S. Podgor, *Criminal Discovery of* Jencks *Witness Statements: Timing Makes a Difference*, 15 Ga. St. L. Rev. 651 (1999) (discussing a survey of when *Jencks* materials are provided by the government to the defense).

torily required, for instance, to "preserve biological evidence that was secured in the investigation or prosecution of a federal offense, if a defendant is under a sentence or imprisonment for such offense,"[41] and to provide witness statements to the accused.[42]

Despite the wealth of ethical obligations, federal rules, statutory authority, and strong case law, courts across the country are continually confronted with discovery violations. One does not need to look far to find the many cases where the government failed to disclose favorable FBI notes,[43] DEA reports,[44] or other exculpatory evidence to the defense.[45] Some cases with *Brady* violations have resulted in convictions being overturned.[46] Others have resulted in the incarceration of innocent individuals who were later exonerated.[47]

In *United States v. Olsen*,[48] Judge Kozinski stated in a dissenting opinion that "*Brady* violations have reached epidemic proportions in recent years."[49] He emphasized that a "robust and rigorously enforced *Brady* rule is imperative because all the incentives prosecutors confront encourage them not to discover or disclose exculpatory evidence."[50] As noted in a recent report that quantifies many of these violations, it is stated that "[i]n courtrooms across the nation,

---

41. 18 U.S.C. §3600A(a).

42. 18 U.S.C. §3500 (commonly referred to as the Jencks Act). This emanates from the Supreme Court's decision in *Jencks v. United States*, 353 U.S. 657 (1957), and is also replicated in Rule 26.2 of the Federal Rules of Criminal Procedure.

43. *See, e.g.,* United States v. Triumph Capital Group, Inc., 544 F.3d 149 (2d Cir. 2008) (finding *Brady* violation for failure to disclosure investigating agent's notes).

44. *See, e.g.,* United States v. Avilés-Colón, 536 F.3d 1 (1st Cir. 2008) (finding *Brady* violation for failure to disclose DEA reports, or evidence developed on the basis of the DEA reports, which could have been used for impeachment).

45. *See* Brief of Amici Curiae the Constitution Project and the Innocence Project in Support of Appellant National Association of Criminal Defense Lawyers, *NACDL v. EOUSA*, 2015 WL 4480886, at *8 (D.C. Cir. July 22, 2015).

46. *See, e.g.,* United States v. Mahaffy, 693 F.3d 113 (2d Cir. 2012) (vacating a property fraud conviction in "light of the government's mishandling of material exculpatory and impeaching material").

47. *See, e.g.,* Connick v. Thompson, 131 S. Ct. 1350, 1355 (2011) (noting the suppression of a lab report); *see also* Peter A. Joy, *The Relationship Between Prosecutorial Misconduct and Wrongful Convictions: Shaping Remedies for a Broken System*, 2006 Wisc. L. Rev. 399 (noting prosecutorial misconduct that led to wrongful convictions); Cynthia Jones, *A Reason to Doubt: The Suppression of Evidence and the Inference of Innocence*, 100 J. Crim. Law & Criminology 415 (2010) (noting the under-enforcement of *Brady* violations).

48. 737 F.3d 625 (9th Cir. 2013) (dissenting from denial of petition for rehearing *en banc*).

49. *Id.* at 631.

50. *Id.* at 630.

accused persons are convicted without ever having access to, let alone an opportunity to present, information that is favorable to their defense."[51]

Recognizing the due process rights required by *Brady* and its progeny, the current failure to adequately resolve DOJ violations, and the enormity of the consequences resulting from these failures, which includes the incarceration of innocent individuals, a strong remedy is necessitated. Hiding behind the Blue Book and claiming it as protected work product within the confines of a FOIA exemption fails to recognize the wider obligations to the criminal justice process. Criminal prosecutions lacking in the fundamental features of fairness and justice represented by the Due Process Clause cross the line from valid exercises of government authority to an abrogation of the great responsibility that accompanies the acceptance of such power. Courts must demand transparency and accountability to assure that actors like DOJ are complying with the constitutional rights guaranteed to those accused of crimes. On remand, the district court in the Blue Book Litigation must consider the effects of DOJ concealing its discovery policies on criminal defendants, especially to the extent that concealment implicates defendants' rights under *Brady*.

While there are certainly nuances within *Brady* that may support arguments for or against the release of particular information or the timing of that release,[52] the clear mandates of due process necessitate transparency to assure both the defense and the general public of the legitimacy of the criminal justice process—the assurance that agency conduct conforms to set rules that mirror societal norms and "shared beliefs."[53]

Finally, DOJ's attempt to justify withholding the Blue Book by distinguishing it from other public agency policy documents like the U.S. Attorney's Manual or other discovery memos fails to recognize the importance of trans-

---

51. Kathleen "Cookie" Ridolfi, Tiffany M. Joslyn, & Todd H. Fries, *Material Indifference: How Courts are Impeding Fair Disclosure in Criminal Cases*, Executive Summary x (2014), *available at* https://www.nacdl.org/discoveryreform/materialindifference/.

52. *See generally* R. Michael Cassidy, *Plea Bargaining, Discovery, and the Intractable Problem of Impeachment Disclosures*, 64 Vand. L. Rev. 1429 (2011) (discussing whether prosecutors have to disclose impeachment evidence prior to the defendant pleading).

53. *See* David Beetham, The Legitimation of Power 20 (1991). For discussion of legitimacy in the criminal justice process, see Ellen S. Podgor, *White Collar Shortcuts*, 2018 U. Ill. L. Rev. ___ (forthcoming), *available at* https://papers.ssrn.com/sol3/papers.cfm?abstract_id=2952212 (discussing aggressive government policies that undermine legitimacy and deterrence); *see also* Anthony Bottoms & Justice Tankebe, *Beyond Procedural Justice: A Dialogic Approach to Legitimacy in Criminal Justice*, 102 J. Crim. L. & Criminology 119, 168 (2012).

parency and legitimacy to the criminal justice process.[54] Strategy and legal advice that is not specific to an individual prosecution requires disclosure, especially when it is created in the format of a treatise that includes the DOJ's methodology on *Brady* compliance. Only by approaching the Blue Book Litigation from this broader perspective of government responsibility can the court properly evaluate the full institutional impact of the DOJ's conduct.

II. Discovery and Administrative Law

The Blue Book Litigation also implicates some important, yet largely overlooked, principles of administrative law. It raises issues of good governance that are in danger of going unnoticed, at least in part, because of the role of DOJ as both administrator and litigant. The DOJ's status as the primary litigating arm of the federal government threatens to conflate its status as a regular party in federal court litigation with its more general role as a law enforcement institution along the lines of any other executive agency. The DOJ's institutional obligations are necessarily broader than those of any private litigant, and they raise the same administrative law issues of effective administration that are faced routinely by the administrative state as a whole.[55] While this dichotomy is certainly not lost on the parties to the Blue Book Litigation, it is

---

54. *See* Notice of Filing of Supplemental Declaration, *NACDL v. EOUSA*, Civil Action No. 14-CV-269 (CKK) (D.D.C. Mar. 14, 2017) (Supplemental Declaration of Andrew D. Goldsmith ¶ 27).

55. The term legitimacy does not necessarily lend itself to a single definition, but as David Arkush has explained:

> Observers have not always made clear what is meant by the term legitimacy, but the ordinary sense of the term often suffices, with its evocation of a set of characteristics related to public perceptions of legality, propriety, and efficacy. The principal reason for concern over the legitimacy of the administrative process is that it often involves the exercise of "substantial public power by unelected agency officials." The lack of public accountability, as well as agencies' poor fit within the constitutional scheme that separates legislative, executive, and judicial powers, means that agency decisions run a higher risk than other government actions of being viewed as unlawful, unsound, or undemocratic.

David Arkush, *Democracy and Administrative Legitimacy*, 47 WAKE FOREST L. REV. 611, 612 (2013). Democratic legitimacy is a species of the broader concept of legitimacy, and focuses on key democratic values of public participation and accountability to justify government authority. *See id.* at 620 (arguing that democratic legitimacy "envisions a high degree of citizen participation in the administrative process, or at least strong democratic accountability for agency officials regarding whether they actively consider public views").

also (understandably) not fully fleshed out due to the focus in that case on the Blue Book's specific status under FOIA.

The Blue Book Litigation thus serves as an example of some potentially unexplored questions about agency decisionmaking and administrative law. More specifically, it highlights the existence of, and challenges presented by, undisclosed agency policies—agency value judgments and interpretations of law that influence government action unbeknownst to the effected public.

Before embarking on a discussion of whether and how undisclosed policies may be justified within the ambit of administrative law, it is important to identify what is *not* at issue. The following discussion does not suggest that all substantive conclusions made within an agency must be available for public consumption. The focus here is on generally applicable, prospective policy decisions by administrative agencies and the underlying principle in administrative law that such policies be publicly disclosed. The most obvious examples of this principle at work are agency regulations (rules), most commonly promulgated through the notice and comment procedures of the Administrative Procedure Act (APA).[56] The APA defines rules as "agency statement[s] of general or particular applicability and future effect designed to implement, interpret, or prescribe law or policy," and sets several criteria for their promulgation, including publishing a full account of the rule in proposed form and then, after opportunity for public comment, the complete text of the rule at least 30 days prior to its becoming effective.[57] Perhaps an even more useful analog is the "general statements of policy" referred to in § 553(b)(3)(A) of the APA. General policy statements are explicitly exempted from the notice and comment requirements of binding regulations, on the theory that they are not legally binding and therefore do not require the same fulsome public participation as obligatory regulations. Despite their different legal effects, the APA clearly anticipates that general statements of policy will also be publicly disclosed. The Attorney General's Manual on the Administrative Procedure Act described such policy statements as early as 1947 as those "issued by an agency *to advise the public* prospectively of the manner in which the agency proposes to exercise a discretionary power."[58]

By contrast, there is a wide range of other agency determinations—individualized adjudications like licensing and enforcement decisions, for instance—

---

56. 5 U.S.C. §551 *et seq.*

57. 5 U.S.C. §§551(4); 553(b), (d).

58. Attorney General's Manual on the Administrative Procedure Act 30 n.3 (1947) (hereinafter "Attorney General's Manual").

that constitute policy determinations and are disclosed to the effected parties, yet are not made public in the same way as more generalized policy statements.[59] Policy determinations that are not yet finalized are another example of agency actions that need not be made public in the same way as binding rules or general statements of policy. This is reflected in the deliberative process protections afforded to government actors both in litigation and under FOIA, and is consistent with theories of open government.[60]

Broadly speaking, the difference between generally applicable policy statements and discreet, individualized policy decisions is not of tremendous consequence in administrative law. Since both species of agency conduct are subject to the same standards of judicial review, we have little occasion to focus on the differences. A problem arises, however, when an agency chooses a particular vehicle for policymaking and then fails to meet expectations as to the appropriate procedures for that vehicle. That is the DOJ's situation in the Blue Book Litigation. In that case, the agency chose to employ a policymaking vehicle that acts generally, prospectively, and finally, yet did not make the public aware of its conclusions—it promulgated a "secret policy". The Blue Book Litigation focused on whether a policy decision pertaining to litigation decisions can be characterized as attorney work product under Exemption 5 of FOIA.[61] The dispute revolved around whether a prospective, generally applicable policy statement about how to interpret prosecutors' discovery obligations under current law was specific enough to a particular litigation event to exempt it from the default rule articulated in the Attorney General's Manual that generalized policy statements are those "issued by an agency *to advise the public* prospec-

---

59. The APA defines adjudication as the "agency process for the formulation of an order," and "order" as "the whole or a part of a final disposition, whether affirmative, negative, injunctive, or declaratory in form, of an agency in a matter other than rule making but including licensing." 5 U.S.C. §§ 551(6), (7).

60. *See* United States Dep't of Justice, FOIA Update: Policy Guidance: When to Assert the Deliberative Privilege Under FOIA Exemption Five (1979) (outlining the deliberative process privilege and explaining that "[t]he main policy reason in favor of the deliberative privilege is to avoid chilling and distorting the candid discussion needed for optimum decision making inside government agencies"), *available at,* https://www.justice.gov/oip/blog/foia-update-policy-guidance-when-assert-deliberative-privilege-under-foia-exemption-five.

61. The DOJ's original decision also relied on the language in Exemption 7 protecting from disclosure those materials "compiled for law enforcement purposes." The court of appeals noted that to the extent any portions of the Blue Book were deemed outside the scope of Exemption 5 on remand, "the court could then consider whether Exemption 7(E) of FOIA would protect any of that material from disclosure." Nat'l Ass'n Crim. Defense Lawyers v. EOUSA, 844 F.3d 246, 258 (D.C. Cir. 2016).

tively of the manner in which the agency proposes to exercise a discretionary power."[62] The D.C. Circuit has so far held that at least portions of the Blue Book qualify as exempt work product under Exemption 5, but remanded the case to the district court for a more granular analysis of whether the Blue Book contains any "non-exempt statements of policy that are reasonably segregable ... and that therefore should be disclosed."[63]

Although not necessarily agreeing with the court's application of FOIA's statutory language to the realities of the Blue Book, it makes perfect sense to follow this regimen. Presented with a dispute over disclosure of public documents, courts should be focused on applying the relevant legal standard to the terms of the disclosure request to determine the proper scope of the parties' rights and obligations. In the administrative law context, however, there are principles at work beyond the straightforward application of law to fact. When a government entity makes a statement of policy, it brings to bear the law enforcement authority of the executive branch. This inevitably raises an issue that pervades (and in many ways is unique to) administrative law—the legitimacy of the agency's exercise of its power within our constitutional democracy.[64]

Because the administrative state is not explicitly provided for in the Constitution, administrative law is under constant pressure to justify agency policymaking in a system where that power has been expressly assigned to the political branches of government.[65] Three core principles of administrative legitimacy are expertise, accountability, and efficiency.[66] Agency expertise is a

---

62. Attorney General's Manual, *supra* note 58, at 30 n.3.

63. *Nat'l Ass'n Crim. Defense Lawyers*, 844 F.3d at 257.

64. According to Habermas, " '[l]egitimacy means that there are good arguments for a political order's claim to be recognized as right and just.... *Legitimacy means a political order's worthiness to be recognized*.' " Gerald E. Frug, *The Ideology of Bureaucracy in American Law*, 97 Harv. L. Rev. 1276, 1287 (1984) (quoting J. Habermas, Communication And The Evolution Of Society 178 (T. McCarthy trans. 1979) (emphasis in original)).

65. *See, e.g.*, Lisa Schultz Bressman, *Beyond Accountability: Arbitrariness and Legitimacy in the Administrative State*, 78 N.Y.U. L. Rev. 461, 462 (2003) ("From the birth of the administrative state, we have struggled to describe our regulatory government as the legitimate child of a constitutional democracy. That is, we have sought to reconcile the administrative state with a constitutional structure that reserves important policy decisions for elected officials and not for appointed bureaucrats.").

66. *See, e.g.*, Jost Delbrück, *Exercising Public Authority Beyond the State: Transnational Democracy and/or Alternative Legitimation Strategies?*, 10 Ind. J. Global Legal Stud. 29, 34 (2003) ("[W]e find several elements and criteria that are held to contribute to the legitimacy of the exercise of public authority.... [S]uch criteria are transparency and efficiency of government (or more broadly, public authority), and actions and accountability.... Fi-

foundational principle of administrative law.[67] It reflects the often highly specific and technical mission of administrative agencies and the corresponding need for government officials with compartmentalized knowledge and experience in their delegated policymaking arena.[68] Accountability, which includes as a prerequisite transparency,[69] is also of paramount importance. Accountability refers to the public's ability to retain control over its government—including its administrative institutions—by judging its representatives on their performance in office. In order for the public to make that judgment in the administrative context, it must be privy to an agency's explanations for its exercise of authority.[70] Transparency is thus a precondition to accountability because it is necessary for the public to have access to the information upon which administrators base their judgments in order to monitor the conduct and competency of those administrators. The efficiency principle acknowl-

---

nally, we may add expertise as a factor that can contribute to the acceptability of acts of public authorities.").

67. Lawrence Lessig & Cass R. Sunstein, *The President and the Administration*, 94 COLUM. L. REV. 1, 94, 99–100 (1994) ("To be sure, many insist on technocratic rationality.... This is an enduring theme in administrative law.... [T]he absence of expertise, or the distortion of expert judgment..., is an important obstacle to a well-functioning system of regulatory law.").

68. JAMES M. LANDIS, THE ADMINISTRATIVE PROCESS 23 (1938) ("With the rise of regulation, the need for expertness became dominant....").

69. *See* CASS R. SUNSTEIN, AFTER THE RIGHTS REVOLUTION 187 (1990) ("The principle of political accountability has an unmistakable foundation in Article I of the Constitution, and it is an overriding structural commitment of the document. The principle has foundations as well in assessments of institutional performance. At the same time, it operates to counteract characteristic failures in the regulatory process."); Molly Beutz, *Functional Democracy: Responding to Failures of Accountability*, 44 HARV. INT'L L.J. 387, 428 (2003) (noting that transparency is a "precondition" to accountability, as "[t]ransparency ... facilitate[s] accountability because citizens need information to know when to hold which leaders accountable for what decisions").

70. Mark Fenster, *The Opacity Of Transparency*, 91 IOWA L. REV. 885, 899 (2006) ("The most significant consequences [of government transparency] flow from the public's increased ability to monitor government activity and hold officials ... accountable for their actions."). *See also Common Cause v. Nuclear Regulatory Comm'n*, 674 F.2d 921, 928 (D.C. Cir. 1982) (Skelley Wright, J.) (describing Congress' purpose in enacting the Sunshine Act to "enhance citizen confidence in government, encourage higher quality work by government officials, stimulate well-informed public debate about government programs and policies, and promote cooperation between citizens and government. In short, it sought to make government more fully accountable to the people"); *but see* Edward Rubin, *The Myth of Accountability and the Anti-Administrative Impulse*, 103 MICH. L. REV. 2073 (2005) (challenging popular conceptions about political accountability).

edges the importance of responsive, timely government.[71] Any system of administrative law must be attentive to these concerns in order to maintain its credibility and usefulness within a democracy.

An agency's decision to keep a policy statement like the Blue Book confidential raises democratic legitimacy issues that are critical to understanding the full nature of the agency's legal responsibilities. Unlike more individualized determinations that are required to be disclosed to the effected parties on due process grounds, there are no similar constitutional-level requirements that prospective, generalized policy statements be made public. That is where administrative legitimacy comes in. Legitimacy concerns provide a higher-order perspective on agency disclosure that mirrors due process and fits within the existing legal structure for agency policymaking created by the APA and FOIA. In light of the importance of these issues for good governance, it becomes imperative for the court in the Blue Book Litigation to consider the effects of the DOJ's decision to withhold the Blue Book not just in terms of statutory permissions and traditional litigation privileges, but in the context of its wider impacts on government opacity on the functioning and credibility of the administrative state.

Conclusion

Discovery concerns may arise when protecting a witness or when needing to secure evidence for an ongoing investigation.[72] But secrecy outside the confines of a specific case, and more importantly as to policies regarding such procedures, remains questionable. It directly opposes the prosecutorial role of being a "minister of justice"[73] and puts prosecutors in an arena of engaging in a "sporting event."[74] To mask itself in the nuances of FOIA, DOJ fails to recognize these important concerns. More importantly, it flies in the face of key administrative law principles of legitimacy: expertise, accountability, and efficiency.

---

71. Glen O. Robinson, *The Making of Administrative Policy: Another Look at Rulemaking and Adjudication and Administrative Procedure Reform*, 118 U. Pa. L. Rev. 485, 516 (1970) ("The goal of efficiency needs no explanation or defense. If it cannot be considered an ultimate concern of administrative law that tasks be accomplished with the minimum expenditure of time and resources, it is nevertheless a matter of large importance.").

72. *See generally Panel Discussion: Criminal Discovery in Practice*, 15 Georgia St. L. Rev. 781 (1999) (discussing practical issues that arise in the context of providing discovery).

73. ABA Model Rules of Professional Conduct, Rule 3.8 Comment ("A prosecutor has the responsibility of a minister of justice and not simply that of an advocate.").

74. *See* William J. Brennan, Jr., *The Criminal Prosecution: Sporting Event or Quest for Truth?*, 1963 Wash. U. L. Q. 279, 285 (1963).

Allowing DOJ to shield its internal or external guidance to prosecutors from the public fails to recognize the importance of government transparency. In the face of growing discovery debacles, transparency is needed to assure that those accused of crimes receive due process. It is also needed to assure the general public of the integrity of the administrative state. As noted by the concurring opinion in the Blue Book Litigation, "the conduct with the U.S. Attorney must not only be above board, it must be seen to be above board. If the people cannot see it at all, then they cannot see it to be appropriate, or more is the pity, to be inappropriate."[75]

---

75. 844 F.3d at 246, 260 (D.C. Cir. 2016).

Russell L. Weaver*

Privacy and Free Expression

The modern movement toward privacy protections is widely attributed to Justice Louis D. Brandeis and Samuel Warren's landmark article, *The Right to Privacy*,[1] written at the end of the nineteenth century. That article forcefully articulated the need to protect the right of "privacy" which was described as "the right to be let alone" and as one of the rights most valued by civilized men.[2] Brandeis carried his privacy crusade into the twentieth century when he argued for extending the right to privacy to protections against police surveillance. In *Olmstead v. United States*,[3] with some prescience, Brandeis expressed concern that advances in technology could one day threaten personal privacy.[4] He believed that some day government might be able, "without removing papers from secret drawers," "reproduce them in court," and "expose to a jury the most intimate occurrences of the home."[5] Brandeis urged the Court to create an "indefeasible right of personal security, personal liberty and private property."[6]

Professor William Prosser's article, *Privacy*, sought to clarify and define the tort of privacy.[7] In that article, he divided the privacy tort into four separate and distinct categories, involving situations in which: (1) defendant portrays plaintiff in a false light; (2) defendant intrudes on plaintiff's seclusion; (3) defendant publicly discloses private embarrassing facts about the plaintiff; and (4) plaintiff appropriates plaintiff's name, image, or likeness for defendant's benefit.[8]

---

* Professor of Law & Distinguished University Scholar, University of Louisville, Louis D. Brandeis School of Law.

1. Samuel Warren & Louis D. Brandeis, *The Right to Privacy*, 4 Harv. L. Rev. 193 (1890).
2. *Id.* at 193.
3. 277 U.S. 438 (1928).
4. *Id.* at 474 (Brandeis, J., dissenting).
5. *Id.*
6. *Id.* at 475.
7. *See* W. Prosser, *Privacy*, 48 Calif. L. Rev. 383, 389 (1960).
8. *Id.*

Brandeis' call for privacy protections has never been fully realized in the United States. Unlike many European countries, which have adopted stringent data protection laws that protect their citizens against both governmental and private invasions,[9] and who reinforce those laws through judicial enforcement,[10] the U.S. has generally provided far fewer privacy protections to its citizens. U.S. jurisdictions have never enacted strong data protection laws, and the courts have restrictively construed the Fourth Amendment to the U.S. Constitution's prohibition against "unreasonable" searches and seizures.[11] As a result, U.S. businesses routinely gather information about their customers, and the U.S. government has been able to develop and maintain a massive and secret cybersurveillance system.[12]

This article examines a further limitation on the right of privacy that is imposed in the United States: the societal interest in freedom of expression.[13] As we shall see, privacy rights and free speech rights are frequently in tension with each other because individuals may have a free speech right to disclose information that impinges privacy interests. This article explores how the U.S. strikes the balance between these two conflicting interests.

---

9. See, e.g., Directive 95/46/EC of the European Parliament and of the Council of 24 October 1995(protection of individuals with regard to the processing of personal data and on the free movement of data).

10. See, e.g., Case C362/14, *Schrems v. Data Protection Commissioner*, Judgment of the Court (Grand Chamber) of 6 October 2015; Case C230/14, *Weltimmo s.r.o. v. Nemzeti Adatvédelmi és Információszabadság Hatóság*, Judgment of the Court of Justice of 1 October 2015; Case C-131/12, *Google Spain SL, Google Inc. v. Agencia Española de Protectión de Datos (AEPD), Mario Costeja Gonzáles*, Judgment of the Court of Justice (Grand Chamber) of 13 May 2014, EU:C:2014:317.

11. See Russell L. Weaver, *The Fourth Amendment, Privacy and Advancing Technology*, 80 Miss. L.J. 1131 (2011).

12. See Henry Farrell, *Hackers Have Just Dumped a Treasure Trove of NSA Data. Here's What It Means, The Washington Post* (Apr. 15, 2017); Matthew Rosenberg & Andrew W. Lehren, *Documents Said to Reveal Hacking Secrets of C.I.A.: WikiLeaks Exposes Tools Agency May Have Used on Smartphones and TVs, The New York Times* A1 (Mar. 8, 2017); Scott Shane, *No Morsel Too Minuscule for All-Consuming NSA: From Spying on Leader of U.N. to tracking Drug Deals, on Ethos of 'Why Not?', The New York Times*, A10 (Nov. 13, 2013); Doug Stanglin; *Snowden Says NSA Can Tap Email Chats, The Courier-Journal*, A3 (Aug. 1, 2013).

13. See, e.g., *Snyder v. Phelps*, 562 U.S. 443, 459-60 (2011) (claimed violation of right to privacy, through intrusion on seclusion, was rejected); *Cox Broadcasting Corporation v. Cohn*, 420 U.S. 469 (1975) (claimed violation of right to privacy, through publication of the name of a deceased rape victim, was rejected); *Time, Inc. v. Hill*, 385 U.S. 374 (1967) (claimed violation of violation of right to privacy, by casting plaintiff in a "false light," was rejected).

I. Free Speech as a "Preferred Right"

Since the U.S. approach to free expression is different from the approach used in most European countries, it is worthwhile to begin by examining the differences in approach. In general, the U.S. treats free speech as unique and exceptional. Unlike some European countries, the U.S. generally treats freedom of expression as a "preferred right" that often prevails over other rights.[14] In general, this means that U.S. courts usually subject most laws that involve "viewpoint-based" discrimination, or content-based discrimination, against speech to strict scrutiny.[15] In other words, such restrictions are subjected to heightened scrutiny, and are likely to be struck down.[16] By contrast, in many European countries, such as France, freedom of expression is treated as one right among many,[17] and is not necessarily given precedence over other rights.[18] The difference between the two continents is amply illustrated by France's Gayssot law which makes it a crime to deny that the Holocaust occurred, and also makes it a crime to challenge the findings of the Nuremberg War Crimes Tribunal (NWCT).[19] The Gayssot law is indisputably viewpoint-based because it permits individuals to affirm that the Holocaust occurred, or to affirm the findings of the NWCT, but criminalizes denial of the Holocaust.

The French approach is founded upon Article IV of the 1789 French Declaration of the Rights of Man and of the Citizen which provides: "Liberty consists for someone of being allowed to do anything as long as it does not harm someone else. As a consequence, every man's exercise of his natural rights is limited only by those limits that ensure all other members of society the benefit of the same rights. The limits cannot be determined otherwise than by law."[20] This statement illustrates the French approach to fundamental rights since the French Revolution, and incorporates the idea of tolerance

---

14. *See, e.g., United States v. Alvarez*, 567 U.S. 709 (2012); *Brown v. Entertainment Merchants Ass'n*, 564 U.S. 756 (2011); *Snyder v. Phelps*, 562 U.S. 443 (2011); *R.A.V. v. City of St. Paul*, 505 U.S. 377, 387 (1992); *Hustler Magazine, Inc. v. Falwell*, 485 U.S. 46, 52 (1988).

15. *See, e.g., R.A.V. v. City of St. Paul*, 505 U.S. 377, 387 (1992).

16. *Id.*

17. *See* Russell L. Weaver, Nicholas Delpierre & Laurence Boissier, *Governmentally Imposed Truth: An Examination of France's Holocaust Denial Law*, 41 Texas Tech. U. L. Rev. 495-517 (2009).

18. *See id.*

19. La loi Gayssot, No. 90-615 (July 13, 1990).

20. French Declaration of the Rights of Man and of the Citizen, Article IV (1789).

and equality for all individuals in the exercise and enjoyment of their rights.[21] However, the Declaration also provides that an individual's rights can be limited when the exercise of those rights intrudes upon another individual's right to enjoy his/her rights.[22] As a result, French court decisions often discuss the need to strike a balance between rights whose exercise leads to antagonism, and the goal of making sure that one right does not violate the exercise of another right in a disproportionate manner.[23] Thus, the French approach envisages limitations on freedom of speech which prevent others from enjoying one or more of their rights.[24] In this respect, French law conforms to the European Convention of Human Rights (ECHR) which allows member states to limit the exercise of ECHR freedoms, including freedom of expression.[25] For example, France restricts free speech in order to maintain public order.[26]

Under French law, the Gayssot law is regarded as a necessary limit on freedom of speech for several reasons. First, the law protects Holocaust victims' and their families' fundamental right to human dignity by prohibiting statements contesting, denigrating, or denying the existence of "crimes against humanity."[27] Second, the Gayssot law is regarded as necessary to maintain public order given that denials of the Holocaust have resulted in public disturbances and sparked tension between ethnic communities.[28] Finally, the Gayssot law is justified on the basis that the Nazis deported Jews from France during the Occupation, and the French fear that these World War II crimes will be forgotten, especially as those connected to the events have grown old or died.

By contrast, as noted, the U.S. tends to treat freedom of expression as a "preferred right."[29] In other words, the U.S. is much less inclined to balance

---

21. *Id.*

22. *See id.*

23. *See* Paris Cour d'Appel, November 16, 2006, Section A, *Esso c/Greenpeace France*; Tribunal de Grande Instance Paris, July 9, 2004, *SPCEA c. Greenpeace France, Greenpeace New Zealand and Internet.fr.*

24. French Declaration of the Rights of Man and of the Citizen, Article IV (1789).

25. ECHR, Article X, Par. 2.

26. French Criminal Code, Art. 433-5-1.

27. Law of 29 July 1881, Article 35-quatre. Http://www.legifrance.gouv.fr/texteconsolide/PCEAA.htm

28. Conseil d'Etat, 27 October 1995, Commune de Morsan-sur-Orge, *Rec.* p. 372.

29. *See, e.g., Snyder v. Phelps*, 562 U.S. 443 (2011); *Falwell v. Hustler Magazine*, 485 U.S. 46 (1988); *New York Times Co. v. Sullivan*, 376 U.S. 254 (1964).

free speech against other rights, and the right to free speech usually prevails over those other rights.[30] Thus, the U.S. Supreme Court has given the right to free speech preference over the right to recover for intentional infliction of mental and emotional distress,[31] as well as over most defamation claims.[32] The Court has also refused to lightly balance away First Amendment rights against other competing rights. In a number of cases, the U.S. Supreme Court has indicated that it will not apply a " 'simple balancing test' that weighs the value of a particular category of speech against its social costs and then punishes that category of speech if it fails the test."[33] The Court has rejected the idea of such a balancing test as "startling and dangerous," noting that "without persuasive evidence that a novel restriction on content is part of a long (if heretofore unrecognized) tradition of proscription, a legislature may not revise the "judgment [of] the American people," embodied in the First Amendment, 'that the benefits of its restrictions on the Government outweigh the costs.' "[34] As a result, the Court has struck down federal laws making it a crime for an individual to falsely claim that he or she has won the congressional medal of honor,[35] prohibiting crush videos,[36] and prohibiting the sale of violent videos to minors.[37] Likewise, a prohibition against Holocaust denial would likely be struck down as a viewpoint-based restriction on speech.

---

30. *See, e.g., Snyder v. Phelps, supra* (right to free speech prevails over right to recover for intentional infliction of mental and emotional distress); *Falwell v. Hustler Magazine, supra* (right to free speech prevails over right to recover for intentional infliction of mental and emotional distress); *New York Times Co. v. Sullivan, supra* (right to free speech requires heightened burden of proof standards in a defamation case brought by a public official).

31. *See, e.g., Snyder v. Phelps, supra; Falwell v. Hustler Magazine, supra.*

32. *See, e.g., New York Times Co. v. Sullivan, supra.*

33. *See United States v. Stevens*, 559 U.S. 460 (2010); *Brown v. Entertainment Merchants Association*, 546 U.S. 786, 792 (2011).

34. *Id.*

35. *See United States v. Alvarez*, 567 U.S. 709 (2012).

36. *See United States v. Stevens*, 559 U.S. 460 (2010).

37. *See Brown v. Entertainment Merchants Association*, 546 U.S. 786, 792 (2011).

II. Free Speech and Privacy

In a number of cases, U.S. courts have been confronted by conflicts between the societal interest in freedom of expression, and the individual interest in privacy. In general, as with other areas of the law, the Court has cut the balance between those interests in favor of free expression. However, in a few instances, privacy interests have prevailed.

A. False Light Privacy Claims

Although there has been a dearth of U.S. Supreme Court cases on the false light prong of privacy, the one major decision cut decisively in favor of free expression. That decision, *Time, Inc. v. Hill*,[38] arose when Life Magazine published an article entitled "True Crimes Inspire Tense Play" with the subtitle "The ordeal of a family trapped by convicts gives Broadway a new Thriller, 'the desperate hours.'" The article was based on a play that purportedly depicted the ordeal of a family that was held hostage by escaped convicts, and who emerged as heroes for the way they handled a brutal and violent ordeal. The difficulty was that the play misrepresented what had happened. In fact, the convicts had treated the family courteously rather than violently. Thus, plaintiffs were portrayed in a "false (although not necessarily defamatory) light."

The family sued under a New York ordinance that made it actionable for a "person, firm or corporation that uses for advertising purposes, or for the purposes of trade, the name, portrait or picture of any living person without having first obtained the written consent of such person, or if a minor of his or her parent or guardian, is guilty of a misdemeanor."[39] Although Time, Inc. sought to invoke a First Amendment defense, by claiming that the article involved a matter of public interest, the trial court imposed a $50,000 damage award in favor of the plaintiffs, as well as $25,000 in punitive damages.

In overturning the damage award, the U.S. Supreme Court articulated a pro-free speech standard that made it difficult for plaintiffs to recover. The Court held that, in order to recover, plaintiff must show that defendant acted with "actual malice."[40] In other words, plaintiff was required to prove that defendant knew that its statement was false, or acted in reckless disregard for truth or falsity.[41] In analyzing the evidence, although *Time, Inc.* might have

---

38. 385 U.S. 374 (1967).
39. ss 50—51 of the New York Civil Rights Law, McKinney's Consol. Laws, c. 6.
40. *Id.* at 391.
41. *Id.*

been negligent, the Court concluded that Time Magazine's report did not involve actual malice.[42] The Court held that plaintiffs could not establish the required actual malice.[43]

B. Intrusion Upon Plaintiff's Seclusion

The typical intrusion upon seclusion case involves a media report that accurately discloses personal, embarrassing, or intimate details about an individual. The question that arises in such cases is whether proof of truth establishes a complete defense to liability. In *Cox Broadcasting Corp. v. Cohn*,[44] the father of a deceased rape victim sued based on a state law that prohibited publication of a rape victim's name.[45] Even though the publication was made

---

42. *Id.* at 392–93:

Prideaux sent photographers to the Hill residence for location photographs of scenes of the play enacted in the home, and proceeded to construct the text of the article. In his 'story file' were several news clippings about the Hill incident which revealed its nonviolent character, and a New York Times article by Hayes in which he stated that the play 'was based on various news stories,' mentioning incidents in New York, California, Detroit and Philadelphia. Prideaux's first draft made no mention of the Hill name except for the caption of one of the photographs. The text related that a true story of a suburban Philadelphia family had 'sparked off' Hayes to write the novel, that the play was a 'somewhat fictionalized' account of the family's heroism in time of crisis. Prideaux's research assistant, whose task it was to check the draft for accuracy, put a question mark over the words 'somewhat fictionalized.' Prideaux testified that the question mark 'must have been' brought to his attention, although he did not recollect having seen it. The draft was also brought before the copy editor, who, in the presence of Prideaux, made several changes in emphasis and substance. The first sentence was changed to focus on the Hill incident, using the family's name; the novel was said to have been 'inspired' by that incident, and the play was referred to as a 're-enactment.' The words 'somewhat fictionalized' were deleted.

43. *Id.* at 393–94:

The jury might reasonably conclude from this evidence—particularly that the New York Times article was in the story file, that the copy editor deleted 'somewhat fictionalized' after the research assistant questioned its accuracy, and that Prideaux admitted that he knew the play was 'between a little bit and moderately fictionalized'—that Life knew the falsity of, or was reckless of the truth in, stating in the article that 'the story reenacted' the Hill family's experience. On the other hand, the jury might reasonably predicate a finding of innocent or only negligent misstatement on the testimony that a statement was made to Prideaux by the free-lance photographer that linked the play to an incident in Philadelphia, that the author Hayes cooperated in arranging for the availability of the former Hill home, and that Prideaux thought beyond doubt that the 'heart and soul' of the play was the Hill incident.

44. 420 U.S. 469 (1975).

45. Ga.Code Ann. s 26—9901 (1972): "It shall be unlawful for any news media or any other person to print and publish, broadcast, televise, or disseminate through any other medium of public dissemination or cause to be printed and published, broadcast, televised,

during the trial of the alleged rapists, the father claimed that the publication involved an invasion of privacy, and the state trial court granted summary judgment on the father's behalf. The Georgia Supreme Court sustained the law on the basis that it provided a legitimate limitation on defendant's right of free expression, concluding that there was "no public interest or general concern about the identity of the victim of such a crime as will make the right to disclose the identity of the victim rise to the level of First Amendment protection."[46] The U.S. Supreme Court reversed, viewing the case as involving an intrusion into plaintiff's right to seclusion.[47] Although defendants sought to cast their defense more broadly, claiming that they had a constitutional right to publish truthful information,[48] however damaging it may be to reputation or individual sensibilities,[49] the Court chose to decide the case on the more narrow ground that the victim's identity had been obtained legally from a public record (the indictment).[50] Emphasizing that there was an unquestioned public interest in the subject of the report,[51] the Court held that the privacy verdict could not stand because it involved an accurate report on a matter of public record:[52] "the interests in privacy fades when the information involved already appears on the public record."[53] The Court flatly stated that it was "reluctant to embark on a course that would make public records generally available to the media but forbid their publication if offensive to the sensibilities of the supposed reasonable man."[54]

---

or disseminated in any newspaper, magazine, periodical or other publication published in this State or through any radio or television broadcast originating in the State the name or identity or any female who may have been raped or upon whom an assault with intent to commit rape may have been made. Any person or corporation violating the provisions of this section shall, upon conviction, be punished as for a misdemeanor."

46. *Cox Broadcasting v. Cohn*, 420 U.S. at 475.

47. *Id.* at 489 ("plaintiff claims the right to be free from unwanted publicity about his private affairs, which, although wholly true, would be offensive to a person of ordinary sensibilities").

48. *Id.*

49. *Id.*

50. *Id.* at 472–73 & 491.

51. *Id.* at 492 ("The commission of crime, prosecutions resulting from it, and judicial proceedings arising from the prosecutions, however, are without question events of legitimate concern to the public and consequently fall within the responsibility of the press to report the operations of government.").

52. *Id.*

53. *Id.* at 494–95.

54. *Id.* at 496.

The Court was confronted by similar issues in two other decisions. *Landmark Communications, Inc. v. Virginia*[55] involved a newspaper report concerning a confidential judicial disciplinary proceeding. Finding that the information not only was truthful, but had been lawfully obtained, the Court sided with the newspaper. For similar and other reasons, the First Amendment prevailed over privacy concerns in *Smith v. Daily Mail Publishing Co.*,[56] a case that concerned a newspaper's publication of a child's name (the child had been murdered) that had been legally obtained. Although the Court refused to establish an absolute privilege for the disclosure of truthful private information, it held that liability for publishing accurate information on an issue of "public significance" could not be established minus "a state interest of the highest order."[57] What constitutes a matter of public significance potentially presents the same challenge to principled line-drawing that has confronted definition of public figures and public controversies in the defamation context.

In another intrusion upon seclusion case, *Snyder v. Phelps*,[58] the First Amendment also prevailed over a privacy claim. That case involved members of the Westboro Baptist Church who believed that God hates and punishes the United States for its tolerance of homosexuality, particularly in its military. The group publicized its views by picketing at military funerals, having protested at some 600 funerals over a twenty-year period. After Marine Lance Corporal Matthew Snyder was killed in Iraq in the line of duty, six Westboro parishioners decided to protest his funeral on public land adjacent to public streets near the Maryland State House, the United States Naval Academy, and Matthew Snyder's funeral. The protesters carried signs with messages such as "God Hates the USA/Thank God for 9/11," "America is Doomed," "Don't Pray for the USA," "Thank God for IEDs," "Thank God for Dead Soldiers," "Pope in Hell," "Priests Rape Boys," "God Hates Fags," "You're Going to Hell," and "God Hates You." The Westboro picketers displayed their signs for about 30 minutes prior to the funeral, and they also sang hymns and recited Bible verses. However, the picketers did not enter church property or go to the cemetery. On the contrary, they were forced to stay at some distance from the funeral and generally out of sight of the mourners. Snyder's father could not read the signs, but rather only saw the tops of the picket signs, even though the funeral procession passed within 200 to 300 feet of the picket site. He did

---

55. 435 U.S. 829 (1978).
56. 443 U.S. 97 (1979).
57. *Id.* at 103.
58. 562 U.S. 443, 459–60 (2011).

see the signs later that evening while watching a news broadcast. In addition, while doing an Internet search, he came across a Web posting (referred to by the Court as the "epic") that was posted several weeks after the funeral that contained religiously oriented denunciations of the Snyders interspersed among lengthy Bible quotations.

Snyder filed suit against Phelps, Phelps' daughters, and the Westboro Baptist Church, alleging five state tort law claims: defamation, publicity given to private life, intentional infliction of emotional distress, intrusion upon seclusion, and civil conspiracy. The trial court rendered judgment against Snyder on the defamation and publicity claims, but the remaining claims went to trial where Snyder testified that he was "unable to separate the thought of his dead son from his thoughts of Westboro's picketing, and that he often became tearful, angry, and physically ill when he thought about it." Expert witnesses testified that Snyder suffered "emotional anguish" and "severe depression" which exacerbated his pre-existing health conditions. Snyder prevailed in the trial court on the intentional infliction of emotional distress, intrusion upon seclusion, and civil conspiracy claims, and obtained judgments against Westboro liable for $2.9 million in compensatory damages and $8 million in punitive damages. However, the punitive damages were remitted to $2.1 million. The trial court upheld plaintiff's verdict for the intrusion tort on the theory that "when Snyder turned on the television to see if there was footage of his son's funeral, he did not 'choose' to see close-ups of the defendants' signs and interviews with Phelps, but rather their actions intruded upon his seclusion."

The U.S. Supreme Court reversed the district court's rejection of the defendant's First Amendment claim, reasoning that defendant's speech occurred at a public place and related to a matter of public concern. The Court also refused to extend the "captive audience" rationale to *Snyder*'s facts in order to allow recovery for the intrusion tort. Plaintiff had claimed that defendants "invaded [Snyder's] privacy during a time of bereavement," when they posted the "epic" commentary on the Westboro website and left it there for Snyder to discover and read. Given the failure of Snyder's counsel to mention the "epic" in the cert. petition, the Supreme Court declined "to consider the 'epic' in deciding the case."

The foregoing cases suggest that the privacy interest will rarely prevail over a First Amendment defense. However, in some respects, the cases are misleading. There are contexts in which the intrusion on seclusion claim is likely to prevail over a free speech claim. For example, suppose that a reporter wants to publish a scoop on a famous personality. In order to gather exclusive information, unknown to other journalists, the journalist breaks into and searches the famous persons home. In that situation, one can assume that the journalist can be criminally prosecuted for trespass, as well as for theft if he removes items from the house. In addition, the homeowner could presumably sue the journalist for trespass and conversion, and perhaps for restitution if any benefit or gains obtained by publication of the story, and arguably an intrusion on seclusion claim would prevail.

In one dramatic case, involving privacy litigation brought by Hulk Hogan against *Gawker* relating to the publication of sex tapes regarding Hogan.[59] In that case, billionaire Paul Thiel allegedly funded the litigation[60] to the tune of $10 million, purportedly because *Gawker* had outed him and several of his friends as gay.[61] The suit resulted in a $140 million judgment for invasion of privacy, and ultimately to a $31 million settlement.[62] The case led to a sale of *Gawker* and ultimately to its demise.[63]

In *Galella v. Onassis*,[64] former First Lady Jacqueline Onassis sued a freelance "paparazzi" photographer (Galella) for, *inter alia*, invasion of privacy. In an effort to produce interesting pictures of Mrs. Onassis and her children, Galella engaged in conduct that was "frightening" ("jumping," "lunging," "leaping," "rushing out," "bumping," "scuffling," "blocking,"), "offensive mouthings" ("grunts," "yells," "strange sounds," and calls), "bogus events" (hiring a costumed Santa to try to force himself close to defendant), "self-aggrandizement" (conniving to have himself photographed with Mrs. Onassis and claiming an intimate knowledge of her every move), seeking a "payoff" in exchange for suppressing his story, and "incessant surveillance" (the threat that he would follow her hour after hour wherever she goes), including "secret agent" tactics (e.g., hiding behind restaurant coat racks, sneaking into beauty parlors, donning "disguises," hiding in bushes and theater boxes, intruding into school buildings, bribing doormen, and romancing maids).

The court flatly rejected the "proposition that the First Amendment gives the press wide liberty to engage in any sort of conduct, no matter how offen-

---

59. *See* Callum Borchers, *Peter Thiel is Totally Not Sorry, People*, The Washington Post, The Fix (Jan. 13, 2017).

60. *See* Katie Rogers & John Herrman, *Thiel-Gawker Battle Raises Some Concerns About Press Freedom*, The New York Times B-5 (May 27, 2016).

61. *See* Barry Meier, *Revenge and the Future of Media Finances*, The New York Times, Media (May 26, 2016).

62. *See* Sydney Ember, *Gawker and Hulk Hogan Reach $31 Million Settlement*, The New York Times, Media (Nov. 2, 2016).

63. *See* Borchers, *supra* note 59.

64. 353 F. Supp. 196 (S.D.N.Y. 1972).

sive, in gathering news,"[65] as well as the idea that the First Amendment gives a newsman the unbridled license to commit torts.[66] Moreover, the court concluded that it was entitled to balance the interest in speech against the intrusion on Onassis' life.[67] In *Galella*, even after applying the balancing test, the court was unwilling to prohibit Galella from taking pictures of Onassis or her children, correctly viewing such an order as a prior restraint on speech.[68] However, the Court held that "the First Amendment does not license Galella to trespass inside private buildings, such as the children's schools, lobbies of friends' apartment buildings and restaurants. Nor does that Amendment command that Galella be permitted to romance maids, bribe employees and maintain surveillance in order to monitor defendant's leaving, entering and living inside her own home."[69] Even though Galella was allowed to photograph Onassis in public, the court held that there is no "general constitutional right to assault, harass, or unceasingly shadow or distress" her when she is in public.[70] The court ended by concluding that Galella had committed assault, battery, harassment, invasion of privacy, tortious infliction of emotional distress, and violation of Onassis' civil rights, and could be subjected to a damage award.[71]

In recent years, a number of jurisdictions have attempted to regulate the actions of paparazzi.[72] Many of these regulations are designed to preserve public safety, and have been adopted in the wake of incidents between famous person-

---

65. *Id.* at 220.

66. *Id.* at 221.

67. *Id.* at 225:

The balancing test is responsive both to the protection of the individual's right to privacy and to the purposes of the First Amendment. Clearly, the First Amendment protects freedom of expression with respect to public affairs-matters relevant to the self-government of the nation. It extends to "all issues about which information is needed or appropriate to enable members of the society to cope with the exigencies of their period." Curtis Publishing Co. v. Butts, 388 U.S. 130, 147 (1967). Doubtless, Mrs. Onassis is a public figure, whose life has included events of great public concern. But it cannot be said that information about her comings and goings, her tastes in ballet, the food that she eats, and other minutiae which are the sole product of Galella's three years of pursuit, bear significantly upon public questions or otherwise "enable the members of society to cope with the exigencies of their period." It merely satisfies curiosity.

See also id. at 226.

68. *Id.*

69. *Id.* at 222.

70. *Id.* at 223.

71. *Id.* at 226–33.

72. *See* Jennifer Steinhauer, *Los Angeles Proposes Restraints on Paparazzi*, N.Y. Times, Aug. 1, 2008, A-12, c. 1–6.

alities and aggressive paparazzi (basically, journalists who follow personalities around hoping to snap interesting pictures). Some of these paparazzi travel in packs, run red lights, and make unsafe U-turns. Because of their aggressiveness, and their willingness to place themselves in the way of personalities trying to avoid them, paparazzi have sometimes caused traffic accidents. In *Raef v. Superior Court*,[73] a lower court upheld a Los Angeles ordinance that increased the punishment for reckless driving and other traffic offenses which are committed with the intent to capture an image, sound recording, or other physical impression of another person for a commercial purpose.[74] Raef challenged the law on First Amendment grounds, claiming that the laws improperly targeted paparazzi, thereby improperly infringing the constitutional rights of news gatherers. In upholding the law, although the court noted that stricter scrutiny is generally required when a law targets the press, the court held that there is no reason to believe that this particular law specifically targeted newsgatherers.[75] The law applied "without limitation, whether the intended image or recording is of a celebrity or someone with no claim to fame, whether it qualifies as news or is a matter of purely private interest, and whether it will be sold to the mass media or be put to purely private use."[76] The court also found that, even if the intent to take a picture is a communicative activity, the law was nonetheless valid because the statute focused not on the communicative activity, but on "the 'special harms' produced by the conduct."[77] But would it be similarly permissible to enact a law providing for "comfort zones" around personalities, when they are out in public, in which nobody may intrude? Such a rule may not sur-

---

73. 193 Cal. Rptr. 3d 159 (Cal. App. 2015).

74. The law contained the following provision: "No person shall wilfully interfere with the driver of a vehicle or with the mechanism thereof in such manner as to affect the driver's control of the vehicle." Section 21703 provided: "The driver of a motor vehicle shall not follow another vehicle more closely than is reasonable and prudent, having due regard for the speed of such vehicle and the traffic upon, and the condition of, the roadway." Section 23103 provided: "(a) A person who drives a vehicle upon a highway in willful or wanton disregard for the safety of persons or property is guilty of reckless driving. (b) A person who drives a vehicle in an offstreet parking facility, as defined in subdivision (c) of Section 12500, in willful or wanton disregard for the safety of persons or property is guilty of reckless driving. (c) Except as otherwise provided in Section 40008, persons convicted of the offense of reckless driving shall be punished by imprisonment in a county jail for not less than five days nor more than 90 days or by a fine of not less than one hundred forty-five dollars ($145) nor more than one thousand dollars ($1,000), or by both that fine and imprisonment, except as provided in Section 23104 or 23105."

75. *Raef v. Superior Court*, 193 Cal. Rptr. 3d at 1122.

76. *Id.*

77. *Id.* at 1128.

vive judicial review since the potential harms from infringing these "comfort zones" are not as great, and such laws might be regarded as vague or overbroad.

One might suspect that there are other situations when an individual might be able to prevail on an intrusion on seclusion case as well. For example, in *Foster v. Svenson*,[78] a photographic artist, who lived in New York City, took pictures of his neighbors in nearby apartments without their knowledge or consent.[79] The apartment building in which plaintiffs lived had a glass façade, and the artist took the pictures by peering through the window using a telephoto lens. When the artist sought to display the pictures as part of an art exhibition, the neighbors objected on privacy grounds. In *Foster*, the Court held that the art constituted speech that was entitled to First Amendment protection. Since defendant had removed plaintiffs' pictures from the exhibit, the Court denied injunctive relief. One might imagine a different court reaching different results, depending on the facts.

C. Right to Publicity

The right of publicity protects an individual's economic interest in the use of his name, image, and talent. It is an interest that is of special concern to athletes, entertainers, and performers. However, protection of name, image, and likeness also imposes restrictions on news gathering and thus implicates First Amendment interests. However, in a number of these cases, privacy interests have prevailed over free speech interests.

One of the more famous decisions was rendered in *Zacchini v. Scripps-Howard Broadcasting Co.*,[80] a case that involved a direct conflict between the right of publicity and the First Amendment. At issue was a television station's broadcast of Zacchini's "human cannonball" performance which lasted about 15 seconds and propelled Zacchini some 200 feet. He performed his act at a fairgrounds that was surrounded by grandstands, making it difficult to see the performance without entering the stands. The case arose when a reporter, who Zacchini had asked not to film his performance, filmed the act from blast-off to landing and showed the entire videotape on the evening news. Zacchini sued, claiming that he was "engaged in the entertainment business," that the act had been "invented by his father," that it had been "performed only by his family for the last fifty years," and that defendant "showed and commercialized the film of his act without his consent," thereby unlawfully appropriating "plaintiff's professional property."[81]

---

78. 41 Med. L. Rptr. 2564 (N.Y. Sup. Ct. 2013).
79. *See Foster v. Svenson*, 41 Med. L. Rptr. 2564 (N.Y. Sup. Ct. 2013).
80. 433 U.S. 562 (1977).
81. *Id.* at 564.

In finding in Zacchini's favor, the Court noted that the right of publicity accounts for two significant societal concerns: the right of an entertainer to trade upon his or her talents to make a living and society's interest in the facilitation of creative energy.[82] Although recognizing news gathering as an important media function, the Court concluded that plaintiff was entitled to damages. Otherwise, defendant's broadcast might rob his performance of all economic value.[83] Moreover, Zacchini did not seek to prevent defendant from airing the performance. He simply sought compensation.[84]

In some instances, rather than arguing that defendant stole plaintiff's performance, privacy suits involve claims that defendant stole plaintiff's name or likeness, often to help advertise defendant's business. For example, in *Davis v. Electronic Arts, Inc.*,[85] former professional football players sued the maker of the *Madden NFL* video game which included avatars that the game user could direct. The goal of the game was to create a level of reality that simulated a real NFL football game. In order to enhance that reality, the game depicted current players for all 32 NFL teams, along with accurate player names, team logos, colors and uniforms. The game maker paid millions of dollars in licensing fees to the players association in order to obtain the rights. However, the game also included certain "historic teams" with the names and likenesses of actual players on those teams. The game maker had no agreements and made no payments for those rights. Some of these "historic" players sued. Although defendant admitted that plaintiffs' likenesses were included in its games, it asserted a "transformative use" defense which shields a work from liability when it "adds significant creative elements so as to be transformed into something more than a mere celebrity likeness or imitation."[86] The Court rejected this defense, noting that the game replicated "players' physical characteristics and allowed users to manipulate them in the performance of the same activity for which they are known in real life—playing football for an NFL team," and therefore the Court did not regard the background and graphics added by the game makers as "transformative."[87] The court also rejected the idea that defendant's use of plaintiffs' likenesses was incidental.[88]

---

82. *Id.* at 573.

83. *Id.* at 575–76.

84. *Id.* at 573.

85. 775 F.3d 1172 (9th Cir. 2015).

86. *Id.* at 1177.

87. *Id.* at 1178.

88. *Id.* at 1180. For cases applying these rules to video games using the images of college athletes, *see O'Bannon v. National Collegiate Athletic Association*, 802 F.3d 1049 (9th Cir. 2015); *Davis v. Electronic Arts, Inc.* 775 F.3d 1172(9th Cir. 2015).

There are a couple of unusual cases that illustrate how the right of privacy might apply in particular cases. In the first, *White v. Samsung Electronics America, Inc.*,[89] game show hostess Vanna White of *Wheel of Fortune* sued Samsung for using her likeness in an advertisement. White claimed that the game show was popular and was watched by some 40 million people per day. The Samsung advertisements depicted a current item from popular culture and a Samsung electronic product. However, the advertisements were set in the twenty-first century and conveyed the message that the Samsung product would still be in use by that time. By hypothesizing outrageous future outcomes for cultural items, the ads created humorous effects. In the *White* case, Samsung videocassette recorders (VCRs) were depicted along with a robot, dressed in a wig, gown, and jewelry that were chosen to resemble White's hair and dress on the *Wheel of Fortune* show. In the advertisement, the robot posed next to a game board, which was instantly recognizable as the *Wheel of Fortune* board, in a stance for which White was famous. The caption of the ad read: "Longest-running game show. 2012 A.D." Defendants referred to the ad as the "Vanna White" ad. White had neither consented to the ads nor was she paid. She sued under section 3344. Section 3344(a) provides, in pertinent part, that "any person who knowingly uses another's name, voice, signature, photograph, or likeness, in any manner, ... for purposes of advertising or selling, ... without such person's prior consent ... shall be liable for any damages sustained by the person or persons injured as a result thereof."[90]

The court held in favor of White, emphasizing that Samsung had not appropriated White's likeness since the advertisement used a robot with mechanical features, rather than "a manikin molded to White's precise features."[91] Nevertheless, it concluded that Samsung might have infringed White's right of publicity by appropriating her name or likeness for commercial advantage.[92] The court held that this tort can arise when plaintiff's identity is appropriated, "as by impersonation, without the use of either his name or his likeness, and that this would be an invasion of his right of privacy."[93] The Court concluded that Samsung's advertisement "directly implicated the commercial interests which the right of publicity is designed to protect."[94] In-

---

89. 971 F.2d 1395 (9th Cir. 1992).
90. California Civil Code §3344.
91. *White v. Samsung Electronics America, Inc.*, 975 F.2d at 1397.
92. *Id.*
93. *Id.* at 1397–98.
94. *Id.* at 1398.

deed, the Court suggested that the advertisement seemed to refer only to Vanna White.[95]

In the second case, *Onassis v. Christian Dior–New York, Inc.*,[96] Christian Dior ran a series of ads featuring the "Diors" (a female and two males), who were portrayed as chic, sophisticated, elite, unconventional, quirky, audacious, elegant, and unorthodox. One of the advertisements depicted a wedding attended by their ostensible intimates—Gene Shalit, the T.V. personality, model Shari Belafonte, actress Ruth Gordon, and a woman (Barbara Reynolds) who looked like Jacqueline Onassis. The copy for the advertisement read: "The wedding of the Diors was everything a wedding should be: no tears, no rice, no in-laws, no smarmy toasts, for once no Mendelssohn. Just a legendary private affair." Of course, what was "legendary" was the presence of this eclectic group, the most legendary of which was Mrs. Onassis, obviously delighted to be in attendance at this "event." Defendants knew that Mrs. Onassis would never have allowed her name or face to be used in commercials, and only rarely allowed it to be used in connection with civic, art, and educational projects. So, defendants sought out Ms. Reynolds who, with appropriate coiffure and dress, looked remarkably like Mrs. Onassis. The ad ran in several upscale publications (i.e., *Esquire, The New Yorker*), and Dior boasted that the campaign caused sales to go through the roof. Onassis sued Christian Dior, claiming that it had appropriated her right of publicity.

In the *Onassis* case, the Court held that Christian Dior had appropriated Ms. Onassis' personality and likeness in an effort to sell its product by using Ms. Reynolds, the look-alike. The Court noted that Dior was attempting to portray its products as " as chic, sophisticated, elite, unconventional, quirky, audacious, elegant, and unorthodox."[97] Knowing that Ms. Onassis would never have consented to appear in such an ad, Dior located Ms. Reynolds through a "celebrity look-alike" agency.[98] Thus, it was no accident that she bore a striking resem-

---

95. *Id.* at 1399:

Viewed separately, the individual aspects of the advertisement in the present case say little. Viewed together, they leave little doubt about the celebrity the ad is meant to depict. The female-shaped robot is wearing a long gown, blond wig, and large jewelry. Vanna White dresses exactly like this at times, but so do many other women. The robot is in the process of turning a block letter on a game-board. Vanna White dresses like this while turning letters on a game-board but perhaps similarly attired Scrabble-playing women do this as well. The robot is standing on what looks to be the Wheel of Fortune game show set. Vanna White dresses like this, turns letters, and does this on the Wheel of Fortune game show. She is the only one. Indeed, defendants themselves referred to their ad as the "Vanna White" ad. We are not surprised.

96. 122 Misc.2d 603, 472 N.Y.S.2d 254(1984).

97. *Id.* at 257 & 605.

98. *Id.*

blance to Ms. Onassis, and the court concluded that Onassis was entitled to protection against this "rapacious commercial exploitation."[99] The Court noted that: "We are dealing here with actuality and appearance, where illusion often heightens reality and all is not quite what it seems. Is the illusionist to be free to step aside, having reaped the benefits of his creation, and permitted to disclaim the very impression he sought to create? If we were to permit it, we would be sanctioning an obvious loophole to evade the statute. If a person is unwilling to give his or her endorsement to help sell a product, either at an offered price or at any price, no matter—hire a double and the same effect is achieved."[100] Of course, the unique aspect of the case was that Onassis sought to enjoin Ms. Reynolds from appearing in the ads using her own face, and the court concluded that she could be enjoined from exhibiting her own face when it was done in such a way as to be deceptive or to promote confusion.[101]

D. Public Disclosure of Private Embarrassing Facts

In the final privacy category, public disclosure of private embarrassing facts, free speech interests often prevail as well. This tort requires proof that (1) defendant published matters regarding plaintiff's private life, (2) the publication would be highly offensive to a reasonable person of ordinary sensibilities, and (3) the matter was not of legitimate public concern.[102] Although the U.S. Supreme Court has mentioned this branch of the privacy tort, it has not ruled on the applicability of that tort, or its relationship to the right to free speech. There have, however, been a number of lower court decisions, and the right to free speech has generally prevailed over the right of privacy.

Illustrative is the holding in *Lowe v. Hearst Communications, Inc.*,[103] in which a newspaper was sued for public disclosure after it published an article about how a woman had bilked several lovers out of tens of thousands of dollars through an internet ad seeking "erotic and intellectual" relationships with men. After the relationships were consummated, her husband would prepare draft petitions and settlement agreements and present them to her lovers, naming them as potential defendants and threatening them with legal action that would publicly expose the affairs. As many as five men ultimately entered into settlement agreements to avoid litigation, paying between $75,000 and $155,000.

---

99. *Id.* at 260 & 610.

100. *Id.* at 261 & 612.

101. *Id.*

102. *See Star-Telegram, Inc. v. Doe*, 915 S.W.2d 471, 473–74 (Tex.1995); *Industrial Found. of the South v. Texas Industrial Accident Board*, 540 S.W.2d 668, 682 (Tex. 1976).

103. 414 F. Supp.2d 669 (2006).

When the woman sued the newspaper, the court concluded that the case involved a matter of legitimate public concern, and therefore denied her request for recovery: "Where the facts published are of 'legitimate public concern,' the right to publish information will overcome privacy rights."[104] Indeed, the "risk of … exposure [of the individual to the public] is an essential incident of life in a society which places a primary value on freedom of speech and of press."[105] On these facts, given that the case involved an alleged blackmail scheme, the Court found that it involved a matter of "legitimate public concern."[106]

Freedom of expression also prevailed in *Gilbert v. Medical Economics, Inc.*[107] In that case, defendant published an article entitled "Who Let This Doctor In The O.R.? The Story Of A Fatal Breakdown In Medical Policing." The article outlined incidents of alleged medical malpractice in which plaintiff's patients (plaintiff was an anesthesiologist) suffered fatal or severely disabling injuries because of plaintiff's acts of alleged malpractice. Plaintiff's insurer settled one malpractice action for $900,000. Following a description of these incidents, the article suggested that the malpractice occurred because of "a collapse of self-policing by physicians and of disciplinary action by hospitals and regulatory agencies." The article further suggested (1) that there was a causal relationship between plaintiff's personal problems and the acts of alleged malpractice, (2) that plaintiff's lack of capacity to engage responsibly in the practice of medicine was or should have been known to the policing agents of the medical profession, and (3) that more intensive policing of medical personnel is needed. The article identified plaintiff by name and included her photograph. When the subject of the article brought a privacy claim, the court rejected it on the basis that the item was newsworthy and therefore protected by the First Amendment.[108]

---

104. *Id.* at 673 (quoting *American Civil Liberties Union of Mississippi, Inc. v. State of Miss.*, 911 F.2d 1066, 1071 (5th Cir.1990)).

105. *Id.* at 673 (quoting *Time, Inc. v. Hill*, 385 U.S. 374, 388 (1967)).

106. *Id.* at 674:

Without question, the facts depicted in the article are matters of legitimate public concern. The article described an alleged blackmail scheme by lawyers who were willing to bend if not break the law to procure money from Mary's unsuspecting paramours. The public is legitimately interested in and entitled to know that two local lawyers, who hold themselves out as pursuers of justice and skilled and vigorous advocates on behalf of their clients, are using the processes of the law in such a legally and morally questionable manner. The article also presented insights into the operation of the legal system and a debate involving the ethics and legality of the Roberts's' scheme.

107. 665 F.2d 305 (10th Cir. 1981).

108. *Id.* at 308–309:

With respect to the publication of plaintiff's photograph and name, we find that these truthful representations are substantially relevant to a newsworthy topic because they

Conclusion

As noted, there is a significant gulf between the U.S. and Europe with regard to the handling of both free speech and privacy interests. Whereas the U.S. is often very protective of speech interests, treating freedom of expression as an interest that is entitled to special or preferred protection, European countries are generally more protective of privacy interests. As a result, in many types of privacy cases (e.g., false light privacy and intrusion on seclusion), it can sometimes be difficult for U.S. plaintiffs to prevail against free speech claims. However, in one area, cases involving appropriation of plaintiff's name or likeness for business or commercial purposes, U.S. plaintiffs have been more successful. Recovery might also be appropriate (in an appropriate case) for intrusion on seclusion.

Of course, there are lots of frontiers yet to be explored. For example, the European Court of Justice declared a "right to be forgotten" and ordered Google to expunge records in appropriate cases. In rendering its order, the court held that privacy rights take precedence over public access to online speech in some cases, and ordered Google to accept requests from European citizens to have their Google results purged of certain types of unflattering information. Whether U.S. courts will be willing to follow the European lead on this issue is doubtful, especially if the plaintiff is seeking to be "forgotten" on a manner related to the public interest. In such an instance, it is not clear that the privacy interest will prevail in the U.S. Indeed, one state court has already rejected the idea that the European Court decision should be applied in the U.S.[109] Likewise, there are emerging issues regarding how to handle so-called "revenge porn."[110] In one case, a woman who sent topless photos to a boyfriend learned that he posted them on a website after they broke up. One can expect some of these scenarios to show up in future privacy litigation.

---

strengthen the impact and credibility of the article. They obviate any impression that the problems raised in the article are remote or hypothetical, thus providing an aura of immediacy and even urgency that might not exist had plaintiff's name and photograph been suppressed. Similarly, we find the publication of plaintiff's psychiatric and marital problems to be substantially relevant to the newsworthy topic. While it is true that these subjects would fall outside the first amendment privilege in the absence of either independent newsworthiness or any substantial nexus with a newsworthy topic, here they are connected to the newsworthy topic by the rational inference that plaintiff's personal problems were the underlying cause of the acts of alleged malpractice.

109. *See Google, Inc. v. Expunction Order*, 441 S.W.3d 644 (Tex. Ct. App. 2014).

110. *See* Nathan Koppel, *Women in Texas Suing a Porn Site*, Wall St. J., Jan. 23, 2013, at A-6.